SPACES *of* IMMIGRATION

CULTURE, POLITICS, *and the* BUILT ENVIRONMENT

Dianne Harris, *Editor*

ALSO IN THE SERIES

World Observation: Empire, Architecture, and the Global Archive of Itō Chūta
Matthew Mullane
Model Schools in the Model City: Race, Planning, and Education in the Nation's Capital
Amber N. Wiley
A Territory in Conflict: Eras of Development and Urban Architecture in Gaza
Fatina Abreek-Zubiedat
Spatial Theories for the Americas: Counterweights to Five Centuries of Eurocentrism
Fernando Luiz Lara
Race and Modern Architecture: A Critical History from the Enlightenment to the Present
Edited by Irene Cheng, Charles L. Davis II, and Mabel O. Wilson
The Architecture of Good Behavior: Psychology and Modern Institutional Design in Postwar America
Joy Knoblauch
Neoliberalism on the Ground: Architecture and Transformation from the 1960s to the Present
Edited by Kenny Cupers, Catharina Gabrielsson, and Helena Mattsson
Building Character: The Racial Politics of Modern Architectural Style
Charles L. Davis II
Improvised Cities: Architecture, Urbanization, and Innovation in Peru
Helen Gyger
Of Greater Dignity Than Riches: Austerity and Housing Design in India
Farhan Karim
Ideals of the Body: Architecture, Urbanism, and Hygiene in Postrevolutionary Paris
Sun-Young Park
Colonialism and Modern Architecture in Germany
Itohan Osayimwese
Modern Architecture in Mexico City: History, Representation, and the Shaping of a Capital
Kathryn E. O'Rourke
Building Modern Turkey: State, Space, and Ideology in the Early Republic
Zeynep Kezer
Re-Collecting Black Hawk: Landscape, Memory, and Power in the American Midwest
Nicholas A. Brown and Sarah E. Kanouse
Designing Tito's Capital: Urban Planning, Modernism, and Socialism in Belgrade
Brigitte Le Normand
Architecture, Politics, and Identity in Divided Berlin
Emily Pugh
Governing by Design: Architecture, Economy, and Politics in the Twentieth Century
Edited by Daniel M. Abramson, Arindam Dutta, Timothy Hyde, and Jonathan Massey for Aggregate
Second Suburb: Levittown, Pennsylvania
Edited by Dianne Harris

SPACES *of* IMMIGRATION

AMERICAN PORTS, RAILWAYS, *and* SETTLEMENTS

Catherine Boland Erkkila

University *of* Pittsburgh Press

This publication has been supported by a grant from Furthermore: a program of the J. M. Kaplan Fund

Published by the University of Pittsburgh Press, Pittsburgh, Pa., 15260

Manufactured in the United States of America
Printed on acid-free paper
10 9 8 7 6 5 4 3 2 1

Cataloging-in-Publication data is available from the Library of Congress

ISBN 13: 978-0-8229-4849-0
ISBN 10: 0-8229-4849-4

Cover photo: Men, women, and children pose among their bundles on a passenger train in Warsaw that will take them to the port in Gdansk. Photograph by Alter Kacyzne, 1921. From the Archives of the YIVO Institute for Jewish Research, New York

Cover design: Alex Wolfe

To Andrew,
Home is wherever I'm with you

CONTENTS

ACKNOWLEDGMENTS

In 2007, I worked as a research assistant for the Irish Mission at Watson House in New York City, which aided more than one hundred thousand immigrant women between the years 1883 and 1954. During my time spent transcribing the mission's record books, something about these women took hold of my imagination, as many of them were around my age and some even shared my name. I wondered about their journey overseas and their time at the mission, where many found their footing on American soil. These daydreams planted the seed for this project. I am grateful to Dr. Maria Iacullo-Bird and Father Peter Meehan for creating this position for me through AmeriCorps. I would also like to thank Diane Richio and Ewa Lada for their companionship, advice, and many cups of tea during my time at the mission.

This book would not be possible without the support and encouragement of Andrew Erkkila. Your brilliant insights, writing prowess, and sharp editing skills are what helped bring this research to life. I am so grateful to be on this journey with you. To our children, Helen, Jane, and Abigail—your creativity, joy, and curiosity are an inspiration. When I struggled with completing this book, thinking of you one day reading it kept me going. I am fortunate to have such a loving and supportive family, including my in-laws, who have always encouraged my work. A special thank-you to Julie Boland Perez, whose breadth of skills is astonishing—you find a solution to any problem with grace, patience, and good humor. My beloved friend Maggie Slepickova Grove kept me sane while I juggled parenthood and career, always sending encouragement and laughs from afar, especially on days when it all felt like too much.

At Rutgers University, I had the immense privilege of working with Carla Yanni, who was the first to warmly welcome me into the architectural history profession. Her steadfast guidance shaped the earliest form of this project, and I've always been grateful for Carla's continued reassurance and advice. The Jacob K. Javits Fellowship allowed me to focus solely on my research as I completed my doctorate. Choosing a career outside academia has made completing this book challenging, but my dear friend and mentor Gabrielle Esperdy boosted my confidence more times than I can count. She and her wife, Julie Herzog, encouraged me to seek my own path—and provided delicious food along the way. Thanks to all my colleagues at the Society of Architectural Historians and University of Virginia Press for your camaraderie. It has been a joy working with you this past decade.

I have encountered many wonderful archivists and librarians over the years, for whom I am indebted. On my first research trip, Joe Piersen of the Chicago & North Western Historical Society Archives in Berwyn, Illinois, found and scanned the immigrant pamphlet for me, which was a huge breakthrough in my research. Marjorie Jantzen Shoemaker generously opened the Mennonite Heritage and Agricultural Museum for a private tour on her day off, when my husband and I passed through Goessel, Kansas, during our move to New Mexico. Thanks also to Jeffrey Dosik, Barry Moreno, and George Tselos of the Bob Hope Memorial Library at Ellis Island—it still amuses me that you remembered the commotion my sister Ann caused on the first day of her internship, when she inadvertently caused a security panic. Patricia LaBounty of the Union Pacific Railroad Museum and Denise Morrison of the Kansas City Museum located images that were critical to my work, for which I am very grateful. Nicholas Fessenden of the Baltimore Immigration Museum generously shared information that helped me solve the mystery of Augusta Koether's boardinghouse. My research on railroad settlements was only possible thanks to the Newberry Library's Short-Term Residential Fellowships for Individual Research. The publication of this book was made a reality by Furthermore: a program of the J. M. Kaplan Fund.

I am grateful to all those who provided critical feedback on this work, especially Paula Lupkin, Timothy Mennel, Susan Sidlauskas, Tanya Sheehan, fellow immigration landscape researcher David Monteyne, and the University of Pittsburgh Press's two anonymous peer reviewers. Marta Gutman and Cynthia Falk expertly edited a portion of this research for publication in *Buildings & Landscapes*, for which I was thrilled to receive the Vernacular Architecture Forum's Catherine W. Bishir Prize. To Dianne Harris, I am honored to be included in the Culture, Politics, and the Built Environment series. Thanks to the ever-patient Abby McAllister and her colleagues at the University of Pittsburgh Press, who shepherded this book from proposal to publication without ever making me feel rushed. I am also indebted to the many open-access digital collections that make humanities research feasible for a broader audience.

This project has been with me through graduate school, cross-country travels, my brief stint in academia, an editorial career at the Society of

Architectural Historians, a historic home gut renovation, and welcoming three remarkable daughters into the world. This book was a labor of love that accompanied me through many stages of my life. It has been inspiring and heartbreaking to read all the personal narratives of those who have left behind one country for another. I wish to acknowledge all the brave souls throughout history who have migrated, whether by choice or by force. Your experiences are an important part of the human record. I also want to thank the dreamers and poets like Robert Louis Stevenson whose art enriches our lives and has preserved a sense of wonder and beauty for the journey ahead.

NOTE ON TERMINOLOGY

In the nineteenth century, the term *emigration* and the corresponding *emigrant* were used by government and railroad officials to denote our contemporary notion of immigration. In architectural plans and company literature, railroad companies labeled the spaces designated for immigrants as "emigrant trains" and "emigrant waiting rooms" until the turn of the twentieth century. To prevent confusion, I have chosen to consistently use the terms *immigrant* and *immigration* and only retain the historical term when it appears in a quotation or in a name or title, for example, the Board of the Commissioners of Emigration or the Union Pacific's Emigrant House in Council Bluffs. In all other instances, *emigration* refers to the act of leaving one's country of origin and *immigration* refers to the act of entering the United States.

SPACES *of* IMMIGRATION

INTRODUCTION

The Journey Begins

It is the summer of 1879, and twenty-eight-year-old Robert Louis Stevenson stands shivering on a train platform in a Jersey City railway station. Exhausted, the lanky and shabbily dressed Scottish author awaits the next leg of his six-thousand-mile journey from Glasgow to San Francisco. Having spent ten days on the SS *Devonia* crossing the Atlantic, he stands among a "babel of bewildered men, women, and children," all waiting for the immigrant train to arrive so they can continue their journey west.[1] Like his fellow passengers, he has come to America hopeful that the life he establishes there will be a prosperous one. Stevenson, a shrewd observer of humankind, documented his journey to the United States in a series of memoirs, published in full in 1895, a year after his death.[2]

These writings provide a rare account of the long and arduous journey through what I call "spaces of immigration." This network of physical spaces—ships, ports, railway stations, train cars, boardinghouses, quarantine stations, and detention buildings—encountered during a migrant's journey has largely been overlooked in scholarship. This is the first book to explore the built environment of the immigration landscape in the United States. During the mid-nineteenth and early twentieth centuries, the vast majority of immigrants entered the United States by steamship, passed through some form of customs inspection, and journeyed via rail to their intended destinations. These physical spaces form a microcosm for many ongoing conflicts in American society, conflicts driven by politics, capitalism, race, and class. Stevenson, who serves as a kind of avatar in this text, was keenly aware of this, and his writings indicate the spatial sorting of travelers, which was often reinforced within the built environment, as architects and designers intentionally established societal divisions at the behest of their public or private employers. How immigrants, including Stevenson, navigated or *were* navigated through these transitory spaces is equally important, and this book examines both the physical and experiential environments from entry into the country through settlement. The fundamental inquiry of this book is how the immigration landscape reveals certain truths about American culture, politics, and capitalism. To answer this question, we must explore not only the design of these spaces, including the interiors, furnishings, finishes, and signage, but also look broadly at archival sources from corporate and government records to oral history, poetry, and memoir in order to recreate these often-lost and transitory spaces of immigration. In so doing, we can begin to understand how the built environment promoted an exclusively white definition of American character, one that pervades our society even today.

This approach to architectural history adds materiality to immigration studies as well as nuance to our understanding of the spatial implications of racial prejudice in the construction of modern, capitalist American culture. Weaving together an analysis of physical structures with a range of archival sources allows a deeper understanding of how people actually experienced their surroundings. This interdisciplinary methodology draws on a variety of fields, including social history, human geography, and especially cultural landscape studies, wherein *landscape* refers not only to open space but also to the spatial and cultural relationships between people and their surroundings.[3] Popularized in the 1950s by John Brinckerhoff Jackson, the field of cultural landscape studies posits everyday built spaces as "significant evidence of social groups, power relations, and culture."[4] Historians such as Paul Groth, Jessica Ellen Sewell, and John Michael Vlach, among others, have skillfully employed a cultural landscape approach to their subjects (residential hotels, women in public space, and plantation landscapes, respectively).[5] *Spaces of Immigration* is unique, however, in that it considers a range of buildings, from award-winning monumental works such as the Ellis Island immigration station to temporary lodging houses built by railroad and immigrant laborers in the Midwestern United States. These structures have their own inherent value, yet studying them within the landscape of immigration—a larger network of transitory spaces—reveals a deeper cultural meaning. More specifically, in placing transportation vessels such as ships and trains, and ancillary buildings like railway stations and government immigration facilities within this larger network, we can begin to understand how this particular built environment illustrates partitioning of and attitudes toward the racial, ethnic, and class hierarchies evident in turn-of-the-century American society. Thus, while high-style architecture (i.e., Architecture with a capital A) is included in this book, different questions are asked of these buildings. The focus is not so much on aesthetics and designers but rather on how these spaces are experienced by occupants, as well as the powerful role of space in the construction of citizenship and identity.

Stevenson arrived in the United States with an exaggerated and romantic view of American democracy, believing he would find an ideal social and politic life. It is perhaps not surprising that the author who would one day pen *The Strange Case of Dr. Jekyll and Mr. Hyde* would penetrate the contradictory heart of social relations in turn-of-the-century America. The east–west transportation network through which Stevenson and millions of others traveled in the late nineteenth and early twentieth centuries forms the basis of this study. Stevenson serves as our guide in navigating not only the literal immigrant journey through ports and the railways but also this complex cultural milieu. He was a man of complexity himself: this "amateur emigrant" could afford first-class passage but traveled in the lower-class compartments on both ship and train (figure I.1). He fancied himself an anonymous pauper and yet came from a wealthy and well-known engineering family. Stevenson's paternal ancestors designed most of the deep-sea lighthouses along the Scotland coast, and his maternal grandfather, Thomas Smith (1752–1815), designed improved street lighting for Edinburgh's New Town. Thus, from a family dedicated to wayfinding comes a young man seeking his own way. Stevenson can be described as a wanderer—traveling to find the right climate for his tubercular lungs, journeying across land and sea in order to escape the life his family had planned for him, and in the case of his journey to San Francisco, for love as he sought to reunite with the American magazine writer Fanny van de Grift Osbourne. This beguiling traveler is candid and sincere in his observations, and yet Stevenson is a gentleman in disguise, documenting the strivings of the masses who escaped their homelands due to poverty, war, or famine, while he himself is profoundly bourgeois and seeking adventure.

Despite the misgivings of family and friends, the quixotic author forged ahead with his travels. Just a year prior to his American voyage, in 1878, Stevenson embarked on a twelve-day, two-hundred-kilometer hiking journey through the Cévennes mountains in south-central France with his donkey, Modestine. At the time, he traveled as therapy—seeking to distance himself from the heartbreak of losing Fanny van de Grift Osbourne, an American woman who had returned to her husband in California. But he also wanted to get his literary career off the ground, and his memoir, *Travels with a Donkey in the Cévennes* (1879), became one of the first works of outdoor travel literature. When Stevenson learned that Fanny was ill,

Figure I.1. Robert Louis Stevenson, 1890–1894. Photograph by James Notman. © National Portrait Gallery, London and that her divorce was nearly finalized, he began his westward journey to San Francisco.

Stevenson's work was met with criticism among his literary circle, and his firsthand experience of an immigrant's journey into the United States so shocked his white middle-class family and friends that the publication was delayed. The first part of Stevenson's journey, by steamship from Europe to New York City, was ready for publication in 1880 under the title *The Amateur Emigrant from the Clyde to Sandy Hook*, but was ultimately withdrawn. Stevenson's family and friends were horrified that he traveled in steerage, and Stevenson's father, Thomas, felt the work was beneath his son's talents. Thomas even purchased all the copies the publisher had already printed to ensure the book would not be released. Yet Thomas's actions were fueled by more than concern for his son's reputation. Thomas maintained a business relationship with the Henderson brothers, who owned the Anchor Line Steamship Company on which Stevenson traveled. Surely a publication revealing the ineptitude of the staff and poor travel conditions would negatively impact the company and Thomas's relationship with its owners.[6] The second part of Stevenson's journey, a train ride from New York to San Francisco, is documented in *Across the Plains*, first published thirteen years later, in 1892. In the final portion of his American journey, published as *The Silverado Squatters* in 1883, Stevenson recounted his and Fanny's honeymoon in Napa Valley, California.

Stevenson is certainly not representative of the typical steerage traveler or immigrant train passenger, but in his narrative, he passed through many of the same physical spaces and endured similar hardships as his fellow travelers. And yet there are notable exceptions, particularly when Stevenson decided to shell out extra cash for a night at a grand hotel—respite from the uncomfortable journey on the immigrant train. While he indulged in a drink and a private room at the Union Pacific Hotel in Council Bluffs, Iowa, his fellow passengers bunked at an austere immigrant boardinghouse or caravanserai, as Stevenson calls it, exoticizing the spare lodgings that, to him, were optional. For the most part, the other immigrant travelers had disparate lifestyles and reasons for migrating. Some traveled for adventure, yes, but most were relocating because it was their only option to advance in life—whether financially or fleeing their home countries for their own safety.

Beginning in the mid-nineteenth century, the vast majority of migrants coming to the United States were from northern and western Europe. The arrival of more than a million poor and starving Irish during the Great Hunger of 1845–1852 and the high number of Germans who poured into the country following the 1848 revolution marked a turning

Figure I.2. "The Immigrant: Is he an acquisition or a detriment?," T. Frederich Victor Gillam, *Judge*, September 19, 1903. This cartoon illustrates the country's varying responses to immigration. Uncle Sam, a contractor, and a politician claim benefits while a citizen, health officer, and workman are threatened. The statesman in the top hat at right claims the immigrant remains a puzzle to him. The Ohio State University, Billy Ireland Cartoon Library and Museum

point in American immigration. At the same time, and into the 1860s, a significant number of Asian immigrants also arrived, seeking fortune in the gold mines of the American West, and many found employment with the railroad companies.[7] This period of mass migration sparked much anti-immigrant prejudice and nativist propaganda, as revealed in the political cartoons of the day. By the time of Stevenson's journey in 1879, the tides of immigration had turned once again. Restrictive legislation against the Chinese and changing conditions in Europe led to growing numbers of immigrants from southern and eastern Europe—people whose unfamiliar languages, different religions, and darker complexions alarmed an Anglo-Protestant citizenry (figure I.2). In nineteenth-century America, the credo of Manifest Destiny emerged in defense of an exclusively white Christian nation, which, as historian Charles L. Davis II notes, "pitted white colonial settlers against Indigenous peoples, formerly enslaved Africans, and other migrant laborers of color."[8]

Indeed, race and ethnic identity as the basis for constructed societal divisions forms a crucial component of immigration studies, particularly in a nation built on colonization. The outmoded concept of the United States as a "melting pot," implying a loss of immigrant culture and assimilationist thinking, has shrewdly been dismantled by scholars.[9] Author and playwright Israel Zangwill coined the phrase in his 1908 play titled *The Melting Pot*. The play's main character, David Quixano, hoped for a world free from ethnic divisions, following the murder of his immediate family in a pogrom that forced him to emigrate from Russia to the United States. To him, America resembled a refuge from persecution: "America is God's Crucible, the great Melting-Pot where all the races of Europe are melting and re-forming. Here you stand [. . .] Germans and Frenchmen, Irishmen and Englishmen, Jews and Russians—into the Crucible with you all! God is making the American."[10] While Zangwill's play emphatically insisted that America was a place where hatred had no home, American novelist Toni Morrison noted that the melting pot metaphor denies inclusion of Black people, who were brought against their will to America and enslaved. She posited instead that Black people *were* the pot, "and everything else was melted together."[11] Scholars such as Grace Elizabeth Hale, Matthew Frye Jacobson, and David Roediger have explored the making of this segregationist culture and how the construction of whiteness, particularly its shifting definition over time and place, has helped shape the United States' immigration policy.[12]

The capitalist framework in which the transportation companies benefited from mass migration was also shaped by racism. Railroad companies, for example, developed settlements in the Midwestern United States during the nineteenth century, and they worked alongside state governments to publish brochures and pamphlets that advertised the benefits of a particular area or region. These advertisements were selectively circulated to only those foreign countries from which railroad and government officials wished to attract settlers—that is, mainly northern European countries. Railroad companies (themselves owned and operated by white men) popularized the notion that white immigrants were the best racial stock for American development. The prejudice evident in these publicity campaigns was also revealed in the physical spaces of the railways. One of the most explicit examples is the segregated immigrant waiting room found in railway stations across the United States—in cities like Baltimore, Philadelphia, Chicago, and Kansas City. These rooms were in stations that received the most immigrant passenger traffic—that is, on the coasts at ports of entry and in the large Midwestern cities where multiple rail lines converged, usually at the aptly named Union Station. These rooms served a dual purpose: on the one hand, immigrants were protected from those seeking to take advantage of them (there were many of these swindlers, unfortunately), and on the other hand, foreign travelers were kept separate from United States citizens who did not want to be exposed to them. Segregated spaces for immigrant travelers were not limited to the stations but also on locomotives themselves in individual railcars or sometimes entire trains. None of this segregation was accidental. These were specifically designed spaces to direct the movement of large groups of people.

Immigrant waiting rooms were a critical part of the entire network of spaces of immigration: not just in the railroad infrastructure—the miles after miles of track laid, the stations, the settlements—but also in the American cultural landscape, where the effects remain well over a century later. The railroads were both a product of an emerging capitalist society and a mechanism of cultural hegemony—a crossroads where commerce also forged culture. The railway system's rapid growth in the nineteenth century, in addition to drastically altering the United States' physical landscape, allowed waves of migrants from eastern states and newly arrived immigrants to travel along rail lines east to west, virtually repopulating the country's interior on lands that were forcibly taken or ceded from Indigenous peoples. To construct a transportation network, railroad companies relied on immigrants for cheap labor and also to purchase land along their completed lines. These people were both potential labor and future consumers. Immigrants were lured by affordable transportation and the chance at a new life advertised to them. For those seeking to escape the poverty, famine, and civil unrest in their home countries, America seemed to offer limitless possibilities. While in many ways the relationship was reciprocal, it was largely controlled by railroad officials, who advertised lands to specific nationalities, determined routes of travel, and denied access based on race and ethnicity. In train cars and station spaces, railway officials drew boundaries, segregating foreign travelers, thus revealing and reinforcing contemporary American prejudices in which immigrants were stereotyped as poor, dangerous, and diseased. Historians Alan Kraut and Amy Fairchild have skillfully revealed how foreigners have continuously been equated with disease and genetic inferiority throughout history.[13]

The physical spaces through which foreigners traveled were also part and parcel of this experience, however—both highly charged and yet largely overlooked in history. It is this gap that this book begins to fill. At the turn of the twentieth century, most European immigrants arrived in New York Harbor, where they gazed at the awe-inspiring sight of the

Statue of Liberty, followed quickly by the stress-inducing inspection procedures of Ellis Island. In early-twentieth-century San Francisco, Angel Island Immigration Station's dreadful conditions were infamous to Asian immigrants, who endured exhaustive interrogation sessions and extended detention periods as a result of the government's racially charged and prohibitive immigration practices during this period. Once immigrants gained entry into the country, a difficult railway journey often bridged their passage from the port of entry to their intended home. In train cars and railway stations, those newly arrived from Italy, Poland, or Russia were segregated from American passengers by virtue of their lower class and national origin. Racial segregation pervaded railway spaces as well, not only for African American travelers in southern and eastern states but also for Asian immigrants and Native Americans in the West. Railway officials carefully monitored immigrant movement through the railway system, both for the travelers' protection—they were often the target of fraud—but perhaps, more significantly, for the comfort and safety of white American citizens. First- and second-generation Americans, as well as those who had immigrated only decades earlier, dissociated themselves from newcomers by virtue of language, skin color, custom, religion, political inclination, and behavior, and projected xenophobic fears of disease and disorder onto them. This is all revealed in the built environment. In Kansas City's Union Station, for example, an isolation room for criminal or diseased passengers is adjacent to the immigrant waiting room, both located at the farthest end of the concourse, removed from the main waiting area. An analysis of the architectural plan reveals a hierarchy of travelers imposed by the railroad companies that owned the station. Railroad officials deemed the criminal and diseased unfit to be grouped, architecturally or socially, with American passengers and are instead put in proximity to immigrant passengers, who were also kept at a distance from other passengers.

Railway companies negotiated the fine balance between addressing the public's concerns and catering to their immigrant customers in the design of their built environment. The railroad served the varied roles of being a business subject to market demands, an intimate space in which passengers came in close contact, and, as historian Amy Richter notes, a "socially diverse and fluid space capable of blurring lines of class and caste."[14] From the railroad officials' point of view, both the American public and immigrants contributed to the companies' profits. Within the spaces of the railways, passengers could potentially converge—upper class and lower class, American citizen and foreigner, white and Black, men and women, Jewish and Christian. They could also be separated from one another.[15]

Cultural historian Wolfgang Schivelbusch wrote that the railways annihilated traditional notions of space and time by establishing standardized time and increasing travel speeds. Increased speeds resulted in a traveler's perception that the distance between places was lessened even though the physical distances remained the same. Schivelbusch terms this travel space the "space in-between."[16] It is within this space that passengers encountered one another, societal divisions were confronted, and the railroad companies attempted to limit those confrontations. The space in-between was far from neutral; it was, in fact, fraught with social meaning. This book expands the notion of the space in-between, which Schivelbusch limits to the railway car, to include the entire network of spaces an immigrant encounters on the journey from one's home country to settlement in the United States. In studying the physical places through which immigrants travel, we can begin to uncover the cultural meaning of the space in-between: while it encompasses the time in passage between stations of arrival and destination, it is also the gap between one national identity and another, and can even be applied to the idea of America itself as a democratic society, one in which the ideals of democracy are often at contradiction with the actions of its government.

The railroads were representative of technological and cultural changes rapidly occurring in Victorian America—an observation that has been well studied in scholarship.[17] Within the space of the railroad, notes Alan Trachtenberg in the foreword to Schivelbusch's *The Railway Journey*, "nineteenth-century people encountered the new conditions of their lives; they encountered themselves as moderns, as dwellers within new structures of regulation and need."[18] Part of these new structures included racial hierarchies, where one group could identify themselves by being placed in opposition to another. Segregation, as historian Grace Elizabeth Hale so aptly describes in her groundbreaking book *Making Whiteness*, "is the product of human choice and decision, of power and fear, of longing, even on love and hate."[19] The space in-between, though technologically modern, relied on historic narratives of race-based subjugation and oppression. Beginning in the post–Civil War era, this opposition revealed itself through the emergence of Jim Crow laws, which legalized racial segregation. American transportation and immigration are both inextricably bound in issues of race and class, and transit was frequently where these racial lines were visibly delineated.

The difference between the segregation of African American and immigrant passengers, however, is significant. In terms of immigrant passengers, the railroads were more often profit-seeking than ideological. Superficially, segregation of Black travelers resembled the segregation of immigrants in the late nineteenth and early twentieth centuries only insofar as both groups were physically isolated from other passengers.[20] Yet immigrant segregation depended largely on class, at least for European immigrants. Cultural historian Matthew Frye Jacobson has demonstrated how, by the mid-nineteenth century, Americans used race as a social construct to establish hierarchies of power and privilege for those of European descent.[21] If Europeans had enough money to purchase passage in the first-class compartments (unlike Stevenson, the majority did not), railroad officials allowed them to ride with other first-class passengers. Black passengers, Native Americans, and Chinese immigrants, on the other hand, were prohibited from riding in first-class cars even if they had the financial means to do so—restricted mobility was thus not only limited to travel space but also within American society. Historian Amy Richter asserts that, as Americans came to terms with the new experiences of public life, "the renegotiation and imposition of racial identities comprised [. . .] one effort to stabilize social and cultural change on the trains."[22] The railways served as a location where white American citizens seized the opportunity to define themselves as moral, healthy, and educated in opposition to people of color and foreigners, who were screened from their spaces and sight by various means. Historian Robert Weyeneth's conceptual framework of racial segregation as a spatial system, notably his concept of architectural partitioning versus architectural isolation, is especially relevant when examining spaces of immigration.[23] Immigrant trains and waiting rooms, in particular, were sites where segregation of foreign passengers was most prevalent.

Travel space, however, was more complex than either accommodating or reinforcing binaries of east versus west, American versus foreigner, rich versus poor; for white populations this complicated cultural landscape could also render identity fluid, making it capable of shifting over time and place.[24] Of particular importance to this study are the nuances of racial identity in the nineteenth and early twentieth centuries. Schivelbusch's space in-between thus also serves as a metaphor for the transient nature of migrants—not only in terms of their geographic location but also in terms of their citizenship and their perceived racial identity. While a clear legal line separated citizens from noncitizens, there were significant inequalities among the noncitizens. European immigrants were on a path to citizenship, if they so desired; Chinese immigrants, on the other hand, and later other Asian immigrants, were denied the promise of citizenship. On the West Coast, segregation of Asians was strictly enforced on trains. Euro-American passengers refused to travel with Asian passengers, conforming to anti-Asian biases then prevalent in American society and immigration policy. As Stevenson notes, in the space of the railways, "hungry Europe and hungry China [. . .] had here come face to face."[25] Although the southern and eastern European immigrants arriving on the East Coast experienced discrimination from American citizens and were segregated on the railways, as they traveled further west, where they encountered Asian, Mexican, and Native American populations, railway officials viewed the Europeans as potential citizens and treated them accordingly. Identity, in this case "whiteness," shifted within the context of physical space. The politics of class are also entwined in this discussion of racial identity, since it was often the lower- and working-class white Euro-Americans who most frequently patrolled these boundaries of whiteness.[26] It was these groups who most often felt threatened by the incoming foreigners, who presented fierce competition in the job market.

This racial discrimination also manifested in American politics. The Chinese Exclusion Act of 1882 is frequently described as the first law to bar immigrants on the basis of their race and class, revealing the xenophobia and racism prevalent in American politics and society at the turn of the century. Yet the lesser-known Page Act of 1875, which prohibited entry of East Asian women (assumed to be coming to the United States for prostitution or polygamy), was actually the first restrictive immigration legislation.[27] Both of these laws targeted East Asian immigrants, and historian Erika Lee describes the 1882 Chinese Exclusion Act as marking the shift from the country's relatively open-door immigration policy to a new era as a "gatekeeping nation."[28] In addition to economic concerns, particularly immigration's effect on the American workforce, the pseudoscience of eugenics (then part of the emerging field of modern social science and now recognized as unscientific racism and justification for white supremacy) was a guiding force behind much of this legislation, a contemptible effort to justify restrictive legislation.

In 1907, the formation of the US Immigration Commission, more commonly known as the Dillingham Commission after its chair, Senator William P. Dillingham, resulted in a forty-one-volume study published in 1911, wherein the recommendations on immigration restrictions were, in fact, more restrictive than its own evidence.[29] Between 1880 and 1924, when the Johnson-Reed Act imposed national origins quotas, approximately twenty-four million immigrants arrived on American shores, and by the time the joint commission was established, many Americans viewed immigration as a national crisis. By the late nineteenth century, for European Americans whose families had already been citizens for a generation or more, foreigners arriving from southern and eastern Europe (as opposed to earlier arrivals from northwestern Europe) were perceived as a public threat to the moral and economic health of the nation. Within a decade of the commission's establishment, the government had imposed a literacy test, a quota system based on national origin (which would not be repealed until 1965), and expanded federal oversight of immigration policy. The Dillingham Commission, which also published *A Dictionary of Races or Peoples*, reinforced the use of eugenics to control immigration by creating a hierarchical scale that equated physical attributes (skin color, facial features, etc.) with moral and intellectual qualities.[30] At immigration stations beginning in 1903, officials briefly used the Bertillon system of identification, an anthropometric system of physical measurements of body parts that was first employed in criminology. The time-consuming (and therefore costly) process was eradicated five years later due to objections from immigrant advocates, particularly from Chinese community leaders in San Francisco, who petitioned against the discriminatory procedures at Angel Island Immigration Station.[31] However, the damage could not be undone. The commission's recommendations continue to have a lasting effect on immigration policy, control, and enforcement.

At the turn of the century, the most lucrative years of the railway age, rates of immigration soared. Most of these foreign travelers had crossed the ocean as steerage passengers and endured cramped and poorly equipped steamship quarters for at least a week. Stevenson paid an extra two guineas to travel in the second-class cabin, "a modified oasis in the very heart of the steerages."[32] Although he was "anxious to see the worst of emigrant life," previous travelers had advised Stevenson to take passage in the second-class cabin, where bedding, dishes, and food were provided. For a single man (of financial means) traveling alone, the difference in price between steerage and second class was nominal, as Stevenson himself notes, yet for families traveling together, first by sea and then rail, the price quickly added up.

The steerage and second-class cabins were, however, close in proximity, separated only by a thin partition through which Stevenson could "hear the steerage passengers being sick, the rattle of tin dishes as they sit at meals, the varied accents in which they converse, the crying of their children terrified by this new experience, or the clean flat smack of the parental hand in chastisement."[33] Just as Stevenson would never fully experience the trials of his fellow migrants, he also did not fully experience their discomfort—he was physically adjacent to them, observing from a short distance. This physical barrier divided social classes on the journey, but the distinction was superficial: "In steerage there are males and females; in the second cabin ladies and gentleman. For some time after I came aboard I thought I was only a male; but in the course of a voyage of discovery between decks, I came on a brass plate, and learned that I was still a gentleman."[34] Stevenson himself remarks on the superficiality of this separation of classes yet indicates that its existence was certainly meaningful. In the second-class cabin, Stevenson was also afforded a table on which he could write his observations. Throughout his ten-day sea voyage, Stevenson often wandered into the steerage compartment to socialize with the passengers and was often taken for a steerage passenger himself, "and there was nothing but the brass plate between decks to remind me that I had once been a gentleman."[35]

It is notable that Stevenson frequently relies on his physical surroundings to assure himself of his identity. One of his biographers, Ian Bell, argues that Stevenson typifies a personality that gravitated toward mutual antagonisms—he lived as a constant exile, belonging to no camp.[36] He was emigrating like the others, certainly, and yet could be separated from his fellow travelers when he wished, spending money to achieve a more comfortable experience. He often spoke of the other passengers from what he believed was his higher station, observing how they "had been unable to prevail against circumstances in the one land, [and] were now fleeing pitifully to another."[37] And yet at other times, Stevenson counted himself among these "broken men of England."[38] In many cases, it seems Stevenson was projecting his own feelings of inadequacy and failure onto his fellow travelers (he had yet to achieve much literary success at this point in his life and relied on his parents for income), and so we must take his musings with a grain of salt. Where Stevenson's text is most useful to this study, however, are his descriptions of travel space. Using these descriptions, we can explore what their design revealed about the society in which they were built.

A discussion of Stevenson's identity is necessary if he is to serve as our guide through this immigration landscape. It is important to emphasize that Stevenson was not one of the foreigners discriminated against by the government and the transportation companies at the time of his travels. A British white male raised in the Protestant faith (although he declared himself an atheist, much to his parents' chagrin), Stevenson was not liable to become a public charge due to his family's wealth, nor was he competition for employment: this sickly man of letters was not in the market for manual labor. And, despite Stevenson's own health troubles, he was not considered a threat to public health. On the contrary, here was a man with the funds to travel to a posh sanatorium in the Alps to regain his strength during the winter months.[39] The passengers with whom he traveled, on the other hand, had drastically different life experiences. Stevenson himself declared the *idea* of immigration—the hope of beginning anew elsewhere—as distinct from the reality of relocation: "Emigration, from a word of the most cheerful import, came to sound most dismally in my ear. There is nothing more agreeable to picture and nothing more pathetic to behold."[40] There was a disconnect between Stevenson's fantasies of what his fellow travelers would be (young and adventurous single men like himself) and what they actually were: "Comparatively few of the men were below thirty; many were married, and encumbered with families; not a few were already up in years; and this itself was out of tune with my imaginations, for the ideal emigrant should certainly be young."[41] Then, like now, most of those relocating were families seeking better opportunities and safer lives than could be found in their homelands. Despite the fact that Stevenson was an anomaly among his fellow travelers, the journey from homeland to the United States was, for the most part, similar for all of those traveling together in the same compartments, which Stevenson largely did.

Dispensing with some of the biographical factors of Stevenson's life—there are many wonderful volumes dedicated to his life and writings—and taking him at face value for what he says he is—an amateur emigrant, a gentleman in old rags, a scribbler—this book aims to strike a balance between the immigrant's individual experience and the larger cultural and societal factors at play during this time period, which, indeed, remain present today. As Stevenson wrote in his travel memoir, "The individual is more affecting than the mass."[42] Following so famous a character, one who is white, male, and privileged, may seem misleading to a study of immigration, race, and class in turn-of-the-century America, yet Stevenson's travel memoir is one of the most complete texts we have that incorporates discussion of the physical spaces through which immigrants travel. His work thus enables us to follow the journey of an immigrant from one country to another, across both the geographic and cultural space of the United States.

At the heart of this study are the coastal ports of entry, where the majority of immigrants arrived in the United States in the late nineteenth and early twentieth centuries, and the transportation networks and settlement patterns that developed to facilitate immigration into and throughout the country. Because the focus is on the transoceanic transportation networks that developed during this period, north–south migration routes through Canada and Mexico are omitted from this book.[43] Government border stations were first erected at the land borders of Canada and Mexico after the establishment of the US Border Patrol in 1924. This book is not meant to be a comprehensive look at the built environment of immigration throughout American history but is rather meant to serve as a model for other architectural studies of historical and contemporary landscapes of immigration. Ports and railways, though seemingly only serving as functional way stations for immigrant travelers, were carefully planned and executed spaces regulated by a combination of profit-seeking private enterprise and national racist and xenophobic practices deeply embedded in the American cultural fabric. Even settlement patterns were frequently directed by both public and private interests. The chapters that follow consider not only buildings but also town planning and discriminatory land-use policies, particularly in the western United States, where federal and state land grants allowed railroad companies to plat towns and sell lands along their lines, altering the natural landscape at an alarming rate. As geographer Deryck Holdsworth suggests, we would do well to examine the broader spatial frame surrounding a particular building, which allows architectural historians to form a more thorough understanding of the building, its owners, and its occupants.[44] Examining this larger transportation network, as opposed to studying isolated structures individually, sheds light on the cultural undercurrents informing the design of the built environment and the spatial experiences of those traveling through it.

This book's structure mirrors an immigrant's journey: from ports of arrival, into waiting rooms and segregated trains, and ultimately to settlements. Like Stevenson, whose quotes from *The Amateur Emigrant* form each chapter's subheadings, we move east from New York to west, ultimately ending up in San Francisco, where we expand our discussion to the treatment of Asian immigrants arriving on the West Coast (figure I.3). The physical journey on the rails thus serves as a metaphor for the immigrant's path to citizenship—a journey made easier for some than others. In New York, the first chapter, the government controlled the immigration facilities, first at the state-owned Castle Garden (1855) and then at the federally owned Ellis Island (1892). In both facilities, multiple railroad companies operated within a pool to form an extensive transportation network that enabled passengers to quickly pass through inspection and onto waiting trains out of the city. This important shift from state to federal control is revealed in the architectural design of the buildings. The crowded and chaotic atmosphere of Castle Garden, a circular fortress turned entertainment venue turned immigration facility, was replaced by the purpose-built, rectilinear design of the station on Ellis Island, wherein passengers were moved through the space in a carefully controlled and efficient manner.

In New York Harbor, the surrounding rail terminals worked in conjunction with the government to shuttle immigrants onto waiting trains. With the high numbers of passengers concentrated at these train stations, the railroad companies erected immigrant waiting areas on the shoreline,

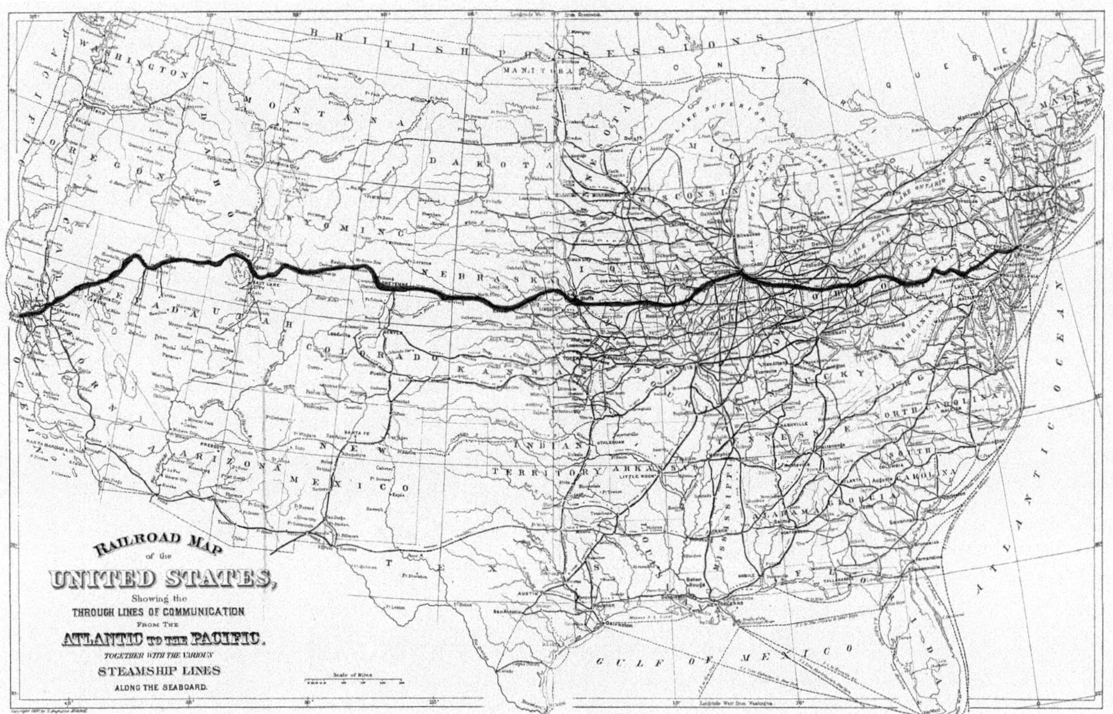

Figure I.3. This 1880 map depicts the country's railroad and steamship network around the time of Stevenson's journey, the route of which is in bold. Today's Interstate 80 follows roughly the same path, except around the Great Salt Lake. Map by S. Augustus Mitchell

separate from the main building. Similarly, in Baltimore, the transportation network between ship and train was a streamlined operation in which immigrants did not come in contact with the local population. These port stations, the subject of chapter two, represent the role of immigration within the railroad's capitalist framework, in which immigrants were shuttled into the country at the same speed and efficiency with which the railways moved freight. While the government and railroad companies worked in tandem in New York, in Baltimore, the Baltimore & Ohio Railroad Company held an exclusive contract with the North German Lloyd Steamship Company for both passenger and freight traffic, and the railroad company owned and operated Baltimore's main port of entry from 1868 until the start of World War I. The economic holdings of the Baltimore & Ohio Railroad enabled the company not only to shape the land, with its transformation of Locust Point, but also to form a significant connection between the American hinterland and European markets.

Railroad officials used the built environment—piers, stations, and train cars—to regulate immigrants' movement and segregate one group from another during the late nineteenth and early twentieth centuries. The third chapter explores immigrant trains and the Midwestern stations where passengers made travel connections. Largely deprived of creature comforts on the steamships, passengers were arguably conditioned to austere travel arrangements by the time they reached American shores. Upon their arrival on the East Coast, European immigrants started their railroad journey by lining up on separate piers, where retrofitted boxcars awaited to carry them from crowded cities to the country's heartland. The physical isolation on the railways would not have been unfamiliar to the immigrants in that it resembled the spatial order of the steamship, in which travelers were sorted by social class; they had merely exchanged one harsh, segregated space for another. The low fares that afforded immigrants the opportunity to relocate resulted in segregated trains, which often ran on a slower freight schedule, were sparsely furnished, and offered little to no amenities. In train stations, segregated waiting rooms were far removed from the main waiting areas, although not banished from the station altogether, as was the case in the port cities (an example of architectural partitioning as opposed to the architectural isolation of the latter). Railroad officials upheld the cleanliness of these white-tiled, sparsely furnished rooms to quell fears of foreign-borne illness.

Some of these passengers were heading to destinations throughout the Midwest, where railroad companies sold them parcels of land on which they could settle. Railroad efforts to establish ethnic enclaves form the subject of the fourth chapter. In the eyes of railroad and government officials, immigration was a profitable enterprise to build the country's infrastructure as well as to spur the nation's industrial and agricultural development. The dispossession and redistributions of Native lands was key to this aspect of wealth-building in the United States, and both the railways and the government wished to control *who* repopulated the American West. Railroad companies advertised and sold their land to targeted white ethnic groups whom they believed to be industrious and skilled, with the goal that the agriculture and goods produced by them would be shipped along the rail lines to domestic and foreign markets, thus perpetuating business for the railroads even after they sold their lands. Along the railways, these flows of capital and commerce moved continuously from region to region, connecting markets in ways that had not been previously possible. William Cronon's concept of Second Nature, in which city and country are linked by the railways and flows of capital, illustrates the profound ecological and economic changes that transpired in nineteenth-century America to modernize a nation mesmerized by its belief in its own manifest destiny.[45] Immigration played a major role in those changes, whereby foreigners settled on the lands that railroad companies had utterly transformed by platting towns onto the sweeping prairie, opening up lands for agriculture, and conquering the land by laying tracks, excavating tunnels, and building bridges, physically shaping the country as it reciprocally shaped American culture, a nation of individuals bound by economic principles of private ownership and industry. The American frontier was declared by Frederick Jackson Turner to be "the line of most rapid and effective Americanization."[46] Railroad companies used rhetorical strategies to invoke the transformative powers of white settlers and farming techniques that could convert the West into a civilized land. Civilization, for nineteenth-century Americans, was defined in terms of opposition to Native populations. The far-reaching hand of American capitalism displaced (or in many cases annihilated) Indigenous peoples and opened up their lands to white settlers. The "blank slate" of the nation was ripe for redevelopment. As millions sat in waiting rooms to repopulate the nation—both as cheap labor and future consumers—the promise of America became obtainable at speeds not yet recorded in history.

In San Francisco, the subject of the final chapter, Stevenson arrives at his destination, yet for the immigrants arriving in the city from Asia, their journey was far from over. Frequently, Asians were detained for much longer periods than their European counterparts, first in pier buildings and later in the federally built Angel Island Immigration Station (1910). Restrictive legislation against Asians, particularly the Chinese, guided the prisonlike design of Angel Island, which was located in proximity to Alcatraz Island. Scholarship on Angel Island tends to focus on interrogation methods, detainment periods, and individual immigrant stories, and while historians have often referred to Angel Island as the physical manifestation of Chinese exclusionary legislation, they have yet to fully examine *how* the architecture of Angel Island Immigration Station communicated exclusion.[47] The extent to which the Chinese were discriminated against pervades every aspect of the station's design, from its island location to its bed furnishings. While often called the "Ellis Island of the West," Angel Island Immigration Station was quite different than its East Coast counterpart. Both immigrant depots were constructed in response to the growing numbers of foreigners arriving on American shores, but these buildings manifested a series of tensions between inclusion and exclusion, between protection of immigrants and protection of Americans, and between veneration of America's immigrant past and rejection of the immigrant present.

The space in-between serves myriad functions and can be interpreted in a variety of ways, from the physical spaces along the immigration landscape to the metaphorical space between cultures, where perception of identity can shift based on surroundings. In the span of a journey, depending on social, cultural, and economic factors, an immigrant could experience the space as purgatorial or a metamorphic transformation as they made their way into the country and progressed by degrees toward acceptance and citizenship (or not). The space in-between was highly regulated and yet as alluring as a dream—hard to define and yet seemingly all-encompassing; full of contradictions and, at the same time, ripe with meaning. A man of contradictions himself, Stevenson is our guide through this liminal space. He was both a product of the Victorian era and, at the same time, thoroughly modern. One aspect many of Stevenson's biographers have in common is that no one can make a statement about him without quickly amending it. He is, at once, a privileged white man and an "amateur emigrant," a constant exile. He referred to himself as the Double Dammed Emigrant, adversely criticized by his peers for his travelogue and not quite part of the group of immigrants with whom he sympathized.[48] And so it is that Stevenson is in many ways a fitting guide through the spaces of immigration, through the space in-between.

NEW YORK

As the *SS Devonia* sailed toward New York, Stevenson's fellow passengers mused about what awaited them. They exchanged stories heard from previous immigrants. The tales ranged from the absurd to the grisly, leaving Stevenson to declare, "You would have thought we were to land upon a cannibal island."[1] These cautionary tales were, as Stevenson noted, so embellished by the time they reached one's ears that they often corresponded to "the least modicum of fact." Yet when one passenger, M'Naughten, shared a firsthand experience, Stevenson took heed. While seeking work in Boston, M'Naughten rented a room at what he later discovered to be a robber's inn—the sparsely furnished room had a secret compartment above the bed (covered by a curtain) where a thief in the next room "could easily take a purse from under the pillow, or even strangle a sleeper as he lay abed."[2] When M'Naughten's travel companion pulled back the curtain, believing it to conceal a window or perhaps a painting, he found three men crouched in the darkness of a small room, waiting to strike. Similar tales spread among the passengers as the *Devonia* came into view of New York Harbor.

Embellishments aside, prior to the establishment of centralized immigrant depots there were in fact few protections for travelers. Ship passengers disembarked at the piers and directly into the eager hordes of swindlers waiting to take advantage of them. Cartoons in contemporary periodicals, such as *Puck* magazine (figure 1.1), portrayed the dangers facing the immigrants on arrival. Fraudulent money changers and baggage handlers, "friends" from the old country, and temptresses are shown as pits into which immigrants might fall. Immigrants lost money on counterfeit railroad tickets or nonexistent accommodations. One of the biggest rackets was set up in the city's boardinghouses, not unlike the one at

Figure 1.1. Cartoon by Frederick Burr Opper published in *Puck*, June 14, 1882. William A. Rosenthall Judaica Collection–Prints and Photographs, College of Charleston Libraries, Charleston, SC, USA

which M'Naughten stayed. Boardinghouse runners, as they were called, typically seized the baggage of newly arrived immigrants and headed off toward one of the city's many boardinghouses. For fear of losing their baggage, the travelers had little choice but to follow. Runners often received a commission for each person recruited, and the boardinghouse owners frequently changed room rates, raising them significantly when they knew the traveler had nowhere else to stay.[3] One Irish immigrant lamented, "I have met with so much deception since we have landed on the shores of the New World that I am fearful of trusting [anyone]."[4] Without specific legislation for immigration and specialized facilities to transfer passengers directly from the ships into the hands of approved agencies, there was no end in sight to the deceptive practices.

In the United States, nineteenth-century immigration was a process governed by international commercial interests, regional powers, and local customs.[5] American borders were not as tightly controlled as they are today, and for most European immigrants, exiting their home country proved far more difficult than entering the United States. Departure procedures varied by country, and only toward the end of the nineteenth century did entry procedures become regularized under federal control. Prior to that, medical inspections took place at the departure ports and also aboard the ships as they sailed into harbor. Immigrants were subject to general quarantine and poor laws or to local ordinances in their arrival city. Just as Stevenson and his fellow passengers were concerned about the deception they might encounter in this new country, American citizens were also wary of immigrants, whom they viewed as threats to public health, as a burden to society (since many were cash-poor), and as competition for employment. New York City received the largest number of immigrants, and due to the influx of mainly Irish and German immigrants in the mid-nineteenth century, the state government established the Board of the Commissioners of Emigration on May 5, 1847.[6] The commissioners, who served without official pay, collected vital statistics, authorized physicians to board and inspect steamships, and were tasked with establishing facilities to contain the incoming foreigners upon arrival.

Concern for public health was an impetus for the development of quarantine architecture. The board of commissioners established and managed an immigrant hospital on Ward's Island, built in 1848, where those with communicable diseases could be quarantined. Another quarantine facility, the New York Marine Hospital on Staten Island, was established in 1799 and burned down in 1858 by angry locals who blamed it for that year's yellow fever outbreak.[7] Immediately following the attack, the *New York Times* noted the irony that "the great problem of the age seems to be, to establish a Quarantine without having it located anywhere."[8] Indeed, this was often the issue with immigration architecture on the whole. The space in-between was, by necessity, a dynamic space that often existed at a crossroads of conflicting goals, both trying to find a compromise that satisfied and facilitated movement *and* was exclusionary. Since no existing location was apparently suitable for quarantine, the state's response was to create artificial islands in Lower New York Bay on which they could locate the necessary facilities. By the early 1870s, New York State had constructed two new quarantine facilities on islands created from landfill on a shoal in the Narrows, just south of today's Verrazzano-Narrows Bridge, about one mile off of Staten Island's South Beach. The four-acre Dix Island (later Swinburne), built in 1870 and comprising rows of long white hospital wards and a crematorium, was the location where those afflicted with disease were sent. The eleven-acre Hoffman Island (1873), which originally consisted of three large brick buildings that were later expanded, was the location where those exposed to disease were held for observation. Isolated from the mainland, these facilities were but one stop along the immigration landscape.

"We Had Accepted This Purgatory"

Aboard the ships, it was the steerage passengers who underwent more thorough medical inspections, since their quarters were overcrowded and unsanitary, and often lacked adequate ventilation—conditions ripe for communicable disease. Passengers in first and second class, like Stevenson, disembarked the ship and ventured directly into New York City. Upon docking, a relieved Stevenson recounted that "we of the second cabin made our escape along with the lords of the saloon."[9] Those in steerage, however, had to remain onboard overnight—out to sea, so to speak—until they could pass through the Castle Garden Emigrant Depot the next morning.

Castle Garden, which the New York State government opened in 1855 to register immigrant passengers, was the first facility of its kind in the United States.[10] Yet the building's design proved inadequate to serve and protect the increasing number of foreigners entering the country, since the commissioners had to accommodate the functions of an immigration depot within this unusual round structure. The massive, circular, open-air sandstone fort was built in 1808–1811 as the West Battery by Jonathan Williams and John McComb Jr. (figure 1.2) Located at the southernmost tip of Manhattan, it was meant to protect against the potential threat from British battleships during the War of 1812 and had openings for twenty-eight guns that could sweep the harbor. This threat from the British was never realized, however, and a few years later, in 1815, the West Battery was renamed Castle Clinton in honor of New York City Mayor (and later governor) DeWitt Clinton. The structure was decommissioned in 1821 and leased to the city in 1824 with the goal of creating space for public entertainment, at which point it was renamed Castle Garden to reflect its new purpose. Over the next two decades, the building served as the location for events such as band concerts, wrestling matches, and fireworks shows.[11]

The facility reached the height of its popularity in the 1840s, when entrepreneurs Philip French and Christopher Heiser renovated the building. They added a stage and seating for six thousand people, and built a roof supported by slender cast-iron columns that fanned out at their capitals along the rotunda's perimeter and around a central domed cupola. The

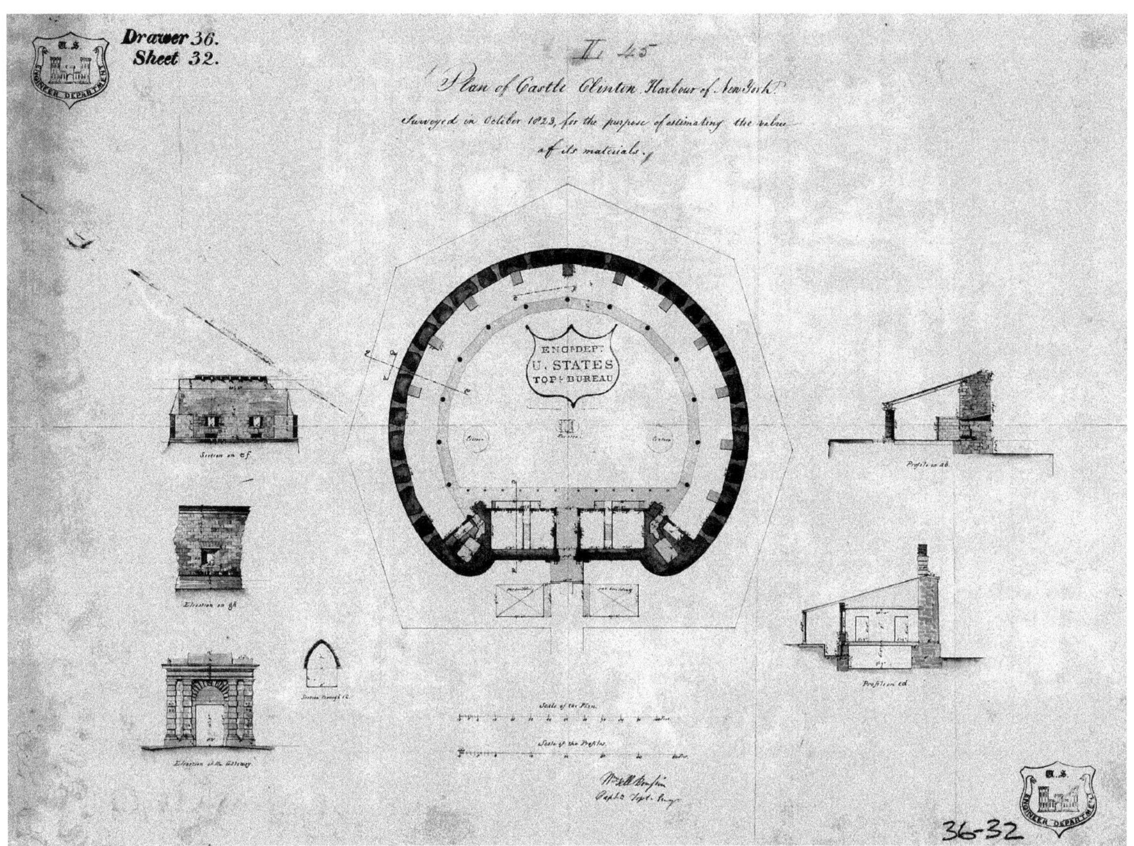

Figure 1.2. Built as the West Battery in 1808–1811, the thick sandstone walls and circular plan made it difficult to adapt the fort for immigration purposes. Courtesy of the Library of Congress, Prints & Photographs Division, Reproduction Number LC-USZ62–22399

former gun embrasures were left open to provide ventilation, while chandeliers hanging from ceiling medallions provided both artificial lighting and an opulent atmosphere; the cupola also provided natural light. To facilitate movement through the space, the rotunda was divided into four compartments, each designated by lamps of a different color. Tickets were printed in corresponding colors, and the ushers carried wands in the respective colors to direct patrons to their seats. The music hall's interior, with its delicate columns, cupola, chandeliers, and ceiling medallions, was a stark contrast to the former fort's austere construction. The renovation was a success and contributed to its selection as the site of Swedish singer Jenny Lind's American debut on September 11, 1850, which became the most successful event in Castle Garden's short history as an entertainment venue.[12] In fact, the vast majority of interior prints and drawings of Castle Garden during its music hall–era depict this singular event (figure 1.3).

Figure 1.3. Interior of Castle Garden as music hall, depicting Jenny Lind's 1850 performance. From the New York Public Library

In the years following Lind's appearance, however, no performance ever attracted the same numbers, and profits declined.

French and Heiser's lease expired in 1854, just as the Board of the Commissioners of Emigration was looking for a facility large enough to contain the increasing numbers of immigrants arriving in the city. When the fort was built, the structure was isolated from mainland Manhattan, accessible only by footbridge. But the area surrounding Castle Garden had been built up by landfill by the early 1850s and became a recreation site ideal for promenades and picnics in the fashionable First Ward (figure 1.4). Lower Manhattan residents and property owners, including shipping and railroad magnate Cornelius Vanderbilt, fervently opposed the renovation of Castle Garden into an immigration depot, fearing that "pestilential and disagreeable odors" would waft into their respectable homes, not to mention the threat of declining property values.[13] The Board of the Councilmen of New York City adamantly opposed the creation of an

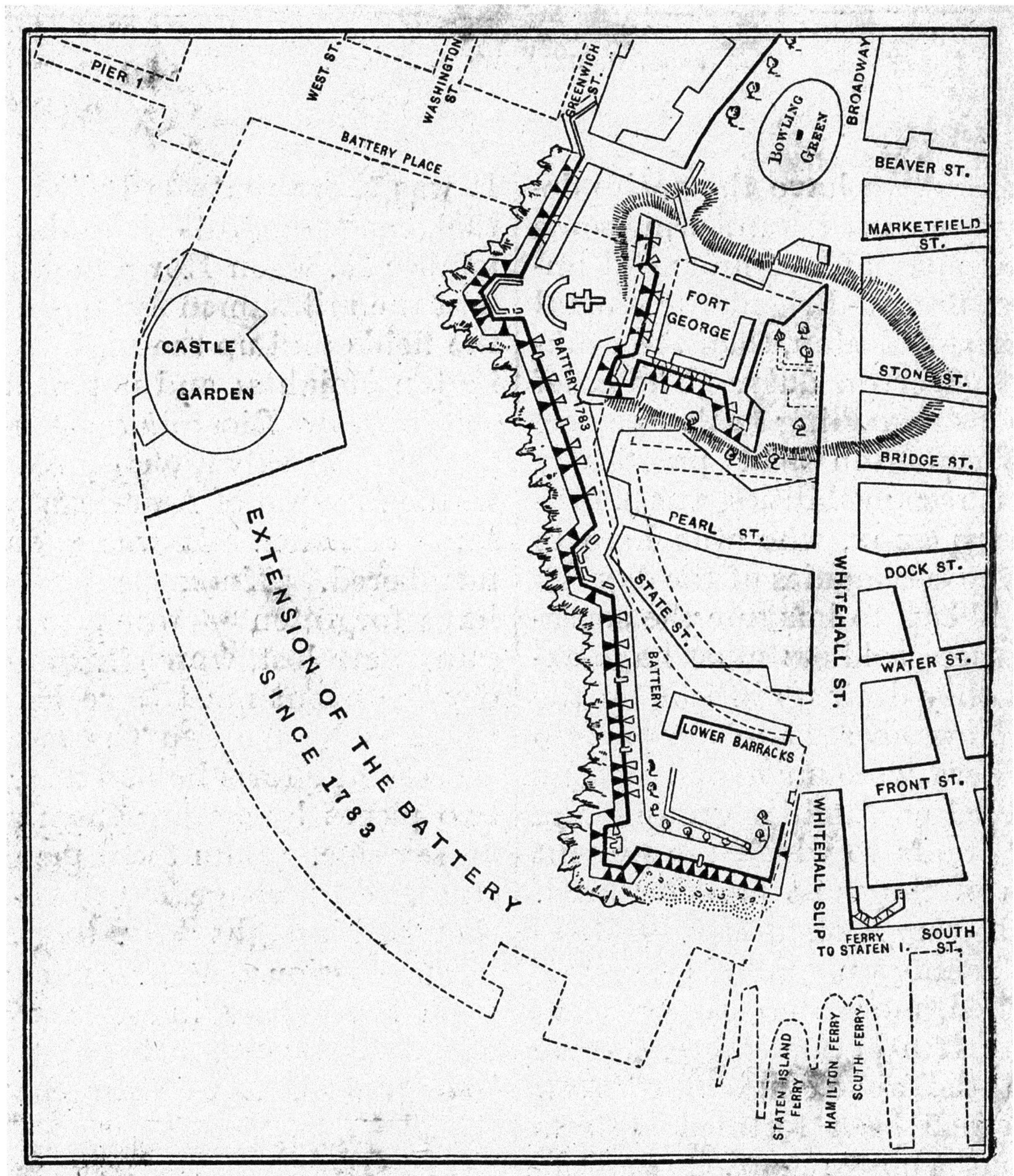

Figure 1.4. The West Battery was originally built 300 feet offshore and connected to Manhattan by a wooden bridge. By 1855, when the Castle Garden Emigrant Depot opened, the area surrounding the former fort had been built up by landfill. From the New York Public Library

immigration depot at Castle Garden as well, citing public health reasons and fewer taxes for the city due to declining property values, and they accused the commissioners of forcing immigrants to pay exaggerated rates for their baggage and railroad tickets.[14] Residents also feared losing their jobs to immigrants willing to work for lower wages. Contemporary newspaper coverage revealed that the mobs holding the noisiest demonstrations against the development of an immigrant depot, however, were led by private interests, including boardinghouse keepers and runners as well as ticket vendors—those whose livelihood was most immediately in jeopardy.[15]

The use of Castle Garden as an immigrant depot was also widely disparaged in city newspapers. The *New York Times* noted the irony that the structure had been "built to keep off the British, and now it is used as a nursery for them," by which the journalist was referring to lower-class English immigrants.[16] An August 14, 1855, *New York Tribune* article described a meeting of boardinghouse runners outside Castle Garden, where they argued that the "next step would be to take possession of the houses of citizens for hospitals," and that Castle Garden was now "a pest-house"—that is, a location for those infected with plague or other infectious diseases.[17] Their fearmongering was based on potential loss of income if immigrants were protected within Castle Garden's walls, and riling up local residents was one way to prevent the facility's opening. Fear that Europe's "riffraff" would congregate around the building led the commissioners to propose enclosing the area with a high board fence. The commissioners' assurance that the facility and its patrons would be isolated from the city did little to quell the fears and disapproval of New Yorkers.

The commissioners moved forward with their plans to convert Castle Garden into an immigration facility, signing the lease in May 1855. Under the skylit domed roof, workers removed the six thousand seats and replaced them with wooden benches to accommodate seating for between two thousand and four thousand people.[18] Where the stage once stood, an iron staircase now rose to the Office of the Superintendent of the Commissioners of Emigration. Signs posted in English indicated the Registration, Information, and Railroad Departments in the rotunda's center at an enclosed quadrangle of desks. Barriers on either side of the entrance encompassed two alleyways and extended to the central quadrangle of desks to ensure all were registered. The cast-iron columns and decorated ceiling allowed the rotunda to retain its air of elegance from its days as an entertainment venue (figure 1.5). Two contemporary accounts describe a fountain in the rotunda, with one reporter stating that its "purifying influence upon the atmosphere is most perceptible."[19] Although

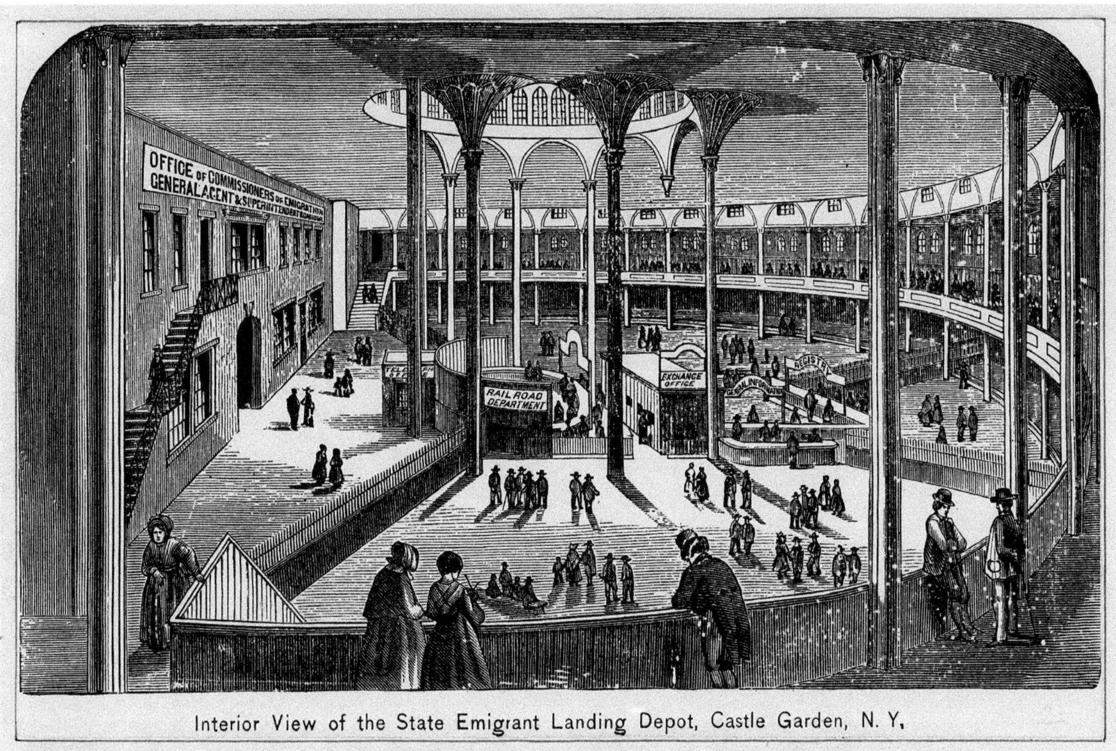

Figure 1.5. "Interior view of the State Emigrant Landing Depot, Castle Garden, N.Y," c. 1861–1880. The fanned capitals and dome remain present from the building's theater days, but the seats and stage have been removed. Where the stage once stood is now the commissioner's office, and the central floor is reserved for the registration, money exchange, and transportation desks. From the New York Public Library

these descriptions include a fountain, contemporary interior prints and drawings do not depict this feature. It is possible the fountain existed near the refreshment rooms closer to the entrance. Unfortunately, any architectural plans for the immigrant depot were likely destroyed during a fire in later years.

For steerage passengers, arrival at Castle Garden meant the long and arduous sea voyage was behind them, and they could perform basic hygiene at the depot to ready themselves for the next leg of their journey. Near the main entrance, the music hall's once lavish refreshment rooms were converted into men's and women's restrooms containing massive twenty-foot-long basins with continuously running water and rows of sinks.[20] In an 1855 article describing the facilities at Castle Garden, the *Albany Evening Journal* emphasized that immigrants were given the opportunity to cleanse themselves before going on to their destinations: "[. . .] soap is not only suggestively handy, but has to be used. Every immigrant landing at the Castle, well enough to stand the process, inevitably is washed clean before he, she or it gets out."[21] The clearly derogatory attitude—referring to a person as "it"—and the sanitary requirements indicate that the amenity was an attempt on the commissioners' part to quell the general public's fears as much as it was an opportunity for the travel-weary immigrants to bathe.

Registration occurred at the building's center, where clerks sat at a quadrangle of desks, facing two lines where multilingual employees sorted the travelers into English and non-English speakers. In ledgers with columns running vertically down each page, the clerks recorded each person's name, former place of residence, intended destination, and the amount of money in their possession. During the registration process, station employees transferred luggage from the ship into Castle Garden to be weighed and stored. Once registered, immigrants proceeded to other agents in the quadrangle to exchange money, have baggage transported to their destinations, buy railroad tickets, or find a job or place to stay from persons or organizations previously inspected and licensed by immigration officials.[22] By 1868, a Labor Exchange (the nineteenth-century name for an employment agency) established an office in Castle Garden to aid immigrants in seeking jobs without falling prey to defrauders waiting outside the walls.

With no separate rooms designated for dining, sleeping, or for those waiting for transportation, throngs of people crowded the rotunda and its galleries (figure 1.6). As described in testimonies from the August 1887 congressional investigations, the building's open plan resulted in an often chaotic and crowded atmosphere. While they waited to depart for the ferries that would take them to the New Jersey railroad stations, immigrants slept on the wooden benches or bare floors. Groups of people gathered in areas, some clustered around benches and some blocked stairways and walkways. This open plan provided a sharp contrast to the carefully organized space that would later be built at Ellis Island.

While initially funded by the state government, in 1882, when the federal government levied a fifty-cent head tax on all immigrants (the first federal law to do so), a portion of that tax was allotted to New York State to maintain services at Castle Garden, the country's busiest port of entry. With these federal funds, the commissioners were finally able to expand the facility. The building's circular plan and six-foot-thick stone walls made it impracticable to expand Castle Garden itself. The unsuitable building plan resulted in administrative chaos as well. Agents were unable to work efficiently to shuttle passengers among the crowds to the appropriate agency. Some immigrants needed to purchase rail tickets and

INTERIOR OF CASTLE GARDEN.

Figure 1.6. Unlike the relatively calm atmosphere in Figure 1.5, this illustration from *Harper's Magazine* (March 1871) depicts Castle Garden's more accurate crowded and chaotic environment. Courtesy of the Library of Congress, Prints & Photographs Division, Reproduction Number LC-USZ62–58658

transfer baggage for further travel; others sought employment in New York; and still others were waiting for relatives to retrieve them.

As demand for more space grew, the commissioners authorized construction of independent facilities around the former fort and most of the property, except for a portion along the shoreline, was enclosed by a wooden fence (figure 1.7). The addition of a baggage house on the main building's south side meant that luggage could be unloaded directly from the ships. It had previously been stored in a small section of the rotunda where, according to the 1858 annual report, "baggage was heaped up in a contracted space, and every person who had a claim, or pretended to have a claim, was necessarily permitted free access to overhaul it, disarrange checks, and thus, too frequently, had opportunity to purloin the property

Figure 1.7. "Castle Garden, view of grounds," stereograph, 1870. Due to increased immigration, various outbuildings were erected at Castle Garden to accommodate increased immigration. From the New York Public Library

of other parties."[23] The expansion of services at Castle Garden aided the steerage travelers until they were either picked up by relatives or ready to depart by rail. This fenced-in facility also ensured, however, that the steerage passengers would be vetted before they were set free on the New York City streets. It was a true testament to the class system, since the first- and second-class passengers, including Stevenson, were not required to pass through Castle Garden. In reality, three-quarters of all immigrants sailing into the Port of New York traveled by rail further into the interior United States to settle, meaning that most, like Stevenson, did not remain in the city for long.

"Here I Was, at Last in America"

Stevenson and other first- and second-class travelers who disembarked the *Devonia* bypassed Castle Garden, instead heading directly into New York City before continuing their journey west the next day. After hearing the tales of M'Naughten and others, "all inquired after the address of a respectable hotel." Stevenson was fortunate to have made friends with someone named Mr. Jones who had already been to New York and was well known at the "humble hostelry" where he and Stevenson would be staying. Reunion House, a two-story, yellow-painted inn located at 10

West Street, about a quarter of a mile from Castle Garden, cost twenty-five cents for a meal and the same price for a night's lodging. Since it was raining heavily, the two men rode in a baggage wagon the short distance to Reunion House, which "took us but a few minutes, though it cost us a good deal of money." The exorbitant costs charged by baggage handlers and many of the city's boardinghouses were notorious, although at least Stevenson was able to stay at a reputable facility that had been vetted by his travel companion. Nevertheless, Stevenson found the room to be eerily similar to the one described by M'Naughten. The small, plain room was furnished with a bed, a chair, and some clothes pegs; the only light came from the hallway and from a window that led to another apartment, where they could see three men sleeping. Jones took the bed and Stevenson camped on the floor, although he had a restless night, never closing his eyes for fear he would be robbed or, even worse, killed. In the morning, Stevenson ran through the rain across an uncovered courtyard to the lavatory, where another Scotsman was washing his face. Stevenson "began to grow sick at heart for my fellow-emigrants," for this was not the first person he had met who was unable to find employment despite searching for months, and who had run out of money.[24]

It rained "with patient fury" as Stevenson completed his errands around the city before departing west. He visited the bank, post office, a bookshop, the money exchange, and the railway office, where he purchased a ticket on the Pennsylvania Railroad. By the time he returned to his room at Reunion House, he changed into dry clothes and decided to leave the soaked ones there, "lay[ing] in a pulp in the middle of a pool upon the floor of Mitchell's kitchen," since he would ruin his other clothes if he packed them, and he had no way to quickly dry them out.[25] The landlord hired someone to take Stevenson's baggage to the ferry depot, where he waited along with his fellow immigrants to cross the Hudson River to the railway station.

Waiting alongside Stevenson on this Monday morning were passengers from four steamships: one ship had arrived on Saturday night, another Sunday morning, Stevenson's own on Sunday afternoon, and still another Monday morning. Since there were no immigrant trains on Sundays, the steerage passengers had to wait in Castle Garden, while others, like Stevenson, occupied the city's boardinghouses. Stevenson purchased his railroad ticket in the city, while the steerage passengers purchased their tickets within the immigrant depot. Since its opening in 1855, the New York Central and the New York & Erie railroad companies sold tickets within Castle Garden, and by the 1860s the Pennsylvania Railroad joined the transportation pool called the Castle Garden Agency.[26] The participating railroads decided on fixed passenger rates and divided the immigrant traffic among themselves: 35 percent each to the New York Central and New York & Erie, and the remaining 30 percent to the Pennsylvania Railroad. This division of immigrant traffic meant that travelers were not always granted tickets on the most direct routes. And, although these three railroad companies sold tickets to all immigrants leaving Castle Garden by rail, their lines did not carry passengers to their destinations in the western United States; the Castle Garden Agency lines had separate agreements with railroad companies further west and south of New York. Trains for the three companies carried passengers to major cities, such as Chicago, where they transferred to other railroad lines to continue their journey—all on the one ticket purchased at Castle Garden. Commissioner Kennedy estimated there were actually more than seventy railroads whose tickets were sold inside Castle Garden, despite the fact that there were agents for only three railroad companies present in the building.[27] Thus, even though these three lines controlled immigrant traffic in the early years of Castle Garden, many other railroad companies benefited as well.

The transportation network in Castle Garden allowed regulation and control of immigration, isolating travelers from the general public while also allowing the railroads to maximize profits. Despite later accusations and corruption charges, the commissioners viewed the railroad pool as the lesser of two evils. They now had some control over the transportation offered to the passengers, whereas previously immigrants were prey to defrauders waiting outside the building. A railroad pool also effectively reduced competition among the railroad companies and allowed them to increase profits by gaining exclusive access to immigrant traffic and fixing their own rates. Yet even though the Castle Garden Agency was under the supervision of the commissioners of emigration, the companies still had some freedom in their operations since they paid rent and the cost of utilities for the area they occupied within the depot. When accused by the media of overcharging immigrant passengers, railroad representatives cited the cost of operating within Castle Garden as the reason for not offering better rates.[28]

Not only was there disorganization in the physical environment at Castle Garden, but there was also administrative chaos. The press launched complaints against the Castle Garden Agency that, because of its efforts to divide traffic evenly and also make a profit, immigrants were often left to draw their own conclusions about routes or told to go a certain route without explanation. The superintendent of Castle Garden, Henry J. Jackson, testified that immigrants arriving with prepaid tickets—that is, tickets purchased in one's native country for both sea and rail travel—did not have a choice of railroad route upon arrival in the United States.[29] Thus, due to the division of traffic between the railroad companies, routes were potentially longer for immigrants depending on which line carried the passengers. Missionaries and immigrant aid societies argued that immigrants paid 20 percent more for tickets at Castle Garden than they would have otherwise and that they were overcharged for baggage. The Castle Garden Agency denied all charges brought against it in state investigations, first in 1858 and then again in 1866, when the commissioner of emigration revealed that the Castle Garden Agency circumvented regulations on immigrant fares by charging low rates on only part of the route. It was also discovered that these segregated trains took longer to reach their destinations than those providing regular service and that this lost time added to the immigrants' overall expense.[30] Operations in Castle Garden largely remained unchanged, although in an attempt to aid travelers, the commissioners employed agents at common transfer points and destinations in New York State to aid in train transfers and offer assistance to those in need. The high cost of this practice led, however, to its discontinuation in 1875.[31]

A fire on July 9, 1876, left Castle Garden almost entirely destroyed, with little left except the exterior walls and a few outbuildings on the northern side—the labor exchange, medical quarters, and intelligence offices.[32] The commissioners temporarily transferred immigrant processing to the nearby Barge Office, located east of Castle Garden at the end of Whitehall Street, where the Staten Island Ferry Terminal now stands. Although neighborhood residents and city newspaper editors argued that Castle Garden not be rebuilt for immigration purposes and that, instead, the area be left as a park for the citizens of New York to enjoy, the commissioners planned to rebuild.[33] Construction was completed just over two months later and cost only half of the purported damages.[34] The reconstructed interior featured none of the former music hall's elaborate decorations. The gallery was not replaced during reconstruction; now only the rotunda's floor was available to the waiting immigrants. The new roof provided better lighting and ventilation than the previous one and the gun embrasures in the structure's walls were enclosed with glass windows for the first time in the building's history. Where the delicate cast-iron columns had once supported the roof and decorated ceiling, thick timber posts with splayed trusses supported exposed crossbeams. It was readily apparent why the reconstruction of this barnlike interior cost far less than the cost of damages. Any remnant of the former music hall was no longer; the facility was rebuilt as rapidly as possible to accommodate the ever-increasing numbers of immigrants arriving in New York. It was a transitory, and necessary, location for moving people through the space as quickly and as economically as possible. A *Harper's Weekly* article from May 27, 1882, likened the registration process' efficiency to that of a factory: "Goethe is said to have pronounced a factory the most poetical sight he had ever seen. In the same sense we may call Castle Garden the most poetical sight a New-Yorker can see."[35] Given the sheer number of people entering the country through New York, efficiency was a necessity.

Immigration continued to rise during the 1880s, as passengers increasingly arrived from southern and eastern European countries. By 1887, the railroad pool had expanded to seven companies under the new name of the Castle Garden Joint Agency.[36] The agency allotted immigrant traffic among its members as equitably as possible; however, this proved difficult when routes were served by several different railroad companies, some of whom contracted agents outside of Castle Garden in an effort to reach their desired passenger percentages. This new agency was part of a larger organization known as the Immigrant Clearing House, which divided and regulated all immigrant traffic from eastern ports. The Immigrant Clearing House, in turn, was part of the Trunk Line Association (founded in the late 1870s), a powerful railroad pool that negotiated rates for numerous railroad lines east of the Mississippi River.[37]

The significance of this railroad pool cannot be overstated. It set fixed immigrant fares and baggage rates, regulated the sale of immigrant tickets, and handled the rail business of combination tickets booked from steamship companies. At port cities, one local agency, represented by an employee called the joint agent, carried out the terms set forth by the Immigrant Clearing House. In New York, the joint agent operated out of Castle Garden and reported back to the Trunk Line Passenger Committee. Therefore, instead of reporting solely to the commissioners of emigration, the Castle Garden Joint Agency was held accountable by this larger organization formed specifically to deal with immigrant traffic. What remained the same, however, was that the new agency continued to charge fraudulent rates and immigrants were not allowed to choose direct routes to their destinations. Several railroads even contracted with steamship lines directly to offer lower immigrant rates than those offered inside Castle Garden in order to secure more passengers than they had been allotted by the joint agent. Other railroads sold tickets outside of Castle Garden at lower rates that threatened the railroad pool altogether.[38]

During the 1880s, the nefarious operations occurring at Castle Garden became a national concern. An 1886 complaint filed on behalf of the American Emigrant Company, an organization whose goal was to assist immigrants in settling in the United States, resulted in a congressional investigation and the railroad pool's termination two years later.[39] One of the allegations was that the thirteen-dollar immigrant rate for railroad tickets from New York to Chicago was unjust and unreasonable since the train accommodations were poor and the journey sometimes took up to sixty hours. By comparison, the second-class fare for nonimmigrant passengers was seventeen dollars and the journey was less than thirty-six hours. Furthermore, the American Emigrant Company claimed immigrants were not given a choice of routes and those traveling together were often separated. An immigrant's journey navigating the complexities of the space in-between, then, was needlessly convoluted due to the slower travel times of the segregated trains in favor of railroad profiteering.

During the investigation, Joseph Pulitzer's *New York World* vehemently attacked the operations at Castle Garden, citing violations of New York laws as well as the Interstate Commerce Act of 1887—the first piece of legislation to oversee the railroad industry's conduct that, until this point, had been privately owned and entirely unregulated.[40] Pulitzer, who had emigrated from Hungary at the age of seventeen, had a personal interest in the treatment of immigrants. He was known for launching crusades against corruption, particularly concentrating on issues of concern to marginalized groups, such as immigrants, women, and the working class—groups whom Pulitzer recognized as potential readers. In one article, the *World* complained that Castle Garden had been established to protect the immigrants arriving on American shores, but instead the commissioners of emigration throw them "into the hands of a heartless railroad pool that treats them most shamefully and squeezes all it can out of them [. . .].[41] Subsequent hearings held in New York revealed charges of immigrant abuse, evasion of laws, and mismanagement. Agents were found to be knowingly charging immigrants twice for baggage shipment; railroads made enormous profit from ticket sales, often selling tickets at higher than usual rates; and money changers did not list rates at market value. Congress determined that Castle Garden's facilities were inadequate for the number of people passing through its doors daily. Investigators and the press alike proposed that the Castle Garden facility be shut down.

The corruption rampant at Castle Garden was but one reason for closing the facility. The structure was not built to accommodate such crowds, and attempts to repurpose the space were inadequate. Not only did the crowded rotunda generate a tumultuous atmosphere, but the need for additional buildings to house separate departments also interrupted the movement of people and baggage through the facility. The immigrant depot was in fact a new building type, and the details of its construction and management were "necessarily experimental and uncertain," as

Superintendent John A. Kennedy observed.[42] A multitude of problems arose in both the depot's physical space and on the administrative level, making it "almost impossible to properly inspect the large numbers of persons who arrive daily," according to the appointed committee's chairman, Congressman Melbourne Ford of Michigan, leaving him to declare "the local administration of affairs at Castle Garden [. . .] was a perfect farce."[43] Ford's report exposed problems not only at New York but also other port cities, citing among its chief issues improper inspection, which led to an overburdening of charitable institutions with paupers and medical cases (including those suffering from both physical and mental health ailments). The issues at Castle Garden, particularly those related to finances, were the impetus for the federal government to take control of immigration from the states.

Immigration remained a fiscal concern, and the new Bureau of Immigration was established as part of the US Department of the Treasury on March 3, 1891.[44] A head tax levied on foreign passengers funded the staff and facility maintenance necessary for immigrant inspection at American ports of entry. It was not until 1903, when all operations associated with business within the Department of the Treasury were moved to the newly established Department of Commerce and Labor, that the Bureau of Immigration was transferred as well. This shift of immigration from state to federal control was part of the federal government's gradual expansion that had begun following the Civil War. In the antebellum years, the federal government's role was relatively minor: it established a network of national banks and promoted agricultural and transportation development through land grants, while individual state actions largely overruled the weaker central government. Disputes over states' rights led to the Civil War in the 1860s, with the crucial issue of slavery polarizing the nation. In the decades that followed, during Reconstruction and beyond, the federal government became increasingly centralized, taking over matters—including immigration—that had once been state responsibilities. The federal government gained even more power with the passing of the Sixteenth Amendment in 1913, which implemented a federal income tax, and the Seventeenth Amendment in the same year, which established direct election of state senators and thus shifted the balance of power from the states to the centralized government.

Federal control of American borders took place during a wave of intense immigration to the United States, when rapid industrialization and the availability of jobs attracted millions of foreign citizens at the turn of the century. New York was ill-equipped to handle this influx due to the insufficient facilities at Castle Garden and the corruption that pervaded its administration. When the federal government took over immigration from the states, it resolved to establish a new immigrant facility in the Port of New York designed to handle the hundreds of thousands of arrivals each year and support a more organized administrative system.

"We Stood Like Sheep"

After his arrival in New York on Sunday, August 17, 1879, Stevenson spent one night at a boardinghouse, but for the steerage passengers who had arrived the night prior, on Saturday, this meant two miserable nights in Castle Garden, since no immigrant trains ran on Sundays. By Monday, August 18, when the weekend's travelers could depart New York City by ferry to reach the New Jersey railroad stations, the ferry depot was even more chaotic than usual. Stevenson was dismayed, observing: "It was plain that the whole system, if system there was, had utterly broken down under the strain of so many passengers."[45] Stevenson received his ticket from the clerk and then waited an hour in the baggage room, which was "crowded thick with emigrants, and [was] heavy and rank with the atmosphere of dripping clothes."[46] When it was time to head to the pier, Stevenson and the others were directed to a long shed leading downhill from West Street to the river. The shed was dark, with the wind blowing through it from end to end. Hundreds of passengers and tons of baggage filled the long space, where passengers "stood like sheep with the porters charging among us like so many maddened sheep boys," pushing carts full of baggage to the ferry slip.[47] In the crowd's choking crush, Stevenson saved a small child from being run over by a baggage cart. But due to the bedlam around them, neither the child's mother nor the porter even noticed Stevenson's heroic act. The frantic and stressful atmosphere certainly had a significant effect on the travelers' spirit. In these miserable conditions, Stevenson realized, "We had accepted this purgatory as a child accepts the conditions of the world."[48] Ferry employees lit the shed's lamps and began nudging passengers forward onto the boat heading to Jersey City. The rain continued steadily, and the strong wind rocked the vessel in sudden waves. Once filled, the ferry, with its "freight of wet and silent emigrants," crept across the river—a strong contrast to the massive, illuminated steamers coming into port at a faster clip, with strains of music heralding their approach.[49]

By the end of the nineteenth century, New York Harbor had become one of the busiest ports in the world. When the federal government assumed control of immigration in 1891, Congress resolved to build a new inspection facility on an island location, a move that set a precedent for the federal immigration facility on Angel Island erected decades later on the West Coast, even though the two would function completely differently. In New York, there were two possible locations from which to choose: Ellis Island, which had been occupied by the navy since the 1790s and used to store ammunition since 1835, and Bedloe's Island (now known as Liberty Island), the site of Frédéric-Auguste Bartholdi's recently erected Statue of Liberty (1886). Not surprisingly, the proposal of Bedloe's Island was met with dismay from the New York press, with the most aggressive attacks coming from Joseph Pulitzer's *New York World*, which had led the campaign to raise money for the statue's pedestal. The *World* even contacted Bartholdi himself, who believed the proposed plan to be a "downright desecration." One editorial claimed that surrounding the statue with buildings "will be to dwarf and humiliate it." [50] Bedloe's Island had become a tourist destination immediately following the Statue of Liberty's dedication on October 28, 1886. Treasury secretary William Windom, the head of the new federal immigrant depot, noted that those opposed to an immigration depot on Bedloe's Island believed "that the Goddess of Liberty would gather up her skirts in disdain and contempt of the immigrants from foreign countries, and that the arrival of the immigrants upon our shores would contaminate her."[51] Ironic, considering that in 1903, a decade after the opening of Ellis Island, the statue took on new meaning as a symbol of liberty for those arriving on American shores. It was in that year that Emma Lazarus's poem with its infamous lines, "Give me your tired, your poor, / Your huddled masses yearning to breathe free, / [. . .]" was mounted on the inside of the statue.

The depot's proposed location on Bedloe's Island presented the same issue as Castle Garden: New Yorkers did not want to be in proximity to an immigrant receiving station. The reason the Treasury Department decided to move the station to an island in the first place was to maintain separation of citizens and new arrivals. Coincidentally, at the same time that the media was attacking Windom's proposal to build on Bedloe's Island, New Jersey legislators and newspaper editors launched a third crusade (earlier efforts occurred in 1869 and 1876), asking Congress to remove the highly explosive naval powder magazine located on Ellis Island. Removing the explosives and erecting an immigration station on Ellis Island would appease both parties—those promoting safety in the harbor and those supporting preservation of Bedloe's Island. On April 11, 1890, President Benjamin Harrison signed the bill to remove the powder magazine and appropriate $75,000 "to enable the Secretary of the Treasury to improve said Ellis Island for immigration purposes."[52] The Ellis Island project cost a total of $500,000 and included several major endeavors:

Figure 1.8. The original Ellis Island immigration station shortly after its completion in January 1892. Courtesy of the Library of Congress, Prints & Photographs Division, Reproduction Number LC-USZ62–58723

dredging a channel for the ships; enlarging the island by landfill to nearly double its 3.3 acres; building more than 850 feet of docks; and constructing a three-story wooden building (approximately 400 by 150 feet) for inspection and registration, with separate structures for a hospital, boiler house, laundry, cisterns, and electric light plant. Wharves on the island's southwest side were arranged so that passengers could disembark from two vessels at once before heading into the administration building on the northwest side.

This administration building, designed by Jacob Bachmeyer of the US Public Buildings Service, was a unique combination of railroad station, hospital, prison, and hotel. Multiple departments, including registration, medical services, transportation, and baggage, would need to be arranged in a coherent manner to facilitate the daily movement of thousands of bodies through the space—all within the two-and-a-half-story rectangular structure, which featured a gable roof and four towers, one at each corner (figure 1.8). The first floor included a baggage room, two private offices, a general office, a customs baggage room and space for the customs inspector, and water closets. Officials examined and registered immigrants on the second floor, which, in addition to the registration room, contained a railroad ticket office, railway clerks' room, information bureau, lunch counter, telegraph office, money changer's office, six waiting rooms, a linen counter, three detention rooms, administrative offices, a vault, and water closets. The third floor or balcony floor contained no room designations on building plans dating from 1896.[53] Although the main building received praise from contemporary architectural critics, the auxiliary buildings were simple wooden structures with little to no decoration. Commissioner Joseph Senner called them "a row of ugly, ramshackle tinderboxes."[54] Some of the existing military buildings on the island, constructed of brick and stone, were remodeled for new purposes. For instance, workers enlarged one of the barracks to form a two-story dormitory for detained immigrants.[55] Bachmeyer initially considered iron construction for the facility; however, he selected Georgia pine as the primary building material in order to lessen costs, a move that the government would regret in just five years' time.

The immigration depot at Ellis Island opened with little ceremony on January 1, 1892.[56] It is possible that with the barrage of media criticisms directed toward them for the conditions at the Barge Office, where registration occurred after Castle Garden's 1890 closure, the government did not want to welcome even more criticism. Government officials and the media alike praised the new facility. A *Harper's Weekly* journalist compared the new management with that of its failed predecessor: "the Federal government does not appear to be overestimating its needs so much as to be putting to shame the neglectful State officials who previously mismanaged the business."[57] The building's layout allowed for a systematic inspection and registration process, one that far surpassed the disorderly procedures at Castle Garden. Those employed with the Immigration Bureau were pleased with both the facility's spacious accommodations and its island site. The only complaints about the new building published at the time were from railroad officials, who believed it to be too large, which required much running around on their part to get various passengers together. A *New York Times* reporter rebuked that given the number of immigrants the facility must accommodate, "finding fault with its size was like complaining of a circle for being round."[58] Various departments each received their own space in the new building, instead of shared space like they had in the Castle Garden rotunda. "The new receiving station," stated the secretary's report for 1891, "besides adding vastly to the comfort, convenience, and sanitary well-being of the arriving immigrants, will enable the inspection officers to perform their duties much more thoroughly, effectively, and expeditiously."[59] The building was a success, and a vast improvement on the facilities at Castle Garden. That success, however, was short-lived.

Shortly after midnight on June 14, 1897, a fire broke out on the island and destroyed the main building and several smaller structures, as well as many New York State and federal immigration records.[60] Word of the fire spread quickly since the completion of cables to New York City for telegraph and telephone communication via Governors Island had been completed only the day before. Medical staff and night guards worked quickly to evacuate the approximately 191 immigrants detained on the island that evening. The rescue and evacuation of all immigrants and employees lasted seventeen minutes from the time a night watchman first sounded the alarm. All escaped unharmed to New York by ferry. The fire's cause was never determined. Commissioner Senner expressed his relief to a *New York Tribune* reporter that no lives were lost and declared that "when the government rebuilds, it will be forced to put up decent fireproof structures."[61] In the five years that the station had been open, nearly one and a half million immigrants had passed through its doors. The purpose-built facility at Ellis Island allowed immigration officials to inspect and register immigrants with increased efficiency and to comfortably accommodate foreign travelers. Yet with seven hundred immigrants arriving in New York the day after the fire, and another seven thousand known to be on ships bound for New York Harbor, the Treasury Department needed an immediate solution.

The Department of Parks for the City of New York (now the Department of Parks and Recreation) had converted Castle Garden into an aquarium in 1896, so those facilities were no longer available for use. Instead, the Immigration Bureau sent arriving passengers back to the Barge Office. The building, however, was far too small for long-term processing. Crowding at the Barge Office was far worse than that at Castle Garden, and unfortunately so was the corruption under the administration of Commissioner Thomas Fitchie and his assistant Edward F. McSweeney.[62] The dreadful conditions at the Barge Office amplified the need for a properly designed immigration station. The *New York Tribune* described the Barge Office as "grimy, gloomy [. . .] more suggestive of an enclosure for animals than a receiving station for prospective citizens of the United States."[63] The new facility could not be finished quickly enough; the federal government was beginning to feel the same pressure the New York commissioners of emigration had felt when the corruption and inadequate facilities at Castle Garden were scrutinized by the press. Ellis Island was thought to be the solution to the problems encountered at Castle Garden, but its wooden construction ultimately proved otherwise.

In September 1897, a few months after the fire, the Treasury Department initiated an architecture competition under the Tarsney Act, which allowed architects in private practice to participate in competitive design programs for federal projects—Ellis Island became one of the first projects

Figure 1.9. Ellis Island aerial view, c. 1920. The government expanded Ellis Island over the years, adding Island Three in 1913 and filling in the area between Islands Two and Three in 1934 [text added by author]. Courtesy of the Library of Congress, Prints & Photographs Division, Reproduction Number LC-DIG-pcrd-1d04667

under this act.[64] Treasury secretary Lyman Gage, under the recommendation of George B. Post, then president of the American Institute of Architects, invited several prominent New York firms to participate, including Boring & Tilton; Alfred E. Barlow; Carrère & Hastings; Bruce Price; and McKim, Mead & White. Washington architect John L. Smithmeyer, who had been hired by the Treasury Department to conduct preliminary studies of the island after the fire, was also invited to join.[65] Supervising architect James Knox Taylor (1897–1912) judged the competition along with Robert S. Peabody of Boston and Theophilus P. Chandler of Philadelphia. They selected Boring & Tilton as the competition's winner.

The requirements set forth by Taylor's office determined much of the new station's character. Taylor called for two separate structures: a hospital building and a main building, with the latter containing annexes for the reception, registration, and examination of immigrants, in addition to sleeping quarters—all to be located on about 20 acres. The island originally encompassed a land area of 3.3 acres, which meant 11 acres of landfill were needed for the 1892 immigration facility. By the time of Ellis

Island's 1954 closure, the island comprised 27.5 acres (figure 1.9). This expansion was necessary to accommodate several thousand immigrants daily in addition to several hundred employees. Of paramount importance was that the new station be fireproof and permanent, unlike its hastily built wooden predecessor.[66]

New York architects William Alciphron Boring and Edward Lippincott Tilton, both graduates of the École des Beaux-Arts in Paris, submitted a competition design with a linear, southwest–northeast axis of three primary fireproof buildings—an immigration building occupying the site of the original main structure, a kitchen and laundry building, and a powerhouse—as well as a new island south of the original, with a ferry slip between the two, on which the hospital would be built. The first island served the public functions of inspection and processing, while the second island served the more private functions of the hospital complex. The main building's size and plan was approximately the same as its predecessor (385 feet long, 165 feet wide, and 62 feet high with the corner towers reaching a height of 100 feet), with the exception that the railroad ticket office was now on the first floor, not the second. The main building opened for service on December 17, 1900, but the hospital did not open until the following year. Throughout the construction process, the architects added auxiliary structures to the original plans, including a hospital laundry and surgeon's house. The total cost was approximately $1.5 million, more than double the original amount Congress had appropriated for its construction. Congress had not only underestimated the new facility's cost but also underestimated how many immigrants would arrive on American shores in the following decades.

Visually and logistically, the main building forms the centerpiece of Ellis Island (figure 1.10). It is the complex's largest and most visible structure as well as the space through which all immigrants entering through the Port of New York had to pass to be granted admission into the country. The dichromatic facade features red brick laid in Flemish bond with limestone trim and quoining. On both the southwest and northeast elevations, massive triple-arch entrances rising two stories emphasize the central pavilion, which is flanked by three-story wings on either side. Four towers topped by copper spires mark the central pavilion's corners. At the time of its completion, the building received praise from both the popular press and architectural critics. The *Architectural Record* lauded the "manner in which the light limestone and the red brick are used together" and noted that the arches function in "relieving and animating the sky line without disturbing it."[67] Boring & Tilton meant for the heavy-handedness of the facade to be read from a distance, to serve as a focal point in New York

Figure 1.10. Ellis Island Immigration Station, c. 1905. Courtesy of the Library of Congress, Prints & Photographs Division, Reproduction Number LC-USZ62–37784

Harbor. The *Record* notes that "the effectiveness of a 'distant prospect' is more important than that of a nearer view. [. . .] The [scale of detail] is so inflated and the fronts so 'scaled up' for the benefit of the distant spectator that, close at hand, the detail undoubtedly takes on a forced and almost bloated aspect."[68] The monumental building is thus experienced differently by the citizens admiring its reassuring presence from a distance and the harsher reality of those passing through its doors. For many immigrants, Ellis Island was a frightening place, one where medical inspectors poked and prodded, where government officials launched a series of questions in an unfamiliar language, and where the fear of being separated from one's family was all too palpable.

Historians have often noted the disparity of conditions for steerage passengers and those in cabin class on overseas journeys.[69] Although the Immigration Act of 1893 required steamship companies to provide detailed manifests or passenger lists for *all* those aboard, it was common practice for employees not to ask cabin passengers the personal questions required upon arrival in New York Harbor. When commissioner of immigration William Williams insisted in 1902 that cabin passengers undergo the same inspection as those in steerage, the Washington office backed him for a brief period of time before pressure on the commissioner-general mounted, presumably from the very passengers this would affect. He instructed Williams that "a literal compliance with the law as relating to steerage passengers and a *reasonable* compliance so far as concerns cabin passengers [emphasis added]" would be the new rule.[70] While established to protect immigrants, Ellis Island was also a physical reminder to citizens that they would be protected from the potential danger—physical and economic—that immigrants posed. Unlike wealthy passengers, who were presumed to be healthy and unlikely to become public charges, the government examined steerage passengers in order to determine their eligibility for American residence. Landing at the Barge Office signaled the end of the overseas journey for wealthier passengers like Stevenson, who passed through customs and continued on their way; however, the journey was far from over for steerage passengers.

"You May Imagine How Slowly This Filtering Proceeded"

Once docked in New York Harbor, passengers disembarked from the steamship and guards guided them onto a ferryboat headed to Ellis Island. The ferryboat filled quickly, and those who did not fit on it were loaded onto barges. Often passengers had to wait tightly packed on the boats and barges, which had no restrooms or refreshments, until all had disembarked from the vessels ahead of them. Upon arrival at Ellis Island, immigrants disembarked from two boats at a time and entered the main building by means of a covered passageway, which sheltered them from the weather as well as from "the observation of the curious," as one *New York Times* reporter noted.[71]

Here began the systematic registration process developed by government officials, where immigrants passed from inspector to inspector, each executing their duties as quickly as possible in order to shuttle immigrants through the building and into the country (or sent back out of it). Once disembarked, each ship's passengers traveled together into the main building so that federal inspectors could cross-check that specific ship's manifest. On the ground floor, large trunks and other luggage were stored in the baggage department, although most kept whatever luggage they could carry, to access it during their journey and so as not to lose

Figure 1.11. Ellis Island Registry Room, c. 1904. Courtesy of the Library of Congress, Prints & Photographs Division, Reproduction Number LC-DIG-det-4a25609

it. From there, guards shouted instructions in multiple languages and arranged people in numerical order according to the numbers printed on the tags and pinned to their coats, which corresponded to each person's respective entry on the ship's manifest. Once lined up, immigrants walked through a dark tiled corridor and climbed up a staircase to the brightly lit Registry Room.

The Registry Room, the site of medical inspection and registration, was a double-height, barrel-vaulted room. The space was the largest in the building at 200 by 100 feet (56 feet in height). Three large arched windows ran the room's length on either side and lunette windows on end walls bathed the interior in natural light. The effect was awe-inspiring as the immigrants ascended the staircase into this vast illuminated space. They were unaware, however, that as they climbed the stairs a medical inspection was already underway. A uniformed medical officer from the US Public Health Office stood at the top of the stairs looking for those with difficulty walking, shortness of breath, or any other visible malady. In oral histories of those who passed through Ellis Island, many immigrants mistook doctors for military servicemen on account of their blue uniforms. Officers marked those with general health problems with a piece of chalk before the immigrants filed on to a second doctor who inspected them for specific diseases such as tuberculosis, leprosy, or a contagious skin disease of the scalp called favus—these were diseases specifically mentioned in the law as grounds for deportation. About two of every ten or eleven immigrants were marked with a letter—B for back, H for heart trouble, L for lameness, PG for pregnancy, X for mental illness, and so forth.[72] A third doctor then inspected the immigrants' eyes for trachoma, a contagious eye infection that caused blindness and was also grounds for deportation. The doctor looked for inflammation on the inner eyelid using his fingers, a hairpin, or a buttonhook. The procedure lasted only seconds but was incredibly painful; immigrants dreaded these appropriately dubbed "buttonhook men." Fannie Kligerman, a young Jewish woman, later recalled, "This I remember well—the eye exam. It was such a fright, such a fright."[73] Inspectors directed those who did not pass medical inspections into an area enclosed by a wire screen, where they waited to be sent to the hospital or to be put on a ship heading back to Europe.

For those who passed medical inspection, registration commenced. Immigrants filed into the rows of iron railings that divided the Registry Room's main floor into narrow corridors (figure 1.11). The press and immigrant aid societies criticized these pens, as they were called at the time, as insulting and inhumane. While providing much-needed order to a complex system, little thought was given to the way in which people would experience the space. Williams addressed the concerns posed by the press and aid societies that immigrants were treated "like cattle" and "herded," stating, "Insofar as this statement may mean that they are at times crowded, and that the portions of the building set over to the use of the railroad companies are inadequate, the statement is correct."[74] Williams finally replaced the pens with wooden benches in 1911. The wait time usually lasted an hour or two on busy days, when up to and occasionally more than five thousand immigrants were processed. Interpreters guided immigrants into adjoining rows as they moved up in line. An inspector sat at the end of each aisle with the ship's manifest in front of him (figure 1.12). He noted the number pinned on each person's clothing and found it on the manifest. For approximately two minutes, the inspector questioned each traveler on their name, profession, destination in the United States, criminal record, and financial holdings. If the inspector was satisfied with the answers, the person received a landing card and proceeded to the Money Exchange

Figure 1.12. Registration desk at Ellis Island, c. 1902–1910. Photograph by Edwin Levick. From the New York Public Library

at the end of the hall before returning downstairs to collect baggage and continue their journey. If not completely satisfied with the answers, the inspector sent the immigrant to the Board of Special Inquiry in an office located in the west wing on the second floor, where three inspectors and an interpreter interrogated the person without the presence of a lawyer, although friends or relatives could be brought in to testify on the person's behalf.[75] Given the sheer number of people passing through the building daily, officials had to make rapid judgments on whether an immigrant's health and responses to inquiries were sufficient enough to be admitted into the United States.

The system established at Ellis Island could only be effective with an appropriate layout of the departments within the building. In contrast to Castle Garden, Ellis Island's architectural plan allowed the inspection and registration of immigrants to become a streamlined process in terms of the physical movement of bodies. Once immigrants completed processing

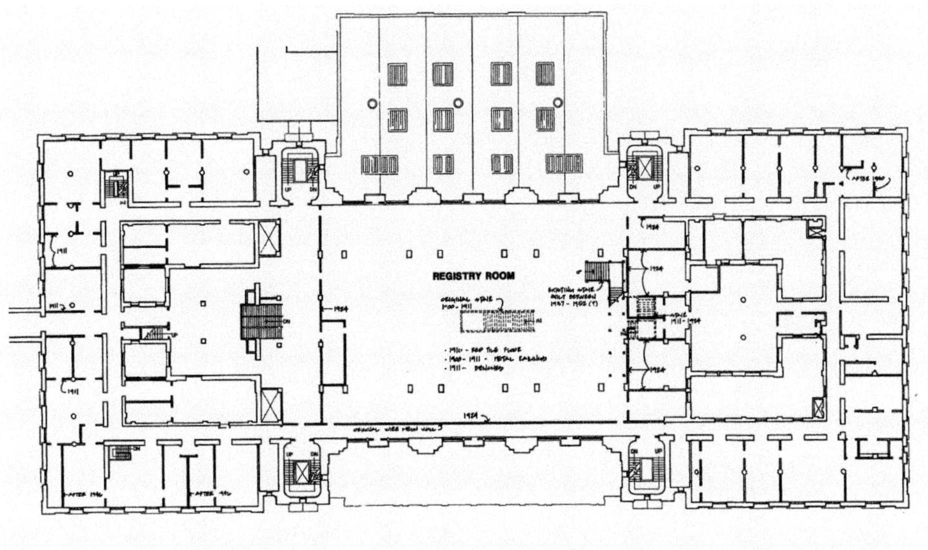

Figure 1.13. Ellis Island first-floor plan, showing the architectural changes over the course of its history. Plan prepared by Beyer Blinder Belle / Anderson Notter Finegold for the National Park Service

in the main building's Registry Room, they exited down a staircase with three doors at the bottom leading to different destinations: the north staircase led to the railroad ticket office and currency exchange; the south staircase brought passengers to the New York ferry; and the central stairs led to the detention rooms for additional inspection.[76] Called the Stairs of Separation, it was here where those who had befriended one another on their overseas journey often separated for the last time. The railroad ticket office and waiting rooms took up most of the ground floor, along with the baggage room and various missionary and immigrant aid offices.

The distribution of people throughout the building and the designated areas for each department allowed a form of organization that was impossible to achieve in Castle Garden's rotunda (figures 1.13 and 1.14). Indeed, the architects' primary concern was circulation. Boring & Tilton's design surpassed the competitors' with its "uninterrupted circulation for a continuous human flow [. . .], not subject anywhere to stoppage or congestion," as a critic for the *Architectural Record* noted in a 1902 article.[77] In the same article, the critic attempted to describe the unique building type in relatable terms: "The closest analogue to it, in familiar buildings,

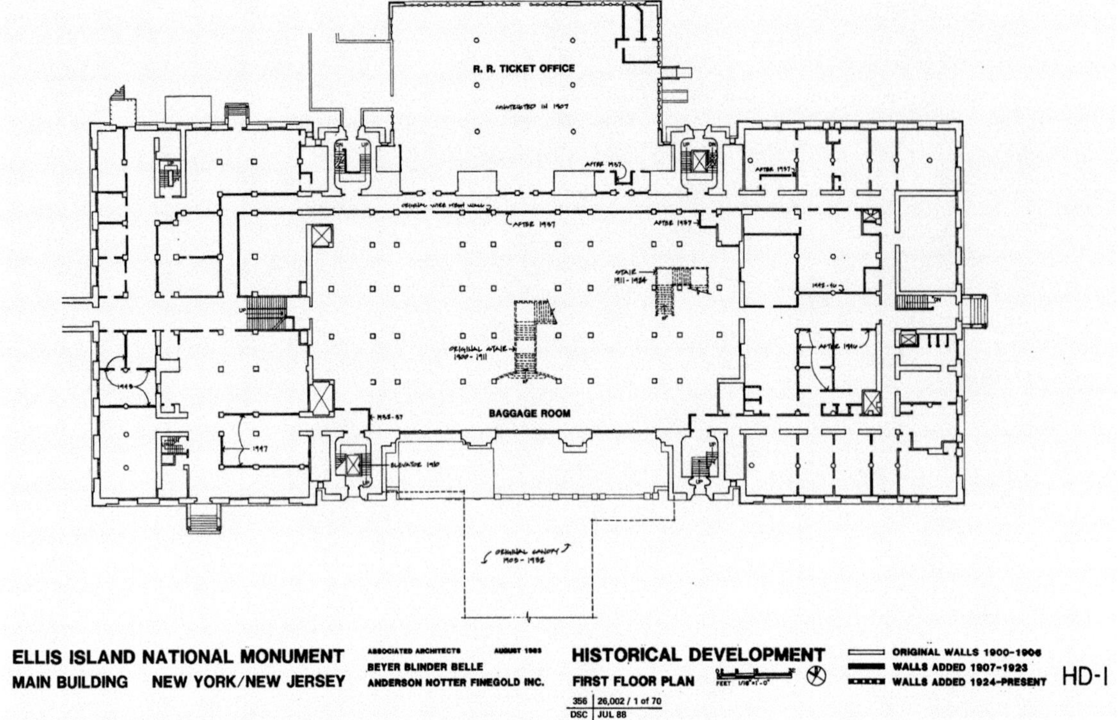

Figure 1.14. Ellis Island second-floor plan, showing the architectural changes over the course of its history. Plan prepared by Beyer Blinder Belle / Anderson Notter Finegold for the National Park Service

is doubtless the railway station [. . .] the requirement which characterizes its main and central features is the same as that of a railway station, the requirements of 'landing,' collecting and distributing great and sudden crowds with a minimum of confusion or delay [. . .]."[78] Yet the design of Ellis Island was even more complex than that of a railway station in that it also functioned as a medical facility, dormitory, and detention center. The press praised Boring & Tilton's arrangement of these functions. The *New York Times* reported "the interior arrangements are what, after all, make the station a model of completeness."[79]

Ellis Island's Beaux-Arts classicism expressed contemporary trends in federal architecture. In typical Eurocentric fashion, supervising architect Taylor expressed aspirations for classicism to become the official national architecture.[80] He insisted it was the style "best suited for government buildings," since "the experience of centuries has demonstrated that no form of architecture is so pleasing to the great mass of mankind as the classic, or some modified form of the classic."[81] This interest was hardly unique to Taylor; the preference for classical forms was heralded by architects at the École des Beaux-Arts and also dominated the 1893

World's Columbian Exposition in Chicago. The desire for monumental architecture at Ellis Island was not only steered by contemporary trends in architecture, however. Treasury Secretary Gage commented that the Ellis Island immigration station "will form what the Treasury Department set out to make it, the model immigration station of the world."[82] Taylor and the Treasury Department succeeded in establishing Ellis Island as a cultural monument, the first purpose-built government immigration station in the country. Ellis Island also achieved international fame. Boring & Tilton's design won awards at three world's fairs: a gold medal for Architecture at the Exposition Universelle, Paris (1900); a gold medal for Architecture at the Pan-American Exposition, Buffalo (1901); and a silver medal at the Louisiana Purchase Exposition, St. Louis (1904).

Despite the architectural success of Boring & Tilton's design for Ellis Island, there was one significant flaw—the facilities were too small to handle the number of immigrants arriving in the early twentieth century. When the first facility was built in 1892, immigration was still on the rise. Nearly half a million immigrants entered through New York that fiscal year. Yet by late August 1892, immigration had slowed due to a cholera scare in Europe. President Benjamin Harrison imposed strict quarantine on all vessels carrying immigrants into the United States, and subsequently, many steamship companies refused to carry emigrant passengers from foreign ports.[83] Congress's approval of stricter laws, particularly the Immigration Act of 1893, also contributed to the decrease in immigration. These reasons, along with the financial panic of that same year and the subsequent nationwide depression, worked concurrently to stem the flow of immigration into the country, reaching a low of nearly 230,000 in 1898.[84] When plans to rebuild Ellis Island were underway in the year after the fire, the commissioner-general of immigration doubted that "immigration will ever reach the volume of past years, notwithstanding the most prosperous conditions in our country."[85] Congress authorized funds to rebuild a facility that, at most, could handle 500,000 immigrants a year. The Immigration Bureau, however, was unaware that a record mass movement of foreigners into the country was about to occur in the early years of the twentieth century.

Once the American economy recovered at the turn of the century, immigration increased once again, with migrants escaping religious, racial, and political persecution in their native countries or seeking relief from famine and economic hardship. Construction crews became a permanent fixture at Ellis Island in the first decade of the twentieth century as the government struggled to expand the complex to accommodate this growth. In 1904, workers built a new dining room and also erected a playground on the roof to occupy detained children. Meanwhile, immigrants occupied sidewalks for several hours a day to alleviate overcrowded rooms.[86] In 1905, commissioner of immigration Robert Watchorn (1905–1909) built a new refrigerator plant and dormitory, the latter accommodating the approximately 20 percent of immigrants who were detained overnight.[87]

The following year, Congress authorized funds for a much-needed addition to the hospital building. Despite this addition, Ellis Island lacked facilities to treat and isolate those with contagious diseases. Those with typhus, cholera, leprosy, or smallpox were sent to the New York Quarantine Station on Hoffman and Swinburne Islands after medical inspectors examined them aboard the ship.[88] The percentage of passengers held in quarantine was quite low. In 1890, for example, of the 370,000 steerage passengers, roughly 0.04 percent (nearly 1,500) were transferred to Hoffman Island. The remainder of passengers continued on to Ellis Island, which received a record number of immigrants in 1907, with as many as 10,000 foreigners arriving daily to a facility that was built to handle 8,000 at most.[89]

"It Is Not by a Man's Purse, but by His Character, That He Is Rich or Poor"

When the new federal station was completed in 1900, it provided better accommodations and a systematic approach to the registration process, yet the employees treated the immigrants in the same manner as they had at the Barge Office and at Castle Garden. In Ellis Island's early years, both national and international press printed tales of mistreatment, including shortchanging at the Money Exchange, filthy conditions in the dormitories, and meager food supplies. The corruption under Commissioner Thomas Fitchie and his assistant commissioner, Edward McSweeney, was highly publicized, including McSweeney's deal with the railroad companies to supply free passes to Ellis Island employees in exchange for ignoring the inflated prices. McSweeney took with him many public documents when he was discharged, some of which would be found incriminating during later investigations.[90]

Immigrant welfare became a top priority for William Williams when President Theodore Roosevelt appointed him commissioner of immigration at Ellis Island in 1902. Williams ultimately served for two terms, from 1902 to 1905, and again from 1909 to 1913. Williams's first memorandum to his employees directed them to treat every immigrant with "kindness and consideration" or else they would be suspended or dismissed from service.[91] And while Williams demanded immigrants be treated well, it is important to note that he also harbored racist views, especially toward those arriving

Figure 1.15. Dining Hall with staff members, c. 1902–1913. Photograph by Edwin Levick. Place settings consist of worn porcelain-enameled plates and a fork and knife. From the New York Public Library

from southern and eastern Europe, such as the Polish, Italians, and Jewish migrants who arrived after 1880, and he fervently supported immigrant restriction.[92] Nevertheless, he sought to improve operations and conditions at Ellis Island. Williams examined firsthand the companies contracted to work there, refusing to renew contracts with the existing food, money, and baggage service companies whom he found guilty of overcharging and mistreatment. He was known to eat in the dining room from time to time to judge the quality of food (figure 1.15).[93] On discovering a telegraph boy had given a counterfeit coin to an immigrant, Williams had him arrested. He issued a notice to employees that "swindling immigrants is a contemptible business, and whoever does this, under whatever form, should be despised [. . .]."[94] Williams preferred to give contracts to companies that would make a profit, since the companies that underbid frequently resorted to shortchanging and exploitation of immigrants in order to make ends meet.[95]

While immigrant welfare was indeed a concern for Williams, he banned missionary and immigrant aid workers from the Registry Room so they did not interfere with the rapid inspection and registration processes. Williams relegated them to the lower floor, where immigrants headed *after* registration. While the general public lauded the presence of immigrant aid societies on Ellis Island, the commissioner had a more reserved view of them. He investigated the various missionaries and aid organizations at Ellis Island to determine their validity, a controversial move that received negative press.[96] These organizations operated independently of the government but were nevertheless monitored by Williams, who noted that some of these so-called benevolent societies were in fact successors of boardinghouse runners, luring immigrants to their businesses under the pretense of protection. His goal was to "draw a line between the true missionaries (of which there are a number on Ellis Island) and the boarding-house runners who, parading under false colors, are for that reason the most dangerous people to whom an immigrant may be turned over."[97] In one case, Williams received word that a Reverend Berkemeier of the Lutheran Mission for Immigrants at 12 State Street in New York City had been taking funds for himself and was making immigrants work for him at the residence. Commissioner-General Sargent castigated Berkemeier in a letter to Williams, stating that the "scoundrel ought to be treated to a coat of tar and feathers and cast off the island, without any regard to his means of transportation to the mainland."[98] Williams subsequently banned Berkemeier from Ellis Island, presumably without the coat of tar and feathers.

The transportation companies at Ellis Island were also scrutinized by Williams. The transportation network that had developed at Castle Garden played a significant role in the operations at Ellis Island, since hundreds of thousands of immigrants passed through on their way to western destinations each year. Williams instated a general policy that no immigrant destined to western points would be allowed to enter New York City under any circumstances, lest they "fall into the hands of unscrupulous people."[99] The government allowed the railroad companies access to Ellis Island, yet government officials were not allowed to interfere with the way those companies ran business. This put the commissioner of immigration in a precarious position; he had authority to deal with agents treating immigrants unfairly but otherwise had no control over the companies. Despite his relative lack of authority over the railroad companies, the commissioner had no qualms about monitoring their activities. Both Williams and his successor Watchorn hired undercover agents to inspect immigrant trains and waiting areas. One undercover inspector, Philip Cowen, took his role quite seriously, going so far as to expend "the amount of $1.50 for false hair, etc." in order to travel as an immigrant; Williams later stated that "the money spent in collecting these reports [was] extremely well spent."[100] The subsequent reports from these operations highlighted areas for improvement and served as a warning to the railroad companies that they were under the federal government's watchful eye. During Williams's two nonconsecutive terms as commissioner, he sent out notices regarding the railroad agents' behavior and practices, directing them to "maintain the same standard of courtesy that is required of Government officials."[101]

The companies involved in the railroad pool at Ellis Island functioned in the same capacity as they had at Castle Garden—as part of the Immigrant Clearing House, which regulated all immigrant traffic from eastern ports. Like the medical officers and inspectors in the Registry Room, railroad agents functioned methodically and swiftly. Agents at Ellis Island sold as many as twenty-five tickets per minute during the busiest times.[102] The majority of tickets sold were based on immigrant rates for travel on segregated trains, although passengers did have the option of purchasing first-class tickets for nonimmigrant trains or rail cars (an option many could not afford). Williams issued strict orders to the railroad companies, however, not to solicit first-class tickets to immigrants for fear that they would be deceived into thinking the first-class rate was the only one offered.[103] With the help of translators from immigrant aid societies, the agents used maps to point out various routes, noting the differences between the fastest routes and the cheapest price. Agents did not always perform their duties to Williams's satisfaction. In another notice from Williams to the railroad agents, he stated: "It has come to my attention that immigrants headed to Chicago took 52–78 hours instead of the less than 36 hours it should take. The cost for the long journey with multiple transfers is $14 but a direct route is only $1 more."[104] He urged agents to be more conscientious when selling their tickets. For the railroad agents, it was a fine line between working swiftly, making passengers aware of all of their travel options, and helping them to take the most economical route.

Even with the help of translators, agents occasionally had a difficult time determining where someone was headed, since the immigrants themselves often had incomplete information or were given an illegible address. A contemporary observer noted that "the spoken name of an American city is apt to be absolutely unintelligible even to the trained interpreter, and often the address is far from legible." One Hungarian woman handed an agent a slip of paper that read "Szekenevno Pillsburs." After puzzling for a few moments, the agent finally deciphered it as "Second Avenue, Pittsburgh."[105] In many cases, agents made educated guesses about an intended destination based on a person's nationality. Large German families typically were traveling to the Midwest, and thus an agent translated "Linkinbra" to Lincoln, Nebraska. This imprecise method, of course, occasionally led to mistakes. In one instance, a group of fifteen Italian immigrants destined for Amsterdam Avenue in New York City were sold tickets to Amsterdam in upstate New York.[106] Victor Safford, a physician at Ellis Island during its initial years, recalled another instance where a Jersey Central conductor accidentally mixed up the destination envelopes for a Syrian woman with plans to meet her husband in Memphis and a Finnish woman meeting her husband in Cincinnati, "to the general dissatisfaction of all four parties generally concerned."[107] Upon arrival, the parties involved realized the error and railroad employees sent the women to their correct destinations. Mistakes such as these were surprisingly few in number, even though there were twelve railroad lines operating out of Ellis Island.

After purchasing tickets at the Railroad Office, immigrants proceeded to the passenger waiting rooms located on the ground floor of Ellis Island, arranged according to destination: one for passengers bound for all points west and south; another for New England; and a third for New York.[108] Immigrants heading to all points west and south took government boats, docked at the main building's rear, to the railroad depots in Jersey City and Hoboken. Those traveling to New York or New England took the ferry back to the Barge Office, where they could meet in-town relatives and friends. Passengers heading north on the New York Central & Hudson River or the New York, New Haven & Hartford lines transferred at the Barge Office to boats heading to Pier 71 at Thirty-First Street and Thirteenth Avenue. There, in compliance with Williams's orders not to expose immigrants to potential threats in the city, the railroad companies boarded the travelers directly onto immigrant trains at the freight yards on West Thirtieth Street instead of boarding them at Grand Central Terminal. While at Ellis Island, immigrants remained the responsibility of the steamship companies that had carried them over. Travelers with a long wait ahead of them in the railroad rooms received provisions at the steamship companies' expense, which they provided sparingly until Williams threatened the companies with fines. While waiting, immigrants could also purchase boxed lunches for their rail journey. On average, these lunches cost fifty cents and provided enough food (meat, cheese, bread, fruit, and beverages) for about three to four meals.[109] In his 1903 annual report, the commissioner noted the urgent need for additional accommodations for those proceeding west by rail, since a growing number of passengers had to wait outside the building.[110] Inadequate space interfered with the ordered arrangement of waiting rooms, and in 1904 the Treasury Department authorized an addition near the main building's rear that expanded the railroad companies' quarters. Immigration officials

Figure 1.16. Getting tagged by railroad official, c. 1905–1926. Photograph by Lewis Hine. From the New York Public Library

pinned numbered tags, referencing the intended rail line, onto the passengers' clothing as they headed into the waiting rooms—another form of spatial sorting (figure 1.16). Railroad conductors used the tags to quickly determine on which rail line an immigrant should be traveling, and where connections should be made. One Hungarian immigrant, Ann Vida, recalled of her journey in 1921 that "when we were getting off Ellis Island, we had all sorts of tags on us. Now that I think about it, we must have looked like marked-down merchandise in Gimbals' basement store or something."[111] In addition to the railroad tags, passengers would also have had tags with their steamship name and the number corresponding to the entry on the ship manifest, as well as any chalk marks on their clothing for certain medical conditions.

Although the transportation network remained virtually the same from Castle Garden to Ellis Island, the shift from state to federal control of immigration did bring about a number of changes in the way officials processed immigrants. At the state-owned Castle Garden, the inspection and registration processes took place in the rotunda's open plan, where immigrants also waited for transportation, searched for relatives, purchased concessions, or sought employment opportunities. The disorganized environment, paired with the corruption occurring at the administrative level, reached such levels that the federal government intervened. When the Treasury Department opened Ellis Island, the building's plan allowed for a systematic inspection and registration process that accommodated more immigrants each day than had ever been possible at Castle Garden.

In many ways, Ellis Island functioned as its own city, with its own transportation network, hospital, lodging, sanitation department, power plant, and so on. Its island location, however, emphasized the isolation of the immigrant population occupying the facility. This isolation pervaded several areas of the immigrants' journey: isolation in steerage on the ships that carried them overseas; isolation from American citizens at the immigrant receiving stations; and isolation from nonimmigrant passengers in railroad waiting rooms and on train cars. The millions of individuals arriving at Ellis Island were, in a sense, treated as one; the speed with which these government officials processed and directed the flow of people moving through this carefully designed space emphasized that notion. This speed was a necessity, of course, since officials had to register thousands of people daily, and it resulted in the majority of immigrants passing through Ellis Island in several hours or within a day.

New York's immigration stations reveal the paradoxical relationship that formed between the government and the railroad companies in the nineteenth century. The railroad pool's presence at Ellis Island, and at Castle Garden before that, protected immigrants from swindlers but also allowed the government to ensure that each person had a specific destination, with money in hand, lessening their likelihood of becoming a public charge. In this way, private and public interests served one another in a mutually beneficial relationship. At the same time, however, the nature of these two parties kept them at odds. Even with the reforms at Ellis Island initiated under Williams's tenure, the profit-seeking railroads still operated independently of government officials. In 1912, Williams noted: "The duty of this office is, and presumably always will be, to execute statutes enacted to restrict immigration, while the interests of the powerful transportation companies represented at Ellis Island demand liberal immigration laws and a liberal execution of the same."[112] While the goals of railroad and government officials may have differed, they worked together to manage the flow of mainly European immigrants into the United States—first on a smaller scale, by directing the movement of bodies through their buildings, and then on a larger scale, by channeling the movement of foreigners throughout the country via a network of segregated spaces.

2
PORT STATIONS

To continue his journey west, Stevenson rode a ferry across the Hudson River from Manhattan to the Pennsylvania Railroad Terminal in Jersey City. At this time, in 1879, there were no tunnels connecting Manhattan and New Jersey (the first would not be completed until 1908). A robust ferry system developed on the Hudson River to shuttle passengers to and from the five New Jersey waterfront terminals built around the turn of the century to accommodate passengers in the country's busiest harbor. Stevenson was overwhelmed, for "the landing at Jersey was done in a stampede. [. . .] People pushed, and elbowed, and ran, their families following how they could."[1] The sickly Stevenson was so exhausted from his journey that he twice had to set down his bags in the hundred yards or so between the ferry dock and the Jersey City train platform, getting further soaked in the driving rain. "A panic selfishness, like that produced by fear, presided over the disorder of our landing."[2] Those around him were also "cold, wet, and weary, and driven stupidly crazy by the mismanagement to which we had been subjected."[3] Stevenson and his fellow travelers were headed toward a drafty, gaslit platform where they would wait for over an hour before the train doors opened.

During their wait, the only refreshment available was from a young boy selling oranges, of which Stevenson bought a half dozen. Only two oranges had any juice, and he tossed the remaining four on the tracks under the train cars. Shockingly, to Stevenson at least (who could afford to throw away food), he beheld "grown people and children groping on the track after my leavings."[4] While this instance is yet another where Stevenson's upbringing and economic class separate him from his fellow travelers, this incident reveals an important aspect of the station in which they were waiting: there were no amenities for the immigrant passengers, no benches, no refreshment, no lavatories. The passengers stood shoulder to shoulder, waiting to continue their travels, lacking any comforts in this space in-between—both the literal space of the train platform and the figurative space of their migration journey.

As more and more people arrived on American shores, especially in New York, transit architecture changed to meet the increasing demand. Railroad companies began including immigrant waiting rooms in their architectural plans as a way to provide some form of amenities to foreign passengers and to enable isolation from the general public—for the protection of those passengers and the comfort of the American public, certainly, but also because this segregation allowed for a more streamlined transportation network. By the time Ellis Island opened in 1892, the surrounding waterfront terminals, including Jersey City's Pennsylvania Railroad, the Central Railroad of New Jersey, and the Erie Railroad; Hoboken's Delaware, Lackawanna & Western Terminal; and Weehawken's West Shore Railroad Terminal, had constructed segregated waiting rooms for immigrant passengers on the shoreline, separate from the main depot building.

In his 1916 book, *Passenger Terminals and Trains*, John Droege recommended that an immigrant waiting room, which he declared was "a necessity in large stations," should be located "in an out of the way place, and may even be a separate building."[5] Throughout Droege's book, which examines every aspect of railroad terminals from design and construction to maintenance and utilization, he places emphasis on the need to guide and reassure travelers through the process of arriving at the station to finally boarding the train. Sociologist Charles Cooley declared in 1909 that technology, which he defined as "the present regime of railroads, telegraphs, telephones and the rest," reinforced democracy and social well-being and produced social order.[6] In many respects, the railway station formed a microcosm of the city—thousands of people coming and going, the presence of commercial activity, a combination of public and private spaces—yet railroad officials attempted to form a hierarchical model of social and architectural order by controlling circulation throughout the space, creating an idealized microcosm.[7] Architectural historian Anthony Raynsford asserts that within the railway station, then, there was potential for an organized, modern, and democratic crowd.[8] Railroad officials contributed to the ordered appearance of this crowd by segregating the lower classes in their large city stations. In New York's Grand Central Terminal, for example, immigrants and laborers were supposed to be "brought into the stations and enter a separate room without coming into contact with other passengers."[9] In cities where a single railroad company had more than one station, no provisions were made for immigrants in stations intended for elite passengers. The Pennsylvania Railroad in Philadelphia, for example, directed immigrant traffic to its facilities in South Philadelphia, not the bourgeois Broad Street Station.[10] In keeping immigrant passengers out of view, railroad officials attempted to create a more homogenous crowd, a crowd unthreatened by foreign passengers. This intention was almost, if not altogether, impossible to achieve since the train concourse was unavoidably a place in which different races and classes converged. Yet railroad officials persisted in this endeavor by directing immigrant traffic to facilities where passengers could be contained until their departure by rail.

"I Do My Best to Keep My Head the Other Way"

In the stations containing immigrant waiting rooms, railroad companies segregated these travelers in two ways: architectural isolation, in which the waiting room was physically removed from the main building, and by architectural partitioning, in which immigrants were segregated within the station's shared space, in a separate room. These distinctions between isolation and partitioning were labeled by historian Robert Weyeneth in his study of the architecture of racial segregation.[11] Throughout the Jim Crow era, isolation and partitioning were architectural strategies for incorporating racial segregation into the public sphere. Weyeneth's concept of racial segregation as a spatial system can be readily applied to the immigrant segregation occurring in railroad stations across the United States. Yet a significant difference must be addressed: Black segregation was a racial caste system that pervaded every aspect of life, from physical spaces to social etiquette, and was enforced through legislation. Immigrant segregation was largely temporary, and mainly dependent on class. It was also at the transportation companies' discretion. Understanding this difference is crucial in studying the development of the American cultural landscape and the complex—and racist—notions of identity and citizenship in the nineteenth and twentieth centuries.

Particularly in New York Harbor, as railroad companies adjusted their services to meet the demands brought upon them by increased immigration, the rail terminals provided immigrant facilities separate from the main depot building—a form of architectural isolation. Passages connected this isolated waiting room to the train concourse, which meant that immigrants did not have to walk through the main station, or head house, to reach their train. Because of the ferry system that developed between Ellis Island and the railroad terminals, of the seven railroad lines operating west from the New Jersey stations in the early twentieth century, each was assigned a day on which it carried all westbound immigrants

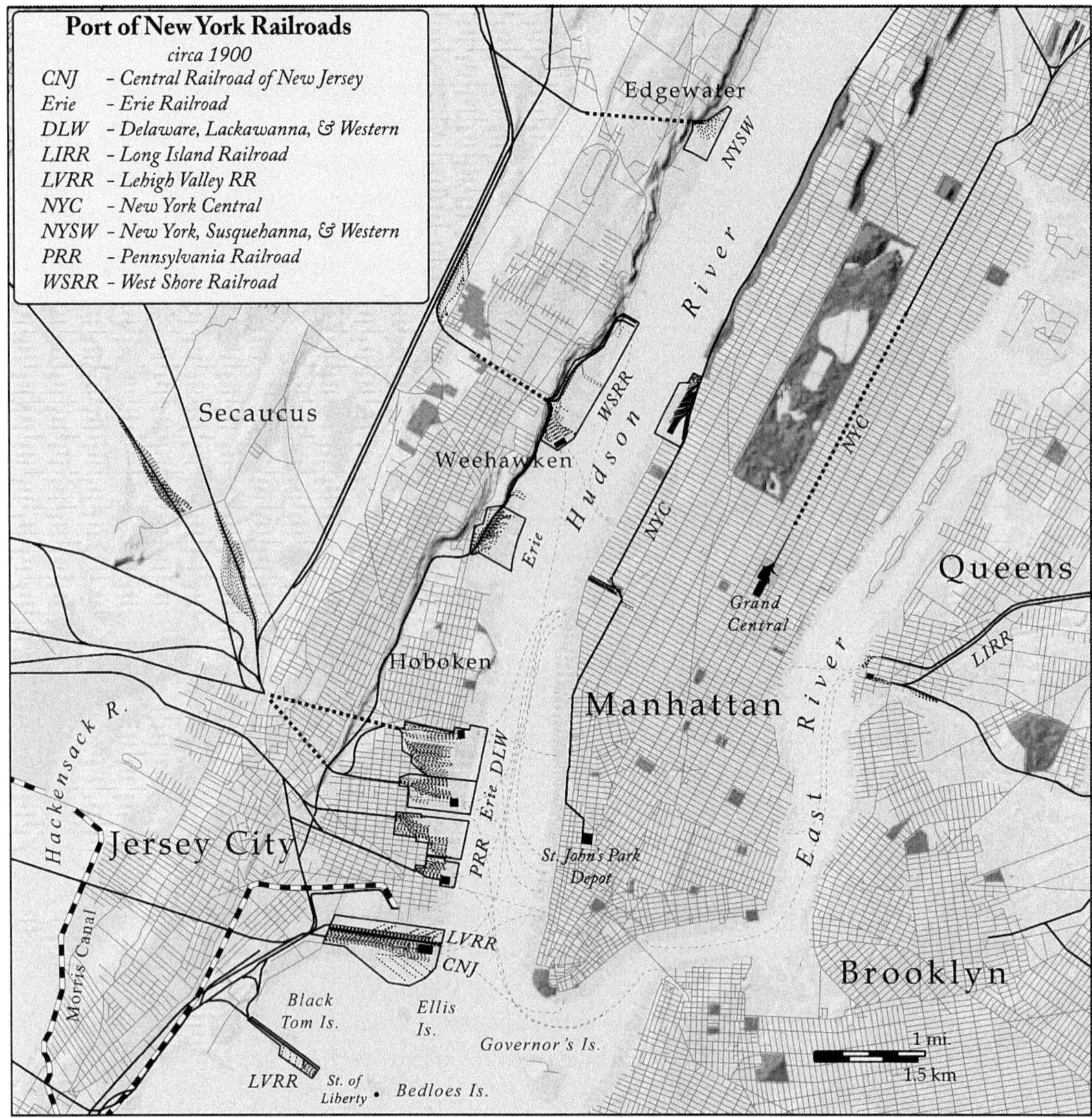

Figure 2.1. Port of New York Railroads, c. 1900. Map by James R. Irwin. Note the proximity of the Central Railroad of New Jersey Terminal (CNJ) to Ellis Island, both located in Jersey City, New Jersey. Courtesy James R. Irwin

from Ellis Island (figure 2.1). These seven railroad companies included the Pennsylvania; West Shore; Delaware, Lackawanna & Western; Lehigh Valley; Erie, Ontario & Western; Baltimore & Ohio; and Central Railroad of New Jersey. Each of these companies had their own terminal, with the exception of the Baltimore & Ohio Railroad and Lehigh Valley Railroad, both of which operated out of the Central Railroad of New Jersey

Figure 2.2. Central Railroad of New Jersey Terminal, Jersey City, New Jersey, Peabody & Stearns, 1889. Photograph by Joe Mabel, 2013. Only the headhouse and ferry slips are extant. The ferry house was demolished in the late twentieth century. Courtesy Joe Mabel

Terminal. Since the Ellis Island ferry traveled to only one station each day, this arrangement simplified ferry traffic and made it less confusing for Ellis Island transportation agents, who would otherwise be responsible for making sure each person arrived at the correct terminal. This also ensured that each railroad company received its fair share of immigrant traffic. By evening, enough immigrants arrived from Ellis Island to that day's station to make up one or more immigrant trains.[12] In 1879, Stevenson and his fellow travelers waited directly on the platform to board the train. Within a decade, the railroads built new waiting areas to streamline traffic and contain the multitudes arriving in New York Harbor.

The Central Railroad of New Jersey Terminal, built in 1889 by the Boston-based architectural firm Peabody & Stearns, was closest in proximity to Ellis Island. The Jersey City terminal, which housed multiple railroad companies, served as the point of departure for the largest share of passengers departing from Ellis Island. The still-extant Victorian headhouse drew inspiration from both the French Renaissance Revival and the Richardsonian Romanesque architectural styles (figure 2.2). With its arched

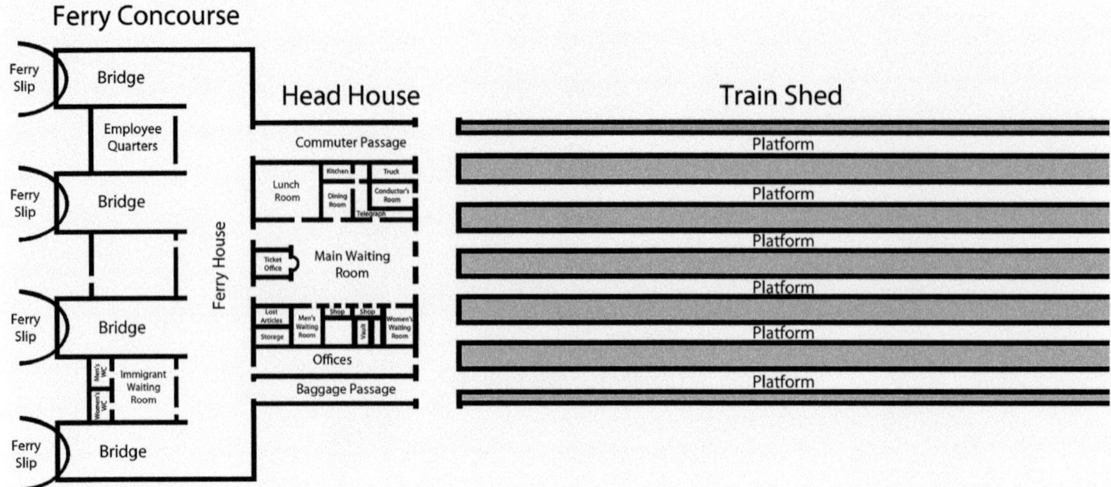

Figure 2.3. Plan, Central Railroad of New Jersey Terminal, Jersey City, New Jersey, Peabody & Stearns, 1889. Redrawn by Julie Boland Perez from Walter Gilman Berg, *Buildings and Structures of American Railroads* (New York: Wiley & Sons, 1893)

openings and picturesque silhouette, the redbrick building with sandstone trim faces the harbor and forms an imposing presence alongside Ellis Island. The facade is divided into a five-part plan: a large, three-and-a-half-story central pavilion with wings connecting to two smaller, two-and-a-half-story pavilions at either end. The building's interior, praised by contemporary architectural critics for its "light and cheerful appearance," featured a sky-lit hall spanned by three wrought-iron tresses and walls veneered with glazed cream-colored English brick.[13] The ground level contained the ticket counter and men's and women's waiting rooms and restrooms, along with numerous amenities such as a lunchroom, dining room, newsstand, telegraph office, and fruit stand. Railroad administrative offices were located along the iron balconies on the central pavilion's upper level.

East of the main station building, on the shoreline, was the single-story ferry-house. It was in this structure where the immigrant waiting room was located, on the dock between the two northernmost ferry slips. Men's and women's toilets were the only amenities available and immigrants waited on wooden benches in this room until their evening departure by rail. The ferry-house architecture was not as complex or grand as that of the headhouse. The timber construction featured simple, low-pitched gable roofs covering the ferry-house and extending over the ferry sheds. Its low profile did not obstruct the view of the headhouse for those seeing the station from across the harbor.[14] Passageways at the northern and southern ends of the headhouse connected the ferry concourse to the train platforms and bypassed the main waiting area (figure 2.3). The wide southern passage, clad in the same glazed brick of the main waiting area, allowed other travelers—commuters traveling to and from New York City—to bypass the headhouse's pedestrian traffic and proceed directly from the ferry to the train concourse and vice versa. Employees transferred baggage from the ferries to the train by means of a much narrower northern passage, which was clad in red brick, a cheaper material than the rest of the interior's glazed brick. It was this passage that also connected the immigrant waiting area to the train concourse and allowed immigrant passengers to proceed directly from the room on the dock to the segregated train waiting area on the north platform, which minimized contact with other passengers.

One of the other prominent stations in the area was the New York, Lake Erie & Western Railroad Station in Jersey City, further north of the Central Railroad of New Jersey Terminal and immediately south of the Delaware, Lackawanna & Western Terminal in Hoboken. The Queen Anne structure was built in 1887 by architect George Archer and engineer C. W. Buchholz. At the time of its construction, the *New York Times* deemed it a "handsome structure."[15] Half timbering on the facade emphasized its wooden construction. Four towers marked the building's corners, with a clock tower rising taller than the others. Skylights and louvered sash windows ran the length of the pitched roof, allowing ample light and ventilation. The station housed a general waiting room, ticket office, ladies' waiting room, restaurant, smoking room, and lavatories. The *New York Times* praised the main waiting area, which was "finished in hard woods in their natural colors," and noted the abundant light that entered the room through stained glass windows.[16] Like the other New Jersey harbor terminals, Erie Railway's immigrant facilities were not incorporated into the main building. Instead, passengers disembarked from the Ellis Island ferries and waited for their train departure in a wooden structure located on Pier 5 (figure 2.4). The two-story building was simple in construction with little architectural embellishment. The brightly colored and ornamented interior of the headhouse's main waiting room starkly contrasted the immigrant room's plain wooden interior, which featured exposed crossbeams and trusses along the ceiling and long rows of wooden benches with cast-iron supports (figure 2.5). Multipaned windows and skylights let in natural light and air to the otherwise crowded space. From the exterior, the pier building gives the appearance of a storage facility—not that of a waiting area for rail passengers.

Figure 2.4. Pier 5 Immigrant Waiting Room, Erie Railway, Jersey City, New Jersey. Photograph c. 1968. Historic American Engineering Record, Library of Congress

The immigrant facilities at the New Jersey waterfront terminals were largely ignored by contemporary sources. If mentioned at all in the terminal's architectural descriptions, authors merely noted the presence of an immigrant area and any description of the space was limited to its dimensions. For example, in historian William Shaw's 1884 book on Essex and Hudson Counties, he describes the West Shore Terminal in Weehawken in detail, noting that the main waiting area is "finely paneled in red cherry and yellow pine wainscoting, and all elaborately ornamented in the Eastlake style."[17] In contrast, his cursory description of the immigrant room is only that it measures sixty by sixty feet. It is a utilitarian space, a transitory yet necessary layover in the long journey of migration. An area of the station in which railroad companies had no desire to spend more on finishes and furnishings than necessary. In city stations, the immigrant room was a far cry from the main waiting area's decorative opulence, which was the public face of the railroad company.

Figure 2.5. Immigrant waiting room, Erie Railway Pier 5, Jersey City, New Jersey. Photo c. 1968. Historic American Engineering Record, Library of Congress

"I Found Myself . . . with More Than a Hundred Others, to be Sorted and Boxed for the Journey"

The isolated shoreline waiting areas facilitated a systematic transfer of immigrant passengers from sea to rail, one in which transportation officials sorted and moved these travelers with a similar efficiency and economy with which they moved freight. At the shoreline, in the space in-between, Stevenson writes that he and his fellow immigrants "had accepted this purgatory as a child accepts the conditions of the world."[18] The architectural segregation that occurred in New York was also present in other eastern port cities. Baltimore, in particular, developed its own streamlined immigration procedures wherein the Baltimore & Ohio Railroad held a de facto monopoly over immigrant traffic until the start of World War I. In fact, the Port of Baltimore serves as a potent example of immigration's role in industrial capitalism in the second half of the nineteenth century. As opposed to New York, where the government—first state and then federal—owned and operated the immigration station, in Baltimore it was a single transportation company who owned and operated the immigration station, although government employees performed the necessary inspections within the facility.

The Baltimore & Ohio Railroad acted as a nexus between the Eastern Seaboard, the nation's interior, and European markets, and established a system to draw immigrants to Baltimore. In 1867, the Baltimore & Ohio Railroad Company established trading links with Bremen, Germany, through the North German Lloyd Steamship Company, exporting raw goods such as the tobacco, cotton, and grain that had been produced in the American Midwest and South and exported through Baltimore and, in turn, welcoming over a million European immigrants (a large percentage of whom were German) to American shores. Baltimore was the third-busiest port in the country, welcoming 1.5 million immigrants, just behind Boston, which welcomed 2 million. In New York, where 22 million people entered, the transportation companies operated within a railroad pool to disperse people throughout the country. In Baltimore, however, the main immigrant transportation network that formed was between a single railroad line and steamship company.

Industrialization in the United States, particularly the railroad system's rise, ultimately changed the nation's landscape, effectively transforming labor and economic markets and reinforcing the cultural division between the regions of city and country. The president of the Baltimore & Ohio Railroad, Philip E. Thomas (1827–1836), declared: "should our present anticipations of the efficiency of Railways be realized, a total change would be produced in commercial and social intercourse in every country where these roads might be introduced."[19] Thomas's comment was prescient of the transformation the railways would ultimately bring to the United States' economic, commercial, and cultural spheres, not to mention the reshaping of the country's physical landscape. As historian William Cronon explained in *Nature's Metropolis*, the railroad altered how the land was used and transformed commodity and capital flows, allowing a symbiotic relationship to emerge between city and country, at once defining the two entities yet inextricably linking them. This symbiotic relationship was especially evident in Baltimore, where the railroad and steamship companies were dependent on industrial and commercial enterprises in the United States. Similarly, immigrants and transportation companies were dependent on one another. This circulation of capital, commodity, and people (both as labor and consumers) inherently linked urban and rural development, enabling each to develop its defining characteristics while still relying on the other for economic prosperity.

The relationship between the Baltimore & Ohio and the North German Lloyd was forged by Albert Schumacher, a German immigrant and son of a Bremen city counselor who had established himself as a successful Baltimore businessman and was on the Baltimore & Ohio Railroad Board of Directors. It was this contract that ultimately allowed the Baltimore & Ohio Railroad to gain control over the immigrant traffic entering the Port of Baltimore. Just a few years later, in 1871, the Pennsylvania Railroad made a similar move in an attempt to attract a greater share of immigrant traffic, establishing the American Line shipping company together with the Philadelphia municipal authorities. In Baltimore, the Pennsylvania Railroad operated its own immigrant station at Canton, across the harbor from Locust Point. With the 1873 financial panic and subsequent depression, however, the Pennsylvania Railroad Company abandoned its effort to establish a steam-to-rail system and sold its steamships.[20]

To secure the North German Lloyd's patronage, the Baltimore & Ohio agreed to several stipulations in the 1867 contract. First, construction of a suitable pier, with covered sheds and the necessary offices and gates, to accommodate the steamships. The Baltimore & Ohio also agreed to construct an adjoining canal yard and warehouse and provide wharves that would be available at all times to the North German Lloyd. Furthermore, the railroad company agreed to "get the vessels exempted from the city-harbor and county taxes" and attempt to obtain for the North German Lloyd a contract for English mail transport. In this way, the Baltimore & Ohio hoped to secure more business for the North German Lloyd and provide reason for the steamship company to conduct business with the Baltimore port. In exchange, the railroad stipulated that "it [be] understood that goods and passengers of and for the ships of the North German Lloyd are to be transported over the roads of the Baltimore and Ohio Railroad Company [. . .]."[21] The steamship company was obligated to provide a Baltimore & Ohio agent at its port in Bremerhaven and to provide two vessels that would each make trips every four weeks for at least a period of five years.

The contract's terms placed the North German Lloyd and the Baltimore & Ohio Railroad in a mutually beneficial relationship: the North German Lloyd had permanent American facilities provided to them by the railroad and the Baltimore & Ohio received guaranteed traffic (both passenger and freight) on their lines. The Baltimore & Ohio's attempts to secure English mail for the North German Lloyd, while seemingly in the steamship company's interest, actually benefited the railroad as well, for once the mail was unloaded at the Port of Baltimore it would be distributed over the rail lines. The construction of new facilities was a considerable financial commitment for the Baltimore & Ohio and indicated the business they expected to incur as a result of their relationship with the North German Lloyd. The Port of Baltimore's geographic advantage, which the Baltimore & Ohio advertised as the "shortest and cheapest path to the sea," in addition to its relationship with the North German Lloyd, would allow Baltimore, in the words of the railroad's President Garrett, "to accomplish the great commercial destiny that awaits her."[22] The aspirations of the railroad's original founders would eventually be realized, since Baltimore did become one of the busiest and successful ports on the Eastern Seaboard, and immigration formed an integral part of those operations.

The contract between the Baltimore & Ohio Railroad and the North German Lloyd Steamship Company enabled a three-part trade between the American hinterland, the city of Baltimore, and Europe. The trade patterns between these regions were marked by flows of capital along transportation routes, demonstrating the larger economic forces at play in a network that architectural historian Paula Lupkin terms *macro-circulation*.[23] In this network, the financial, industrial, and commercial realms between regions—Baltimore and the Midwest, Baltimore and the South, and Baltimore and Europe—were linked by a transportation system that enabled goods and people, and thus capital, to move along its lines.[24] The city of Baltimore forms the center of the exchange between the interior United States and the European markets. The capitalist framework that supported a transportation system between these regions also enabled the mass circulation of goods and people across the sea and throughout the country.

The raw materials and merchandise produced in the western and southern United States were shipped along the Baltimore & Ohio Railroad for distribution in the eastern states and abroad. The North German Lloyd brought immigrant passengers from Bremerhaven to Baltimore. Those traveling further into the country boarded Baltimore & Ohio trains from the Locust Point terminal. Many of these immigrants, once settled in their new cities and towns, contributed to the production of freight shipped along the Baltimore & Ohio's lines through their own agricultural, industrial, and commercial labor. Dock employees at Locust Point loaded the North German Lloyd's steamships (once emptied of their passengers) with freight arriving in Baltimore and intended for international markets. Tobacco was one of the largest export industries, but cotton and timber were also significant exports to Germany throughout the nineteenth century. The ships sailed back to Germany and distributed their holdings throughout greater Europe.

Local manufacturing and regional agriculture stimulated Baltimore's urban growth, and with that growth came increasingly more foreigners to its shores.[25] Immigration to Baltimore followed similar trends seen in other eastern port cities, with Europeans driven to the United States due to economic hardship, social and political upheavals, and persecution in their home countries. The arrival of immigrants to the Port of Baltimore was not entirely based on the immigrant's choice, as historian Dean R. Esslinger has pointed out.[26] Rather, it was a result of the city's trade patterns with northern Europe; immigrants departing from a specific European city (typically the port city closest to their homeland) were limited to the routes taken by steamship lines departing from that particular port. The established trade between the Baltimore & Ohio and the North German Lloyd meant that immigrants departing from Bremen were bound for Baltimore. After the contract between the two companies, nearly ten thousand immigrants arrived in the Port of Baltimore compared to the nearly four thousand who had arrived the year prior.[27] It is for this reason that the Baltimore & Ohio Railroad received a significant number of German immigrants who had departed from Bremerhaven and traveled on the North German Lloyd steamships. Furthermore, the connections between the two companies allowed for relatively easier travel accommodations; passengers on a North German Lloyd ship purchased a single ticket for their entire voyage, transferring to rail once they arrived in Baltimore. American railroad companies also formed contracts with immigrant agencies in the United States who had agents in Europe to offer special rates for passengers in exchange for the agents' agreement not to sell tickets to immigrants over competing rail lines.[28]

The immigration station built by the Baltimore & Ohio Railroad Company at its Locust Point marine terminal enabled ease of transfer from the steamships to train cars (figure 2.6). Per the agreement with the North German Lloyd Steamship Company, the Baltimore & Ohio Railroad constructed three piers in 1868–1869 to serve the passenger and general cargo business. On the first pier, the company erected a single-story brick building to serve as the immigrant facility. The 600-by-75-foot structure quickly outgrew its purpose as immigrant numbers rose, and in 1872, Piers 8 and 9, each of which handled immigrant traffic, were both extended 106 feet in length and 100 feet in width to accommodate the increased business; they were extended again in 1880 and 1881.[29] Baltimore & Ohio officials claimed their facilities were superior to Castle Garden in New York, since immigrants disembarked the steamships and were able to connect to their trains directly at the pier, instead of having to transfer to a train station elsewhere. During the second half of the nineteenth

Figure 2.6. Pier at Locust Point, Baltimore, Maryland, 1872. The Baltimore & Ohio Railroad Company connected shipping and rail at its extensive marine terminal. Division of Work and Industry, National Museum of American History, Smithsonian Institution

century, New York was infamous in the press for the con artists who preyed on newly arrived immigrants. Stevenson and his fellow passengers were regaled of many horror stories that circulated the ships during their Atlantic journey. The Baltimore & Ohio Railroad Company intended to eradicate this issue by containing the immigrant station within the company's marine terminal, one of the many pier structures that enabled foreign trade. Since the station was isolated from the rest of the city, there was little opportunity for swindlers to practice their occupation. The contract with the North German Lloyd allowed the Baltimore & Ohio to integrate immigration into its transportation network in a way that moved travelers quickly along, from sea to rail, all the while keeping them contained.

"The Workman Dwells in a Borderland"

By the late 1880s, a new purpose-built immigration facility was constructed on Pier 9 to handle the increasing number of passengers arriving in Baltimore. It was completed in December 1887 but the Baltimore & Ohio Railroad Company staged the ceremonial opening on February 22, 1888. A party of city and customs officials, transportation officers, and the press welcomed the German steamship *Hermann*, although the ship had in fact docked much earlier than the party's arrival at the pier and the 850 immigrants on board had already disembarked.[30] The facility consisted of two buildings, and the steamer docked alongside them. A long, wooden structure with a pitched roof stored cargo at the end of the pier, with a train track running through its center, facilitating convenient transfer of goods from ship to rail and vice versa. In front of the cargo building, and alongside the railroad track, was the immigrant processing station, a long, two-story brick structure, measuring 180 by 60 feet, with a pitched roof. Passengers walked from the ship's deck via gangplanks directly onto the immigrant station's second-floor balcony and into the main waiting area. As steamships increased in size over the ensuing years, the Baltimore & Ohio relocated the landing platform to the roof, and immigrants walked down a stairway to reach the main waiting area.

Passengers had already undergone medical inspections at the German port prior to their departure because the steamship company would incur the cost of transporting deported immigrants back to Europe if they failed to pass inspection at American ports, and thus medical officials only needed to conduct cursory examinations on arrival. Limited medical inspections took place aboard the ship as it slowly sailed into the harbor to berth. One steamship employee, a German man who later immigrated to the United States, recalled: "The quarantine men boarded the boat on its way up the bay. Every immigrant went through a quick medical examination. Checking of the luggage by Customs was a quick and cursory affair. From that point, most of the immigrants who landed in Baltimore stepped aboard B. & O. trains and traveled on to Chicago, St. Louis or Cincinnati."[31] Passengers disembarked on the station's second floor, and customs officials registered the new arrivals using the ship's manifest. Once landed, passengers purchased or picked up their railroad tickets and gathered in the large open waiting room. Throughout the space were signs written in several languages, including English, German, and Polish (reflecting the period's immigrant demographic), directing foreigners where to purchase railroad tickets, exchange money, or find instructions on how to continue their journey. The Baltimore & Ohio hired multilingual agents to work in the immigration station and direct the new arrivals. When ready to board their train, passengers left the waiting area for the downstairs baggage area, where employees transferred luggage directly from the ship while the customs process occurred upstairs. From here, passengers boarded trains directly outside the building; their baggage was also loaded onto the waiting train.

One journalist covering the station's opening remarked that, because the train platform was adjacent to the building, "the new arrivals are under no necessity of touching the soil of America—or Locust Point either—from the time they leave their native land until they are put down in their future homes."[32] Whether this was for the immigrants' benefit or the Baltimoreans is unclear. What is significant, however, is that, within the physical space of the immigration station, officials handled the immigrants much like the freight that moved daily between sea and rail at the Baltimore & Ohio's Locust Point marine terminal. They were commodities moved along this transportation network, contributing to the railroad's profits. The Baltimore & Ohio's agreement with the North German Lloyd Steamship Company, in which passengers made one ticket purchase, allowed immigrants to travel via steamship to Baltimore and board the train west directly from the pier. The journalist further noted that "the Baltimore receiving-house [could] handle 1,000 passengers in four hours, or at the rate of about 3,000 for a working day."[33] An astonishing number, indeed, for a single railroad company.

In New York, the railroad companies operated in a pool, dividing the passenger traffic among themselves and working in conjunction with government officials (first state, then federal). In Baltimore, however, the Baltimore & Ohio held the monopoly on immigrant traffic and the railroad operated the immigrant station as a profit-driven business. Government agents interviewed the arriving immigrants as they entered the building, asking the standard questions of name, age, city of birth, occupation, and amount of money in the immigrant's possession (a question that determined a person's liability of becoming a public charge). Yet this was the extent of the government presence at the Baltimore port in the 1880s. It was ultimately the transportation companies who were in charge of the arriving immigrants. The process to register, inspect, and release immigrants was considerably more relaxed than the stricter procedures occurring in New York, where the numbers of immigrants arriving annually was significantly higher than in Baltimore.

The Baltimore & Ohio marine terminal was the embodiment of continuous transportation, moving goods and people between modes of transportation, allowing maximum benefits for the railroad's capitalist enterprise. The majority of immigrants arriving by ship continued their journey by rail. At first, three-quarters of immigrants landing at Locust Point traveled to another destination immediately. By 1900, that number rose to 90 percent.[34] Anyone requiring overnight accommodations found space at one of the local boardinghouses. Augusta Koether ran a successful business at 1108 Towson Street for three decades, directly across from the immigration pier. She and her first husband, John Marousek, purchased the saloon and boardinghouse in 1883. After Marousek's death in 1885, Augusta married the German-born William Koether, who worked as an interpreter at Locust Point from 1895 until his death in 1900. Any passengers subject to deportation or who were detained for other reasons found a room at the three-story brick boardinghouse at the corner of Towson and Marriott streets. Koether purchased two adjacent vacant lots in 1903 and 1904 and expanded her business. The property included a toilet and washroom in the backyard, while the boardinghouse itself comprised twenty sleeping quarters, a dining room for steerage passengers, and a dining and sitting room for cabin passengers. The separation of classes aboard the ship was thus maintained at the detention house. For deported passengers, Koether received payment for their room and board from the North German Lloyd Steamship Company, since the steamship companies were responsible for the foreign passengers until they departed from the landing pier. Koether received her first boarders on March 23, 1869, when the SS *Baltimore* landed at Locust Point with 350 steerage passengers.[35]

The boardinghouse was necessary if railroad and government officials wanted to validate their claim that Baltimore was a much safer port of arrival for immigrants than New York's Castle Garden, which was ultimately shut down in 1890 once investigations by Congress revealed its inadequacies. The *Baltimore Sun* credited the Baltimore & Ohio Railroad's immigration station with the protection of the arriving foreigners: "In the history of the immigrant business of this port [. . .] it is said that no sharper [defrauder] has ever approached the piers of landing."[36] Whereas Castle Garden opened out onto the streets of New York City and the nearby rail lines did not extend directly to the immigration station, the adjacent railroad tracks and Koether's boardinghouse allowed immigrants to remain within the confines of the Baltimore & Ohio marine terminal, effectively shielding them from the rest of the city. It also meant that passengers did not have to venture too far from the immigration pier to find reputable boardinghouses, like Stevenson had. In fact, by the 1880s, both the city government and railroad officials boasted that Baltimore's immigration pier surpassed Castle Garden "in the advantages offered and protection afforded those who come to America."[37] Like in New York, various missionaries and aid societies offered assistance to the newcomers.

Other boardinghouses in the neighborhood, including that of the German Reformed Church on Beason Street, welcomed those in need of housing who were not in the transportation companies' care.[38]

"I Descended the Platform Like a Man in a Dream"

By the beginning of the twentieth century, the Baltimore & Ohio immigration station had become too small to contain the tens of thousands of immigrants arriving annually and the ships had outgrown the old pier building. The railroad company constructed a new landing station on piers east of the older immigrant station, which could accommodate four of the new large steamships simultaneously. The old immigrant station was used for storage thereafter, as its long, open-plan construction readily accommodated cargo. The new building's design, while purpose-built for immigration, nevertheless resembled a warehouse-type structure—an economic design that kept costs low for the Baltimore & Ohio, a profit-driven company that did not have to project the type of political message that the federal government's Ellis Island facility did.

On the occasion of the new immigration station's opening in July 1904, an article in the Baltimore & Ohio's monthly publication, *The Book of the Royal Blue*, described the new station in detail and emphasized the old pier's inadequacies, where "each successive [landing] platform designat[ed] the growth of the ships, till the last landing was built on the roof itself, and from there it was necessary to walk down the stairs to the entrance of the pier."[39] The earlier building undoubtedly suffered growing pains but the new facility was built in a similar economic fashion, just at a larger scale. Upon the building's completion, the Baltimore & Ohio Railroad advertised it as "America's Largest Immigrant Pier"—not to be confused with the largest immigrant *station*, which was the title held by Ellis Island in New York. The two-story pier building was of simple construction: a wooden interior frame, corrugated iron exterior siding, windows along the length of the first and second floors, and skylights and ventilation turbines running the length of the pitched roof. The second floor was where inspection and registration occurred, while the first floor contained the train track and platforms, in addition to the baggage room. Much like at the earlier building, immigrants disembarked from the ship via gangplanks connected to the second story. Crowds of passengers packed the main deck, eager to disembark with their belongings packed in bundles, baskets, and boxes, and proceeded into the large open room on the new immigrant station's upper level, which featured wooden support beams and trusses and was lined with long, wooden benches.

Figure 2.7. In this 1904 photograph, immigrants are separated into groups and wait in fenced-in areas called separation pens at the Baltimore & Ohio Locust Point facilities. Maryland Center for History and Culture, MC4733–4

As passengers entered this room, medical inspectors checked for signs of visible disease, particularly trachoma, a contagious eye disease. With this new facility, the medical inspections (a necessary procedure once the federal government took over immigration) occurred on land, not aboard the ship as had been the practice with the nineteenth-century Baltimore immigrant station. Even still, however, medical inspections remained cursory since the steamship companies conducted more thorough examinations at the port of departure. The ship's manifest had already been sent to immigration officials at the pier prior to the ship's arrival (via a faster steamer) and officials in Baltimore grouped the passengers by destination to ensure the travelers boarded the correct trains—each group was assigned a different letter. These groups were guided into separation pens, surrounded by waist-high wooden fencing, to await their turn for registration (figure 2.7). As each group was called, the immigrants filed into the long lanes formed by iron railings, at the end of which a government inspector questioned them and confirmed their entry into the United States.

Upon viewing this procedure, one Baltimore & Ohio Railroad employee observed that the immigrant processing "at times seems similar to that of the manipulation of cattle or sheep."[40] This comparison of moving livestock was in no small part a result of the immigrant pier's design. The immigrants were in fact separated into *pens*—a term used by the railroad officials themselves—and then shuttled through registration and ultimately onto trains headed west. The Baltimore & Ohio Railroad had established its marine terminal to efficiently handle and move cargo between rail and sea; they had also designed an immigrant building in which to shuttle foreigners in the same way. Because of this efficiency, and in addition to the ventilation and sanitary requirements, the commissioner-general of immigration, Frank P. Sargent, who had inspected the station several times during construction, commended the Baltimore & Ohio Railroad for the building's design.[41] What the immigrants thought of the space, however, is unknown as firsthand accounts of this particular facility are rare. After a long sea voyage and before the railroad journey that lay ahead, the brief time at the immigrant station was most likely a hurried and stressful affair, despite government praise for the building's design.

Once immigrants completed inspection and registration, they proceeded to the railroad ticket window. In most cases, tickets for the immigrant trains departing from the Baltimore & Ohio station were sold in conjunction with a passenger's steamship ticket. At the railroad window, passengers picked up their tickets, which agents would have had ready upon receiving the orders from the steamship company prior to the ship's arrival at port.[42] Next stop was the money exchange counter, also on the second floor, where currency exchange rates were listed on signs written in several languages (figure 2.8). With American currency and railroad tickets in hand, the immigrants proceeded to the baggage department. Customs officials inspected the contents of each immigrant's baggage, a time-consuming and frustrating process for the travelers, who then had to quickly repack their belongings (figure 2.9). One journalist, in a 1905 article, declared the baggage inspection to be "one of the most disagreeable features to the immigrant of the entire entrance proceedings [. . .], the seeming impossibility of again getting into their original compass the mass of his belongings. Packed in their homes abroad where time was not considered, these bundles when taken apart present for re-assemblement [*sic*] a puzzle worthy a place with the 'Age of Ann' [a well-known contemporary riddle]."[43] Once the inspection was over, railroad employees checked the

Figure 2.8. Money exchange booth at Locust Point, 1904. Information for various exchange rates is listed on a sign above the booth, including information for English, German, French, Russian, and Austrian currencies, reflecting the largest immigrant groups at the time. Maryland Center for History and Culture, MC4733–8

Figure 2.9. Immigrants with their baggage at Locust Point, c. 1904. Maryland Center for History and Culture, MC4733–6

passengers' baggage and weighed it. Much like airline travel today, if the weight exceeded that covered by their ticket (each passenger received a freight allowance), the railroad charged the difference in cost. Employees then loaded the baggage onto the train when it arrived at the station.

While immigrants waited for their trains on long wooden benches in the main sitting area, they could purchase refreshments at the lunch counter and socialize with one another (figure 2.10). The railroad painted a picture of this waiting period as idyllic, no doubt in an effort to present their facilities as superior to other immigrant stations and attract potential customers: "Accordions are requisitioned and the songs of their native land are played. Sometimes a group of Swiss mountaineers will break into the peculiar yodel songs of their native hills and peasant women sing their babies to sleep with the folk song of their country."[44] Yet the Baltimore & Ohio author belies his intentions, instead revealing his disappointment

Figure 2.10. Main waiting room of the Baltimore & Ohio Immigrant Station, c. 1904–1910. Maryland Center for History and Culture, MC4733-2

that, in his eyes, the immigrants were not, in fact, as quaint as those arriving in decades past: "The costumes of the immigrants of the present day are not nearly as picturesque as those worn eighteen or twenty years ago. The wooden shoes of the lowlands of Germany are never seen now, and it is difficult to guess their nationality from their dress alone. The total absence of hats is conspicuous, for the women all wear handkerchiefs, generally of gaudy colors and often of silk. Now and then can be seen short skirts and boots to the knees, but the majority have no striking mode of dress."[45] The author prefers the earlier model of foreigner, the parochial immigrant out of place in a new land and thus easily discernible from American citizens. The idea of immigrants as "picturesque" turns these people into curiosities for the American public, emphasizing their otherness, which was a convenient way of identifying who was foreign at first glance.

Figure 2.11. Pier 8, Locust Point, c. 1910. The Baltimore & Ohio trains boarded at the marine terminal, allowing ease of transfer between ship and rail. Division of Work and Industry, National Museum of American History, Smithsonian Institution

Although their dress may not have distinguished them as foreigners, the railroad company reinforced separation from the American citizenry by shuttling the immigrants directly onto segregated trains and keeping them contained on the pier while they waited to leave Baltimore, a policy that allowed the railroad company to maximize efficiency and, consequently, its profits. The Baltimore & Ohio stated that "nearly one-half of the upper portion of the big pier is used for a depot; the trains are pushed up an incline directly into the pier and the entire business of the Immigration Bureau is confined directly to the structure, thus obviating the use of the barges, as at Ellis Island."[46] This not only lowered operational costs but also benefited the immigrants, for whom the transfer process from sea to rail was more direct (figure 2.11). In the eyes of railroad officials, this segregation protected the immigrants and it also allowed for a streamlined system wherein the transportation companies could maximize profits.

"It Was Plain the Whole System, if System There Was . . . Had Utterly Broken Down"

The federal government did not interfere with the privately owned facility and even praised the Baltimore & Ohio Railroad for providing a sanitary and safe landing pier for incoming immigrants, reflecting the early twentieth century's free market economy and laissez-faire economics. The Baltimore & Ohio Railroad largely controlled immigration to the Port of Baltimore and it was not until the second decade of the twentieth century, as immigration numbers swelled, that Congress began advocating for a federally owned and operated immigration station in Baltimore. Efforts to restrict immigration had been growing since the 1880s, with the introduction of the Immigration Act of 1882, which set a precedent for barring categories of individuals from entry, and subsequent efforts of various groups like the Immigration Restriction League, a nativist organization, put further scrutiny on the country's immigrant stations. In 1912, Honorable J. Charles Linthicum of Maryland introduced a bill asking for funds for a federal immigration station and hospital to be located on the government-owned lands surrounding Fort McHenry, further east of the Baltimore & Ohio immigrant station. Linthicum argued, "At no other port along the coast does the railroad run into the immigrant station" and that, as a result, the Baltimore & Ohio Railroad has "absolute control over it at this time, and the Government has nothing to say."[47] This was undeniably a problem for government officials, for whom there was increasing pressure from the public to get a handle on the numbers of foreigners entering the country annually. In another congressional hearing, the Honorable James H. Preston, mayor of Baltimore, declared that "the immigrant question in Baltimore is practically in the hands of the Baltimore & Ohio Railroad. [. . .] The narrow and contracted quarters here for immigration purposes, with only one railroad station, has been practically determined by the Government to be inadequate."[48] The main issue, however, was not the facility itself—the railroad had in fact arranged the process quite efficiently, and the agents were able to move people through customs and inspection rapidly—but rather the monopoly the Baltimore & Ohio held on the port's immigration procedures. With a profit-seeking company at the helm, it was in their best interests not to limit immigration.

Congress approved construction of a federal station just northwest of Fort McHenry and opened it in 1914, a decade after the Baltimore & Ohio had opened its most recent immigrant station at Locust Point. During the congressional hearings on the new immigrant station, Henry G. Hilkens, representative for the North German Lloyd, was questioned as to whether the company's choice of landing pier had subsidized the Baltimore & Ohio Railroad. Hilkens affirmed this statement. Since about 85 percent of the North German Lloyd's passengers traveled further west and south via the railways, the Baltimore & Ohio received the bulk of those passengers. However, he made it clear that the immigrants were under no obligation to travel via the Baltimore & Ohio; passengers bound for stops along the Pennsylvania Railroad departed from that company's station in the Inner Harbor, although it was less convenient.[49]

In support of a federal immigrant station in Baltimore was the Southern Settlement and Development Organization, a group established in 1911 by state governors and southern businessmen to promote settlement in the postbellum South, historically a region that was least settled by newly arrived immigrants.[50] The vice president and general manager of the organization, W. H. Manss, argued, "We need more people to work our farms and we ought to have such facilities as will induce the boats to come here with their passengers and freight, and we need such facilities of rail and water as to enable these people to go into the south, southwest, and southeast portions of the country. Baltimore is the natural port of entry for immigrants. Unless we have adequate facilities for landing immigrants the steamship companies will not bring their passengers here."[51] Even though there was an immigrant station in Baltimore, the fact that it was operated by the Baltimore & Ohio Railroad, whose trains most frequently traveled west to Chicago and St. Louis—not to the South—meant that the southern states lost potential business. Efforts to build capital throughout the South was thus dependent on a transportation system that fostered competitive business. It was in the Southern Settlement and Development Organization's best interest, and certainly that of the southern state governments, for a federal station from which multiple railroad lines could operate, rather than allow immigration to remain in a single company's hands.

The selection of a site near Fort McHenry allowed the government to use land it already owned, thus lowering the new facility's total cost, but the land selection was not without controversy (figure 2.12). Fort McHenry held an important place in American history as the site where the Americans successfully defended Baltimore Harbor against the British during the War of 1812. Some citizens, such as A. C. Hubbard, were vehemently against appropriating this site as an immigrant station. Hubbard had been involved in a 1910 celebration in which the Daughters of the American

Figure 2.12. Aerial view of Locust Point, 1937. The Fort McHenry grounds originally covered the entire tip of the peninsula but the federal immigrant station encroached on those grounds, consisting of the first several piers on the right. Note Locust Point's extensive rail development. Fort McHenry at Baltimore, 1937, 1970200_09867, J. Victor Dallin Aerial Survey collection (Accession 1970.200), Audiovisual Collections and Digital Initiatives Department, Hagley Museum and Library, Wilmington, DE 19807

Revolution unveiled a statue honoring Francis Scott Key. He wrote a letter to the editor of the *Baltimore American* arguing that "this unweeded crowd is proposed to be landed on one of the most sacred spots of American soil on no less a spot than that which holds the fort where floated the flag which inspired 'The Star Spangled Banner.'"[52] Similar rhetoric had been employed first in the selection of Castle Garden for an immigrant station, and then the federal proposal to build a facility alongside the Statue of Liberty. Citizens like Hubbard, who were opposed to the use of Fort McHenry grounds for immigration purposes, wanted to defend the site from foreigners yet again—except this time they were unsuccessful.

Coupled with attempts to set restrictions on immigration, by the early twentieth century, American anxiety toward foreign disease continued to grow, especially given the cramped and unsanitary conditions in the steerage compartments of oceangoing vessels. In the first decade of the twentieth century, when ten to eleven immigrants arrived per one thousand residents each year, immigration reached its zenith.[53] During congressional hearings to determine what sort of facility the government would build, US Public Health officer Dr. J. A. Nydegger declared a hospital essential at the new immigration station, as Baltimore hospitals refused to admit immigrants with certain illnesses. Using the example of measles, Dr. Nydegger declared that "no other hospital in the city of Baltimore will take these cases" and that "in all the large cities they have their own Government hospital."[54] Not only would the new federal station take immigration procedures out of the Baltimore & Ohio's hands, but it would also address public health concerns, much like the hospital facilities at Ellis Island.

Congress authorized the construction so that "the proposed station will be absolutely independent, not under control of any one company, but equally accessible to all through lighterage [train cars transported via barges], and over the tracks of the municipal railway, part of which is already constructed."[55] Either by means of a city railway or by barge, the Baltimore & Ohio would no longer hold the monopoly of rail traffic, and thus, immigrant traffic, on Locust Point. Construction began in 1913 and the federal immigrant station opened in 1915. Designed in the supervising architect of the Treasury's office, the facility included a main administration building with the space to inspect and register 1,200 immigrants, a 124-bed dormitory (which effectively put Koether's boardinghouse out of business), and a 65-bed hospital.[56] Yet the new and larger station was built too late. With the start of World War I, immigration virtually came to a halt and would not begin to increase again until around 1925. Instead, the War Department moved into the new facility. In 1922, only 163 immigrants were admitted through the Port of Baltimore, a drastic decrease from the 20,000 arriving annually between 1909 and 1914.[57]

Likewise, in New York, immigration drastically decreased at the start of the war, although by that time the federal government and railroad companies had been working together for over two decades. The railroad station's ideological role as the modern city gateway contained even deeper meaning at these port stations, which served as the literal and metaphorical point of departure for immigrants in their new country. Yet the foreigners who departed from these terminals were denied the symbolic passage through the opulent main stations. Instead, the railroad companies built separate pier buildings—a form of architectural isolation—to keep the immigrant population contained. This was a practical measure, to be sure, since it allowed those traveling on segregated immigrant trains to be corralled in a single area, where they would be unmolested by potential swindlers and prevented from getting lost in an unfamiliar land. It was also the outcome of a capitalist enterprise that enabled low-cost accommodations for large numbers of people within a transportation network meant to be operated as efficiently as possible to keep costs down for the companies. On a cultural level, this segregation was part of a milieu in which xenophobia was a sober reality, particularly during a time when immigration reached its zenith in the early twentieth century. The architecture of the immigrant transportation network adjusted to meet the cultural and capitalist demands. At the time Stevenson entered the country through New York in 1879, the port stations were undergoing a transformation that allowed them to architecturally isolate the foreign arrivals and usher them into the country at nominal expense and with minimal contact with American citizens.

Figure 3.1. Norfolk & Western Railway boxcar, c. 1863–1864. Freight cars typically featured no windows; when they were converted for passenger use, as seen here, the railroad company added windows to the cars. Civil War Photographs, Prints & Photographs Division, Library of Congress, LC-B811–2657

IMMIGRANT TRAINS AND WAITING ROOMS

In the fierce wind of the Pennsylvania Railroad's drafty train platform, Stevenson huddled in the cold rain with his fellow immigrants for over an hour. On this bleak New Jersey stopover, San Francisco was still a distant dream. In his memoir, Stevenson declared that the rail journey between New York and the West Coast was "the second and far less agreeable chapter of my emigrant experience," far worse than his experience on the transoceanic passage.[1] Without a second cabin to retreat to, now nothing separated Stevenson from the crowd, and he experienced their raw and unmitigated suffering. However, true to character, Stevenson continued to consciously divorce himself from his fellow travelers. He states that when, "at last we were admitted into the cars, utterly dejected, and far from dry," that while the other passengers were so exhausted they "composed themselves to sleep," Stevenson took the time to vigorously run a clothes brush over his soaked trousers "till I had dried them and warmed my blood into the bargain."[2] He lent the brush to his neighbor but noticed, somewhat surprised, that no others took the same precaution. Like his abandonment of wet clothes at the New York boardinghouse and carelessly tossing oranges onto the tracks, Stevenson's bourgeois background set him apart from his fellow passengers. Despite his innate sense of privilege, his description of his rail journey provides significant detail about the accommodations provided in segregated immigrant trains.

In the United States, immigrant trains existed as far back as the founding of the railroad itself.[3] The Baltimore & Ohio Railroad was one of the first major companies to use special immigrant cars when it offered reduced rates to German immigrants in the 1840s, and several other companies followed suit. By the 1850s, most lines running from eastern port cities utilized immigrant trains. These services increased ridership, and the cheaper immigrant fares legitimized the lack of comfortable accommodations that were afforded other passengers. Although railroad and government officials made the case that segregated travel offered protection for the immigrants at an affordable rate, in reality, the accommodations on board, particularly in the eastern states, were hardly favorable. Immigrants were able to travel economically—this is true—but their journey was often difficult.

Railroad companies used outdated passenger cars for immigrant trains or, more frequently, they permanently converted boxcars into passenger cars by installing wooden benches and adding windows to the car doors (figure 3.1). Boxcars did not have the same spring construction as passenger cars, since they were not meant for human traffic; consequently, they produced a jolting ride.[4] It should be noted, however, that the earliest passenger trains were also quite uncomfortable until construction improved in the mid-nineteenth century. One Norwegian immigrant wrote, "Travel by rail—on the main immigrant routes, at least—was especially rugged because most newcomers [. . .] rode in immigrant cars, which were ordinary springless boxcars equipped [. . .] with crude benches for seats and providing neither bunks nor other furnishings, much less personal services."[5] Some lines, such as the Illinois Central and Michigan Central, temporarily converted grain cars by installing seats for immigrants on the trip's westbound leg and then removing the seats to transport freight back east, which maximized their use.[6] Like steamship companies, the railways maximized profits by transporting passengers in one direction and freight in the other. To discourage passenger travel back east, railroad companies offered cheaper fares for westward journeys only.[7] Stevenson characterizes the American train car's typical construction as a "long, narrow wooden box, like a flat-roofed Noah's ark, with a stove and a convenience, one at either end, a passage down the middle, and transverse benches upon either hand" (figure 3.2).[8] As space allowed, railroad officials kept families grouped together on the immigrant trains while men traveling alone occupied a separate car.

Conditions on these immigrant trains were unpleasant, to say the least. Railroad companies did not provide any cushions for the hard wooden benches; immigrants had to provide their own, sit uncomfortably on bare wood for the journey's duration, or purchase cushions when available at stops along the way. Lack of upholstery both minimized costs for the railroad companies and allowed for easy cleaning. In contemporary railroad manuals, employees are instructed to hose down the wooden seats and floors after a journey.[9] Ease of cleaning, as opposed to passenger

Figure 3.2. Interior, immigrant train car. *Harper's Weekly* 18 (January 1894): 76. Courtesy Wisconsin Historical Society

comfort, was the priority for these cars, on which passengers paid less to travel. Stevenson noted the immigrant train car's "extreme plainness," constructed of nothing but wood and furnished only with dim lamps. At five feet ten inches tall, Stevenson remarked that "the benches are too short for anything but a young child. Where there is scarce enough elbow-room for two to sit, there will not be space enough for one to lie."[10] The bench construction was such that two faced each other, and then in the evening the upright boards would be removed and laid across the benches to make a flat surface wide enough for the two passengers to lie down side by side. Of course, this plan was impossible when the train was crowded, which Stevenson pointed out. The other factor this arrangement relied on was the mutual agreement of two strangers to share the cost of the straw-filled cushions for sale aboard the train. In the family cars, this was not an issue, but riding in the bachelor car, as Stevenson was, meant that the cushion salesman served as "a most active master of ceremonies, introducing likely couples, and even guaranteeing the amiability and honesty of each."[11] Of course, the more people the salesman matched, the more money he made. He had difficulty matching Stevenson, however, who began to feel the pain of rejection as another passenger declined to sit with him. He was soon matched with a "curly-haired Pennsylvania Dutchman," with whom he split the fees for the cushions. As the day faded and the lamps were lit, travelers began preparing their beds for the night ahead. But the train soon pulled into the station, and the car became crowded with locals selling beds at twenty-five cents a cushion. Before the train departed again, the price was lowered to fifteen cents, one-fifth of what Stevenson had paid at the previous stop, much to his annoyance.

Given the multiday westward journeys, passengers typically tried to sleep when possible but the jolting ride and noisy and crowded conditions made it difficult. Along with physical exhaustion, most passengers likely experienced a distinct form of mental and emotional fatigue. Leaving one's home—unsure of when or if they would ever return—is challenge enough for any person. This, followed by a stressful journey first by sea and then rail into a country where the customs and language (for many) were completely foreign, was compounded by the stress of navigating the transportation network: safeguarding belongings; finding basic necessities like water, food, and restrooms to perform basic hygiene; and being surrounded by strangers while sharing intimate moments of mealtime and sleep must have surely intensified any feelings of alienation. Within this shared liminal space of travel, there was also the individual's own emotional "space in-between." Grief over the lives they left behind, uncertainty of having made the right decision to relocate, anxiety about the future. Passengers occupied their minds in various ways, through games, reading, conversation, as well as music. One of Stevenson's fellow passengers played a cornet to entertain those in the car. Spirits were high and the mood was jolly, but when the musician began to play "Home Sweet Home," the general mood in the car turned to melancholy as passengers were reminded of the homes and people they had left behind. "An elderly, hard-looking man" bade the performer to stop playing the song and "give us something about the good country we're going to."[12] A momentary joyous mood was quickly deflated as the travelers were once again reminded of their liminality. This travel space, the space in-between, was where they had to reckon with the loss of their previous lives and the future that awaited them in a new country. Stevenson's own way of handling this was to immerse himself in the history of the country to which he was relocating. He carried with him six volumes of George Bancroft's *History of the United States, from the Discovery of the American Continent*, one of the colonial period's most comprehensive texts, which he had purchased at a bookstore in New York. Bancroft began publishing his text in 1834, and by 1890 he had completed numerous editions. In 1876, he republished the ten-volume series as a six-volume publication for the country's centennial, which was the edition that Stevenson carried on his journey. Throughout his memoir, Stevenson makes reference to the weighty tomes, which took up much of his limited baggage space. Imbued with the spirit of Romanticism, but also chauvinism and racist overtones toward America's Indigenous population, Bancroft's history was a continuous bestseller during most of the nineteenth century. Today Bancroft has been largely forgotten, mainly because, at the time of his death in 1891, American historiography was transitioning to a more pragmatic and professionalized school of thought, as opposed to Bancroft's own sentimental, rhetorical, and nationalistic way of writing.[13] No doubt Bancroft's style would have appealed to a Romantic like Stevenson, who had his own idealized notions of what defined America, the very qualities that drew immigrants like himself to the country's shores. The hardships of migration, however, led Stevenson to keenly understand the realities of the arduous journey.

"Civility Is the Main Comfort That You Miss"

Before the introduction of the immigrant sleeper car in the 1880s, amenities such as water, toilets, lighting, and stoves for cooking were minimal, if present at all. Stevenson noted the "inefficacy of the lamps, which often went out and shed but a dying glimmer even while they burned."[14] Sharing items, like the bed cushions, was one way for passengers to save money on the journey. On the immigrant trains, sometimes a newsboy walked the length of each car, selling entertainment like books and newspapers, in addition to essentials like soap, towels, tin dishes, coffee pitchers, and food products like canned beans or hash, coffee, tea, and sugar. Stevenson and his bedfellow, who referred to each other as Shakespeare and Pennsylvania, respectively, decided to pool their money with a third companion, whom they called Dubuque, to purchase a tin washing-dish, towel, and brick of soap to share among themselves. Washing one's face was a precarious task: each would take turns filling the dish with water from the faucet near the stove, then carry it across the car to the platform, where he would kneel down and support himself against the wall or with an elbow crooked about the railing to wash his face—"a cold, an insufficient, and, if the train is moving rapidly, a somewhat dangerous toilet."[15] The three men also pooled their funds to purchase coffee, sugar, and a coffee tin, so they could make a pitcher of coffee using the stove in the train car. At the day's first station stop, locals boarded the train to sell milk, eggs, and cakes for the passengers to eat on their bed boards.

In addition to locals boarding the trains to sell goods, at stops along the journey immigrants were also able to use the station restrooms and purchase food and water from the restaurant or bar. This had its disadvantages since stops lasted only about twenty minutes and many immigrants complained of not having enough time to get a meal.[16] One Dutch immigrant recalled, "We had a burning thirst, and only at the stations, whenever the train stopped, could we get water. As the train did not wait for us while we filled our jugs, we always had to hurry."[17] Stevenson noted that he kept an eye on the train even while eating, since "the train stole from the station without note of warning."[18] On standard trains, conductors alerted passengers with a resounding "All aboard!" yet conductors of immigrant trains pulled away without alerting passengers, and the passengers, understandably, feared being left behind. Observing this practice, Stevenson declared, "Equality, though conceived very largely in America, does not extend so low down as to an emigrant."[19] Indeed, Stevenson and many other travelers encountered rudeness and disrespect during their travels. In one scenario, a conductor refused to answer Stevenson's question of what time the train would stop for dinner. Knowing the immigrant trains' erratic schedules, which were often waylaid for other rail traffic, it is likely the conductor could not give an exact time but instead declared that it was his principle not to answer questions like that, because they led to endless other questions. Where the conductor was reticent to share information or put passengers at ease, the newsboy was often the opposite. The boy who rode on the train with Stevenson from Ogden to Sacramento befriended the passengers, telling them when and where they would be able to eat and how long the train would stop, and also made sure they were not left behind when the train departed. These small kindnesses were much appreciated by the weary travelers. It especially meant a lot to Stevenson, who was quite sickly at this point in his journey, and the newsboy, seeing how ill Stevenson looked, offered him a pear at no cost and lent him newspapers to read while Stevenson sat near the door, holding it open to escape the train car's stifling air and take in whatever fresh breeze he could.

There was another notable difference between immigrant cars and standard passenger cars—the opportunity to view the passing landscape. Unlike standard passenger cars, where travelers could enjoy the vista through large glass windows, the converted boxcars, or "economically constructed" cars, as one 1889 source described them, offered little in the way of scenery.[20] On his 1872 journey from Omaha to San Francisco, William B. Stockton wrote that windows on the immigrant train were "small peek-holes high up on the sides where one at a time might stand to see out."[21] Since these cars transported freight east while bringing passengers west—the priority here was ensuring a full carload of grain or whatever commodity would be sold in the East or overseas. Not only did the small openings offer little fresh air but the immigrants were also denied the panoramic views available to other passengers, for whom the speed of travel offered a continuously moving landscape.

German philosopher Dolf Sternberger termed the latter form of viewing *panoramic perception* and attributed its creation to the railroad: "The railroad transformed the world of lands and seas into a panorama that could be experienced. Not only did it join the previously distant localities by eliminating all resistance, difference, and adventure from the journey: now that traveling had become so comfortable and common, it turned the travelers' eyes outward and offered them the opulent nourishment of ever changing images that were the only possible thing that could be experienced during the journey."[22] It is with this panoramic perception that "the traveler saw the objects, landscapes, etc. *through* the apparatus which moved him through the world," explained cultural historian Wolfgang Schivelbusch.[23] These views were inaccessible to immigrant passengers, or only partially visible. One immigrant passenger traveling from Boston to Milwaukee remarked, "Surely any person with plenty of money would be happy to travel for days through such beautiful and ever changing scenery. But travelling as we did on an immigrant train [. . .] was a sore trial, enough to make us downhearted."[24] Just as they would be allowed only partial use of the railroad stations, on the train—the space in-between—immigrants could only catch glimpses of the land that would be their new home.

"When I Awoke . . . the Train Was Standing Idle"

The railroad journey was long and uncomfortable for immigrant passengers, not only because of poor accommodations but also because of slow service. Immigrant cars were often attached to freight trains, which ran on a slower schedule than express, passenger, and mail trains, to which railroad personnel gave the right-of-way on tracks. Stevenson's own train was waylaid on the second day of his rail journey. He awoke at daybreak to an idle train somewhere in Pennsylvania. Since he was in the last carriage, he opened the door and stepped out onto the platform. Other passengers were milling about outside. They were surrounded by an open landscape—neither station nor signal nearby, only some locust trees and a field of corn. Stevenson stood in awe of the sunrise, "more purple, brown, and smoky orange" than those he was accustomed to seeing in Europe. Soon after, the reason for their stop became evident when a train whisked by, horn blaring, and the passengers were summoned to board the train again. Since there had been an accident the evening before, traffic had been disrupted and those in the immigrant train suffered the consequences. Stevenson reveals, "We paid for this in the flesh, for we had no meals that day."[25] There was some fruit for sale on the train, but otherwise the passengers had only a few moments at a station, where all that was offered were some rolls and sandwiches, although not nearly enough to meet demand. Though Stevenson tried to elbow his way to the counter at each stop they made, the food and coffee were always exhausted by the time he got there.

The slower journey added further discomfort and expense for immigrants. Longer travel time meant that immigrants put more money toward purchasing additional food and also toward boarding, if they had to seek overnight accommodations when transferring trains. For many immigrants, finances were running low by the last leg of their journey. John Remeeus, a Dutch immigrant traveling with his family to Milwaukee in 1854, was rerouted to Boston instead of New York, as his steamship ticket indicated, and purchased railroad tickets there to travel west. In addition to the ticket cost, checking his baggage cost him eighteen more dollars than he had expected. At an overnight stop in Albany, his family stayed at a boardinghouse that cost six dollars—"a large sum for a poor immigrant," Remeeus noted. When Remeeus arrived in Chicago, he had only one dollar left in his pocket and with it he had to support his family until they arrived to their relatives in Milwaukee.[26]

Immigrant aid societies and the press were often critical of the railroad companies' methods to transport immigrants. In 1887, an article in the *World* condemned the New York emigration commission and the railroads, stating that instead of protecting and caring for immigrants until they reach their destination, "the immigrants are not only huddled like cattle in the uncomfortable and foul-smelling cars of this unlawful pool, that run on a freight schedule, taking two days instead of one to reach Chicago, but they are deprived of the right to select by which one even of the pool lines that shall purchase their tickets, and are charged exorbitant rates for baggage."[27] Furthermore, Senate investigations in 1871 discovered that the railroad companies ran "slow 'extra' trains for the immigrant" and that "engineers were not responsible to the company for arrival at any certain time."[28] The practice of giving other trains the right-of-way and delaying or rerouting immigrant trains occurred more frequently in the east than on the longer transcontinental journeys, since passenger and mail trains did not run as frequently further west as they did in the East.[29] The eastern trains, cramped with immigrant passengers, became a focus for immigrant aid societies. Their criticisms, however, did not effect change in the same way as it had at the government-owned immigrant receiving stations. The railroad companies were private enterprises with the aim of capitalizing profits. For them, immigrant traffic was a huge source of revenue. Yet even though the western railroad companies had more to gain from their immigrant passengers, the conditions and services were far inferior to the accommodations provided to middle-class travelers.

"I Was That City's Benefactor, yet I Was Received in a Third-Class Waiting Room"

For many traveling by rail from the East Coast, Chicago was a major point of transfer. The most important rail center in the country, more rail lines radiated out from Chicago than any other city (see figure I.3). Stevenson's train reached Chicago on a Wednesday evening, his third day of rail travel. To him, "Chicago seemed a great and gloomy city."[30] After the Great Chicago Fire of 1871, in which 3.3 square miles of the city burned, including more than 17,000 structures, Stevenson, like many moved by the city's plight, had contributed a nominal sum to the city's rebuilding efforts. As the train rolled into Chicago, he saw "street after street of ponderous houses and crowds of comfortable burghers," and he felt owed restitution by the city, "or, at the least, to entertain me to a cheerful dinner." Never mind the fact that it had been nearly a decade since the fire, or that Stevenson had only contributed sixpence to the rebuilding efforts. After a long and exhausting journey from New Jersey, Stevenson was dismayed that, upon his entrance to the city, he was received in a third-class waiting room. Even though he was traveling on an immigrant train, Stevenson must have expected to have full access to the large city stations where he made his transfer. On the contrary, immigrant travelers remained segregated in their own waiting rooms in large Midwestern train stations, but instead of the separate and vastly inferior pier structures, as was common in the eastern port terminals, the railroad companies included the immigrant waiting areas in the main building plan—that is, segregation by architectural partitioning as opposed to architectural isolation.[31] The immigrant room's design and location sustained the segregation present on the trains.

In stations where the immigrant waiting area was located within the main building, there was an increased chance for contact between immigrants and other passengers, particularly in the space of the train concourse. This contact, however, was carefully monitored by railroad officials. Designated immigrant agents hired by the railroads directed immigrant passengers to their waiting room and to the trains. For all of their passengers, railroad companies provided physical spaces to control passenger circulation and limit interaction. For its white passengers not riding on the immigrant fare, larger stations typically offered a main waiting area, ladies' waiting room, and men's smoking room—the latter two being standard in the late nineteenth and early twentieth centuries as they conformed to contemporary notions of middle-class gentility and respectability.[32] Segregated waiting rooms for immigrants or for Black passengers, particularly in the American South, were not separated by gender, suggesting that societal notions of femininity and respectability only applied to white American citizens. Not all railroad stations contained immigrant waiting rooms, and those that did were usually located in large cities where immigrants transferred trains. At union stations where several railroad lines converged, in cities such as Indianapolis, Chicago, and Kansas City, immigrant facilities were included in the building but partitioned from the main waiting areas.

Advertising superior facilities was one way for railroad companies to attract immigrant passengers while simultaneously demonstrating to the public that the immigrant population would be segregated within the space of the station. The Chicago & North Western Railway Company went to great lengths to describe and promote the facilities and services available to immigrants in their new Chicago terminal, which opened in 1911. The five other stations servicing Chicago in the early twentieth century housed between three and eleven carriers each; the Chicago & North Western Terminal was the only Chicago station dedicated to one

Figure 3.3. Immigrant waiting room, Chicago and North Western Terminal, Chicago, Illinois, c. 1910–1920. Courtesy of the Library of Congress, Prints and Photographs Division, Reproduction Number LC-DIG-det-4a24209

railroad company, which perhaps explains the company's extensive advertising campaign that included postcards, brochures, and booklets.[33]

The Chicago & North Western published a thirty-two-page booklet entitled *The Care of the Immigrant in the New Passenger Terminal* in an effort to promote the railroad line to potential immigrant passengers.[34] The booklet, published in English, French, German, and the Scandinavian languages, was distributed in the United States and Europe. Additionally, the Chicago & North Western published several pamphlets with pertinent statistics for immigrants on employment, geography, housing, and so on. This was not unusual; in fact, many railroad companies and state governments published pamphlets such as these to promote immigration to the United States. By providing this information to immigrants, the Chicago & North Western Railway declared that they "hoped that those

Figure 3.4. Washtubs and clothes dryers in the immigrant waiting area, Chicago & North Western Railway Terminal, Chicago, Illinois, 1912. Courtesy of the Chicago & North Western Historical Society

who are deeply interested in the development of the Western States will aid and appreciate the labor and expense incurred by the railway company in these publications, by extending their patronage, and advising their friends when traveling to patronize the Chicago & North Western Railway."[35] The company described the immigrant facilities in their Chicago station as "unequalled in any other railway station in the world."[36] They offered such amenities as tubs in which to bathe, sinks and dryers to launder clothing, a lunch room to purchase food, and tables to sit and write letters to loved ones (figures 3.3 and 3.4).

Although the Chicago & North Western rightfully presented their immigrant rooms as a space that far exceeded any other railroad's immigrant facilities, for which they were commended by immigrant aid societies, there was a marked difference between the immigrant rooms and the areas of the station provided for nonimmigrant passengers.[37] The immigrants' facilities had none of the grandeur associated with the rest of the building. Passengers entered into the public lobby through the colonnaded entrance of the Renaissance Revival structure designed by the architectural firm

Figure 3.5. Main waiting room, Chicago & North Western Railway Terminal, Chicago, Illinois, 1915 postcard. Courtesy of the Hagley Museum and Library

Frost & Granger. From there, first-class passengers ascended a staircase to the massive waiting room on the track level. The main waiting room was a lavish space: abundant light streaming in through lunette windows along the sides and ends of the barrel-vaulted roof, light pink Tennessee marble walls and pilasters, columns of pale green Greek Appollino marble, bronze light fixtures, and mahogany seats (figure 3.5). It was vividly colored and opulent—a stark contrast to the sterile immigrant waiting room. Immigrant passengers did not ascend the staircase to this waiting room but instead an agent hired by the railway directed them to the waiting room accessed by the suburban concourse between Clinton and Canal streets, about halfway along the length of the building (figure 3.6). The immigrants, although allowed to enter the main building, were kept at a far distance from the other passengers, a large number of whom were commuters.

Other Chicago stations advertised their immigrant facilities to potential customers, although they did not go to the same lengths as the Chicago & North Western Railway in their attempt to secure immigrant passengers. For example, the railroad officials at Chicago's Grand Central Station described the immigrant facilities in this way:

Figure 3.6. Chicago and North Western Railway Terminal, Chicago, Illinois, Frost & Granger, 1911 [text added by author]. Courtesy of the Library of Congress, Prints & Photographs Division, Reproduction Number LC-USZC4–14769

> Poverty and luxury are closely allied, they say, and so it is that just beyond the kitchen of the restaurant is a long, clean, well-lit and well-ventilated hall, where the West-bound immigrants rest and wait for their cars. Unlike other places one could name, the Grand Central Passenger Station seems to have immigrant accommodations suitable for human beings, and though, of course, there is not the glitter of marble there, nor does the cheeriness of a hickory fire help to brighten the prospects of the foreigners in search of new lives; still they can have their comforts there. There they can feel, at least, that they are coming to a land where there is room for all and comfort, and through the windows they can watch the tides of traffic and trade as they wait the cars that are to carry them to the farther, wider West.[38]

In so many words, the officials at Grand Central Station claimed that their immigrant accommodations were superior to the inhumane quarters of other (unnamed) railroad stations but admitted that this space was in fact inferior to the main waiting areas. This passage speaks more to the concerns of other passengers at the station than it does to the immigrants' own interests, although the latter is certainly addressed. The railway assures passengers that immigrants are out of the way and will not inconvenience the public; it also assures immigrants that its facilities are better than those of their competitors.

As immigrants traveled further into the country, western railroad companies offered them the opportunity to cleanse themselves—literally—of their old world. John Droege, general superintendent of the New York, New Haven and Hartford Railroad, recommended that the immigrant room be "furnished with complete sanitary equipment, and, if possible, tubs for washing clothes and dryers. [. . .] Immigrant rooms should be well ventilated and the interior of them so designed that they may be easily cleaned."[39] Throughout their promotional booklet, the Chicago & North Western Railroad referenced the cleanliness of the space with descriptions of the "sanitary waiting room," "shining white porcelain bath tubs [and] sanitary towels," "sanitary bubbling drinking fountains," and notes that "its construction of vitrified brick and cement makes scrupulous cleanliness possible."[40] With these descriptions, the Chicago & North Western Railway directly responded to public fears that immigrants bore filth and disease. Immigration officials, certain politicians, and writers for the popular press often viewed foreigners as carriers of infectious diseases and associated them with poor hygiene.[41] The design of these spaces expressed the railroad companies' attempts to control the circulation of foreign-borne illness. In describing the white-tiled, sterile areas of the immigrant waiting room, railroad companies sent the message that other travelers could be protected from the assumed filth and disease the immigrants carried. Offering a sanitary space in which immigrants could bathe and launder their clothing meant that they could continue their rail journey cleansed—something immigrants surely *wanted* to do after several days in the train car.

The opportunity for immigrants to cleanse themselves of the Old World as they traveled to their new home had figurative meaning as well. Railroad companies sought out the "settler who has 'staying qualities.'"[42] The Chicago & North Western viewed new foreigners as potential citizens and thus urged employees to "do our share—prompted not alone by our sense of duty to the Company but by genuine humanitarian considerations—in helping to shape the bewildered foreigner into the ideal of American citizenship."[43] By offering clean facilities and improved amenities (or at least better facilities than the competitors') railroad companies hoped to impart their own standard of morality on immigrant passengers, who were not yet integrated into American society. As Charles L. Davis II explains, the transcontinental railroad in the United States became a "physical emblem of white cultural nationalism," with idealized white settler culture viewed as the source of American culture as a whole—in politics, commerce, literature, and art.[44] In the eyes of railroad officials, immigrants could begin to shed their foreign ways as they traveled by rail to their new home and, once settled, could eventually become model citizens. The Chicago & North Western Railway cautioned its employees to treat every immigrant well since "as we do not know from sight the future winners of the yet unwon West, wisdom advises us to treat all as prospective winners, for we shall want the good will of the man who sticks when he finally comes into his own."[45] The treatment of immigrants was thus tied up in the potential profit to be made by the railroads. Although the Chicago & North Western Railway went to great lengths in their humane treatment of immigrants, ultimately the better the treatment they gave the immigrants, the more profit to be gained—a fact not lost on railroad officials.

In stations with a high number of commuter passengers, like the Chicago & North Western Terminal or the Central Railroad of New Jersey Terminal in Jersey City, the immigrant facilities were removed from general waiting areas, either within the main building or outside of it entirely. At Union Station in Kansas City, Missouri, however, the majority of traffic was through passengers—not suburban commuters.[46] Most of the rail lines terminated at Union Station and thus a large number of the twenty thousand to thirty-five thousand passengers that passed through the station daily were there to transfer trains. Many of the lines that traveled through Union Station, such as the Atchison, Topeka & Santa Fe Railroad, catered to large numbers of immigrant passengers who traveled west in segregated sleeper cars. The low number of commuters at the station meant that the immigrant room did not need to be completely isolated from the main waiting areas. In fact, the immigrant room in this station was adjacent to the main waiting room with a lunchroom separating the two areas (figure 3.7).

The construction of the Beaux-Arts Union Station, designed by architect Jarvis Hunt and completed in 1914, was initiated by the Kansas City Terminal Railway Company, a corporation owned equally by the twelve railroads that would occupy the station.[47] At the time of its completion, it was one of the largest stations in the country.[48] The T-shaped masonry structure opened onto a southern public plaza and the stem of the *T* projected north over the tracks. The steel-framed building was covered with Bedford limestone and trimmed in Maine granite. Three deeply recessed arches, separated by double columns, faced the plaza and marked the grand entrance to the neoclassical building. There were two entrances to the building, one located in each of the end archways, which flanked the semicircular ticket office in the lobby. Service areas included a telegraph office and telephone booths on either side of the ticket office; an octagonal information booth and similar booth for the transfer company were located in the east and west ends of the lobby, respectively. The east wing contained a restaurant and lunchroom, women's waiting room, and

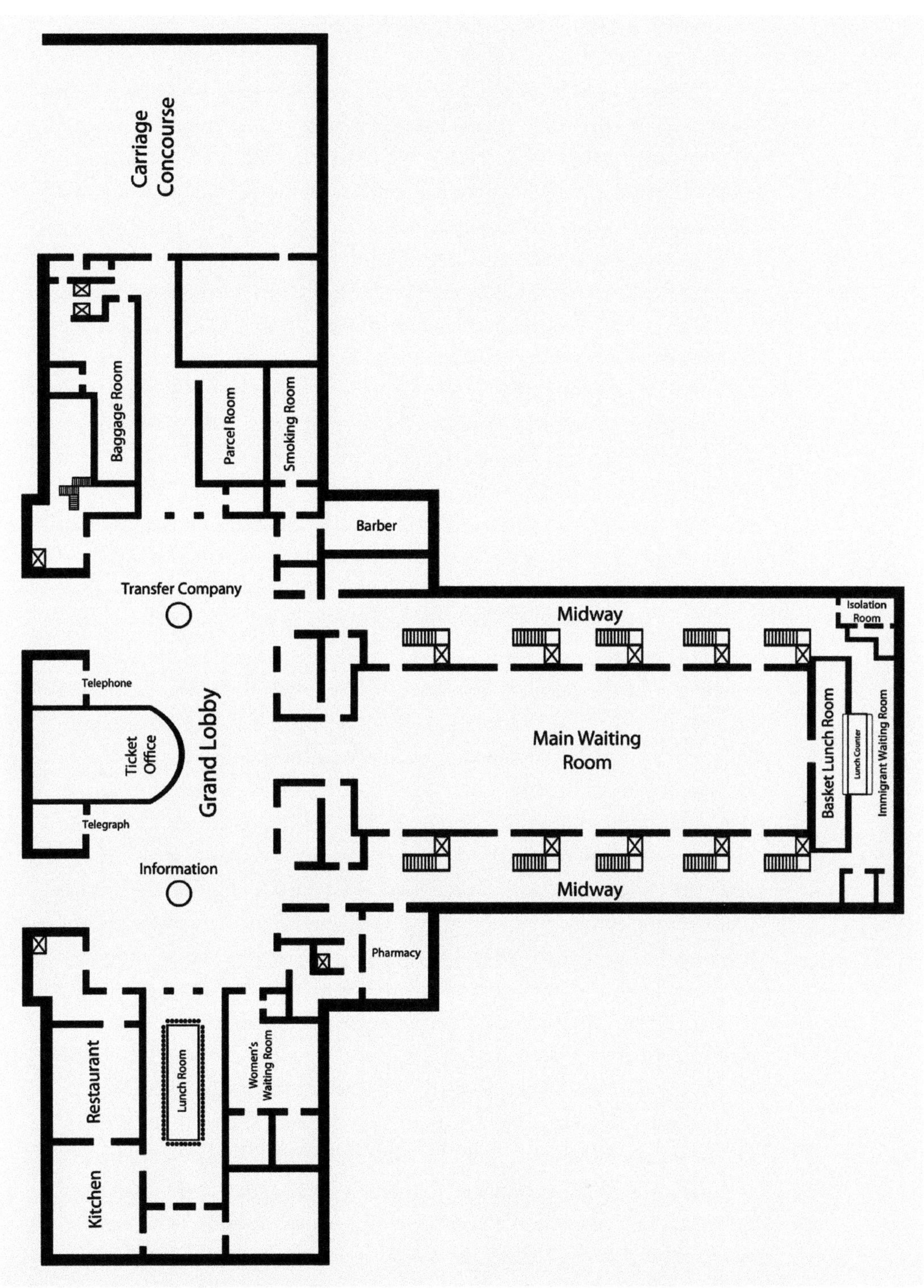

Figure 3.7. Plan of Union Station, Kansas City, Missouri, Jarvis Hunt, 1914. Redrawn by Julie Boland Perez from John Droege, *Passenger Terminals and Trains* (New York: McGraw Hill, 1916)

pharmacist, while the west wing housed the baggage and parcel rooms, a men's smoking room, and barbershop.

The grand lobby opened into the main waiting area, which had eight train gates on either side. These gates opened onto a concourse called the Midway, with stairways to track level. The Midway also led to the grand lobby, allowing incoming passengers to pass directly into the lobby and out the main entrance without having to walk through the main waiting area, a grand space featuring forty-four double mahogany benches, terra-cotta walls with a base of Great Bend marble, a paneled plaster ceiling, and large triple windows over each train gate. Its design and decoration far surpassed that of the immigrant waiting room, located north of the main waiting area. Its walls were capped with a plaster cornice and were constructed of the same buff-colored bricks that were used in the Midway. The room, which had a 150-person capacity, was sparsely furnished with oak wood benches and the interior illuminated by bands of metal-framed windows high on the north and south walls. The brick construction of the immigrant room, as opposed to the marble and terra-cotta walls of the main waiting area, is a reflection of the lower status of the room's occupants (figure 3.8). Hunt intended future expansion of the station and designed the north end so that the brick immigrant room could be removed and the building extended to the north (with the decline of rail travel beginning in the 1920s, this extension was unnecessary and thus never built). A marble-topped lunch counter on the south wall of the room was duplicated on the other side of the brick wall for the station's nonimmigrant passengers. A small kitchen area separated the two counters, although passengers at one counter were partially visible to the other side, an encounter that would have been impossible at stations where the immigrant room and dining areas were physically separated from the main waiting areas by solid walls, entire rooms, or even entire buildings. At these lunch counters, commuters and immigrant passengers visually confronted one another but remained segregated within their respective waiting rooms.

Many immigrants traveled the railroads of the Kansas City Terminal Railway Company to reach their new homes, located on land likely purchased from the railways in Kansas, Nebraska, Texas, New Mexico, and elsewhere. With a minimal number of commuters, there was less of a need for railroad officials to protect the local population from any real or imagined threat posed by the foreign passengers. Yet the Kansas City Terminal Railway Company did address the threat posed by passengers with contagious diseases or criminal records. These passengers were contained in the isolation room adjacent to the immigrant waiting room. The

Figure 3.8. "The Immigrant or Second Class Waiting Room," *Kansas City Star*, March 5, 1912. Customers are seated at the lunch counter in the center [Illustration edited for clarity by Julie Boland Perez]. Courtesy *Kansas City Star*

Railway Age Gazette reported in its description of Union Station's facilities that "the isolation and immigrants' waiting rooms are connected directly with the concourse on each side, eliminating the necessity for this class of passengers passing through the main waiting room or coming in contact with other travelers.[49] Through a close reading of the architectural plans, the hierarchy of travelers is made evident: railroad officials deemed the passengers confined to the isolation room unfit to associate with those passengers in the main waiting area and in this contemporary description are grouped—architecturally and socially—with immigrant travelers. In contrast to the port cities, in the Midwest, where immigrant travelers were viewed by the railways as customers and potential landowners, they were no longer completely isolated from other passengers, yet they were still associated, however tenuously, with criminals and the diseased.

In a floor plan from the Kansas City Terminal Railway Company printed in the *Railway Age Gazette* prior to the building's completion, the waiting room at the rear of the structure was labeled "Second-Class Waiting Room."[50] After the building's completion, in both the *Railway Age Gazette* and Droege's *Passenger Terminals and Trains*, the same space is renamed the "Immigrant Waiting Room."[51] The change in terminology suggests that the Kansas City Terminal Railway Company had originally labeled the space according to the class of travel—not by singling out passengers for their foreignness—but upon completion of the building the company conformed to the segregation of immigrant travelers evident in other railroad stations. Only immigrant passengers could be in proximity of the criminal and diseased, who were possibly migrants themselves, whether newly arrived to the country or from eastern states.

"Now I Was to be Branded Once More, and Put Apart from My Fellows"

Railroad companies operating west of Chicago had more to gain financially from the immigrants than the East Coast lines. For western companies, immigrants were viewed not only as travelers but also as land buyers, settlers, and customers for the railways' subsequent services. Improved conditions on immigrant trains occurred in 1879—the year of Stevenson's journey. With the introduction of the immigrant sleeper car, which was modeled after the fashionable Pullman sleeper cars and allowed, as the name suggests, room to sleep during the journey, travel conditions improved for foreign passengers.[52] For Stevenson, the transfer from the Union Pacific cars to the Central Pacific was a welcome one: "The cars on the Central Pacific were nearly twice as high, and so proportionally airier; they were freshly varnished, which gave us all a sense of cleanliness as though we had bathed; the seats drew out and joined in the centre, so that there was no need for bed-boards; and there was an upper tier of berths which could be closed by day and opened by night."[53] Nevertheless, although related in principle to the Pullman design, these immigrant sleepers lacked the amenities and luxurious interiors of Pullman cars—plush

Figure 3.9. Interior of a Pullman Palace Car, 1893. Note the ornate interior, light fixtures, plush seats, curtained windows, and decorative wood throughout. Courtesy of the Newberry Library, Chicago. Call #MMS Pullman 13–01–01, Box 16, Folder 723

cushioned seats, carpeting, mattresses and linens, brass fixtures, and separate cars for seating during the day (figure 3.9). Instead, the immigrant car featured a plain oak wooden interior, hard wooden seats, and cast-iron fixtures (figure 3.10). Yet Stevenson, and likely the other passengers, were

Figure 3.10. Interior of Immigrant Sleeper Car, 1893. At left, the upper berth is pulled down for sleeping passengers; the first two upper berths on the right are closed. Passengers on the lower berths could lay down or remain seated upright. From the New York Public Library

initially pleased with the upgrade from the eastern lines. The versatility of the interior, with the lower and upper berths, the latter of which could be closed during the day for more room and lowered down, supported by iron rods, at night, allowed for more space. After occupying the cars for the night, however, for those in the upper berths, fumes and lack of air threatened to suffocate passengers. "I think we are human only by virtue of open windows," Stevenson declared.[54] While attempts to improve ventilation had been ongoing since the railroad's earliest decades, it would not be until the introduction of air-conditioning in the 1930s that ventilation improved significantly.[55]

Since no mattresses or cushions were provided on the immigrant trains, passengers had to supply their own, or on some lines, like the

Santa Fe Railroad, they could purchase them on board. In fact, the Santa Fe Railroad prided itself on its immigrant accommodations and advertised that their sleeper cars included lamps, water, a stove, and separate toilet facilities for men and women.[56] Like the trains operating in the eastern states, there was no dining car and passengers could either bring their own food or purchase it at stops along the journey. Immigrants deemed these sleeper cars far superior to the immigrant cars of the eastern lines, where passengers had less room and had no choice but to sleep on the uncomfortable seats, on the floor under the seats, or even in the aisles.[57]

The companies that traveled west of Chicago offered improved accommodations on sleeper trains in the hopes of enticing passengers to purchase land owned by the railroads—Native lands that had been appropriated and redistributed by the United States government for the construction of the transcontinental railroad as part of the Pacific Railroad Act of 1862 (and its subsequent revisions).[58] The continued colonization of Native lands was expedited by the railroad companies, who offered special incentives to prospective settlers, such as applying the train fare toward land purchased, offering discounts to large groups of settlers, or giving free tickets to families of those traveling west to purchase land. Improved conditions on western lines did, in fact, attract more immigrant passengers, who comprised a high percentage of passenger traffic on western lines. For example, in 1888 Union Pacific operated eighty-four immigrant sleeper cars and only fifty-three Pullman cars. Other lines such as the Santa Fe and the Northern Pacific also had a higher number of immigrant cars.[59]

The segregated spaces of the railways not only expressed American prejudices toward newly arrived immigrants but also revealed, and effectually reinforced, a racial hierarchy present among the settlers themselves. Railroad companies tried to increase immigrant traffic by catering to prejudices among the travelers, going so far as to advertise the fact that they did their best to keep members of the same nationality together. Immigrants sometimes expressed annoyance at traveling in train cars with ethnic groups other than their own. Dutch immigrant John Remeeus and his family "were much annoyed during the night by strange Irish people," whom he harshly described as "a low class who had attained only a slight degree of civilization."[60] The Santa Fe Railroad promised to "take special pains to locate passengers of the same nationality, and whose manners indicate that they would prove congenial, in the same car, so that all may be associated with agreeable traveling companions."[61] The Chicago & North Western Railway also noted in their promotional booklet that immigrants traveling on their line are "carefully distributed according to the departure of their trains in family groups, or according to nationalities."[62] The degree to which this promise was fulfilled is unclear; however, the fact that it is documented in railroad promotional literature indicates that this was intended as a selling point for those purchasing tickets from that particular company. Given the close quarters in the train cars and the fact that many travelers, like Stevenson and his companions Dubuque and Pennsylvania, frequently shared items like sleep cushions, soap, and coffee, traveling with passengers familiar with one's language and customs was one way in which the railroad companies intended to put their passengers at ease.

Yet the attempts to group passengers according to nationality extended well beyond an attempt to make passengers comfortable. These efforts also reinforced racist practices evident in the country at the time. Stevenson noted that in the space of the railways "hungry Europe and hungry China [came] face-to-face."[63] As he traveled further west, Stevenson encountered immigrant trains that had separate train cars for Chinese passengers. The train cars were segregated first by families, then by single men, and then Chinese passengers. Stevenson remarked in his travel journal that the Chinese car was, in fact, the tidiest of all the immigrant cars and that the Chinese travelers' "efforts at cleanliness put us all to shame." While Stevenson and the other white travelers "wet our hands and faces for half a minute daily on the platform," he observed that the Chinese passengers, in contrast, took every opportunity to clean themselves: "You would see them washing their feet—an act not dreamed of among [ourselves]—and going as far as decency permitted to wash their whole bodies."[64] Yet prejudice prevailed, and in Stevenson's account, the Chinese received the most scorn from their fellow immigrant travelers, who claimed that they were the filthiest and most foul-smelling of the other passengers, an unfounded bias that resulted in segregation of these passengers. Obviously, this segregation was racially motivated: not only were Chinese passengers isolated from other immigrants but the Chinese car was also the passenger car closest to the engine and thus the most dangerous location on the train. Due to the often-crowded nature of these immigrant trains, however, in which there were typically a higher number of white men traveling alone (as was the case on Stevenson's train), the cars for single men were quickly filled and the other solo white male travelers either rode in the family car or in the Chinese car, depending on where there was enough room. The segregation, then, was sometimes merely superficial, and the limitations of travel space did not always rigidly adhere to contemporary societal divisions.

This racial hierarchy also extended to other groups, including Native Americans. In the western United States, in particular, Native Americans also rode the rails. In Nevada, for example, Shoshoni and Paiute Indians were relegated to the immigrant cars. However, when the immigrants complained that the Native Americans were dusty and unwashed, railroad officials forced them to ride in the baggage cars or on the boarding steps.[65] This meant that Native American passengers were not even afforded the courtesy of a seat; instead, they were treated as subhuman by other passengers and railroad officials. Whereas immigrant passengers had the potential to become citizens and assimilate to American cultural norms, many nineteenth-century American citizens doubted Native Americans could ever *fully* assimilate, despite the federal government's most fervent and extreme efforts, which included establishment of boarding schools, suppression of Native religions and promotion of Christianity, and introduction of agriculture, among other practices.[66]

The same system that provided immigrant trains and waiting rooms also supported Jim Crow train cars and architecture.[67] Black passengers, even when able to pay the higher fare to ride in first-class cars, were not afforded the right to move from segregated cars.[68] Ladies' cars were only available to white women, even if Black women and children paid the first-class fare. Instead, with a first-class ticket Black women and children were forced to ride in the men's smoker car—a place where no respectable white woman would travel, according to the etiquette of the time. The protection of white American women from men (of all races) and from Black and immigrant women conformed to the Euro-American Victorian standards of respectability and femininity.[69] Most southern railroad stations maintained segregated areas for Black passengers. These southern stations, however, typically did not feature immigrant waiting rooms since the vast majority of immigrants entered ports further north or west. Union Depot in St. Paul, Minnesota, designed by architect Charles Frost and completed in 1918, is a unique example of a station containing segregated waiting rooms for both immigrant and for Black passengers. Race dictated the space of Black travel, as well as Chinese travel, but for European immigrants, segregation from other passengers was predominantly an issue of class, since those able to pay higher fares were not forced by railroad officials to travel in immigrant cars (most, however, could not afford the higher fare).

The American railway system differed from railways abroad in that it did not explicitly label varying classes, giving a veiled appearance of democratized travel. Britain set up three classes of travel and the rest of Europe followed suit; in Africa and India there were often four or more classes of travel.[70] In the United States, the immigrant car was the lowest class of travel, both in cost and accommodations. For trains departing from eastern cities, however, the high number of immigrants usually warranted full immigrant trains without accommodations for other passengers. For those who could afford it, American railroad companies offered parlor cars, ladies' cars, men's smoking cars, and coach cars instead of "first-class" or "second-class"—terms used abroad for the same accommodations of travel.[71] The immigrant car was roughly equivalent to British third-class travel. British travelers to America noted the lack of official class difference but recognized the divisions all the same. In an 1885 article in *Harper's Monthly* comparing British and American railways, the author asserts: "Your palace cars are only another form of first and second class carriages. [. . .] Why not admit the class distinction as openly as you adopt it?"[72] Despite attempts at democratizing travel, American railways clearly responded to contemporary cultural ideals in the regulation of public space. Hierarchies of class and race were evident in the placement of the cars on the train. Immigrant cars were located closer to the engines (the Chinese car being the closest) than the other passenger cars, which railroad officials placed further from the engine in order of increasing ticket cost. Not only did those passengers closest to the engine experience higher levels of fumes and noise, but they were also most in danger if an accident occurred. By the 1870s, railroad officials realized the safest part of the train was actually the center; however, the cultural order had been set by that time and despite the danger, railroad companies and passengers defined the proper place for white ladies and gentlemen to be the rear of the train.[73] The organization of space within the train, even though it was not marked as first, second, or third class, nevertheless established class and racial distinctions.

Railroad officials balanced their own needs with those of the public and in so doing perpetuated prejudices toward foreign populations. Railroad company advertisements promoting superior accommodations on their trains and in their stations were directed toward specific immigrants, those who had the potential to become model American citizens. When immigrants first entered the country, they were isolated from American citizens at government receiving stations. The ideological role of the railroad station as the modern city gateway contained deeper meaning at the New Jersey terminals, which were gateways to the country for immigrants arriving in New York Harbor. These stations served as the literal and metaphorical point of departure for immigrants traveling further inland to their new homes. Yet the immigrants who departed from these terminals were denied the symbolic passage through the main building. Further inland, where immigrant traffic was a lucrative business for the railways, foreigners were allowed to enter the headhouse but remained segregated from other passengers. Railroad officials believed that the immigrants purchasing their land and settling along their lines had the potential to assimilate to American life and become citizens. Traveling to their destination, however, they remained outsiders. The transitory spaces of the train cars and railroad stations, in which the immigrant is marked as foreign and inferior, symbolized the transient state of the immigrants themselves—no longer part of their homelands and not yet citizens of their new country.

Stevenson himself embodied these physical and figurative realms of liminality. Even though his fellow migrants "were speaking English all about me, [. . .] I knew I was in a foreign land."[74] One evening, at the Union Pacific Transfer Station on the outskirts of Council Bluffs, Iowa, Stevenson grew weary of his foray into poverty. While his fellow passengers were to spend the night at an inn specifically for immigrants, or "caravanserai" as Stevenson called it, he "gave way to a thirst for luxury" and decided instead to spend the night at the Union Pacific Hotel. The two-story transfer station and hotel, built of brick and stone in a Renaissance Revival style under the direction of Union Pacific superintendent Silas H. H. Clark, had opened on the west end of town in 1878, a year prior to Stevenson's journey. The first floor of the transfer station featured a black walnut and pine interior with twenty-foot-high ceilings. On the main level, five express companies occupied the south wing, while the north wing contained an elegant dining room for 200 guests, a lunch counter, saloon, barbershop, newsstand, and waiting rooms for men and women, respectively. New York–born Thomas Swobe operated a hotel on the second floor, which featured forty rooms and large, elegant parlors at either end of the 207-foot-long hallway. The hotel offered modern improvements, including hot and cold water. It was here where Stevenson opted to spend the night. His fellow immigrant travelers retired to a simple wooden, two-story inn just west of the depot, which was also operated by Swobe and built by the Union Pacific (figure 3.11). In George Crofutt's *Overland Tours*, an early guide of rail travel through the western United States, the Emigrant House in Council Bluffs is described as containing "70 rooms comfortably furnished, accommodates 200 persons, and charges only sufficient to cover cost; plain substantial meals, 25 cents each."[75] Meals at the hotel, by contrast—where Stevenson chose to stay—were around 75 cents each. The Emigrant House also housed a land office, where travelers could learn about and purchase available land in the region.

Crofutt assured his readers they would be safe traveling along the Union Pacific since "'runners' and 'hoodlums' are not allowed about the premises" of the transfer station. The Union Pacific, along with other

Figure 3.11. Council Bluffs Transfer Station, Council Bluffs, Iowa, c. 1877–1878. The Union Pacific Hotel, seen from the rear at left, is where Stevenson opted to spend the night. His fellow immigrant passengers stayed at the two-story wooden lodging house at right. Courtesy Union Pacific Museum

western rail lines, sought to protect their investments—that is, the travelers who were potential land buyers along their rail lines. Crofutt's guide was written for tourists but also those seeking to migrate to the American West. It provided specific information about travel and baggage rates, transfer connections, and stations along the way, like the Union Pacific Transfer Station. As the location from which the transcontinental railroad commenced westward, Council Bluffs held an important place in railroad history. In addition to the hotel and Emigrant House, the grounds also contained grain elevators and large stockyards, since Council Bluffs had grown into a major shipping point for grain and western livestock by the late nineteenth century. In another 1882 travel guide, Council Bluffs was described as "the great grazing belt of the continent."[76] As more and more settlers arrived in the Midwest, the agricultural industry continued to expand and this transfer station became an important part of a larger capitalistic landscape—one of many in the region—in which immigration played a major role. Many people, both from abroad and from the eastern states, traveled west on the railroads seeking land on which to earn a living. Around six o'clock in the evening on Friday, August 22, 1879, Stevenson's train rolled out of the transfer station, "across the wide Missouri River to Omaha, westward bound."[77] Though he would continue his journey across the country to San Francisco, many of Stevenson's fellow travelers would remain in the Midwest to begin the newest chapter of their lives.

MIDWEST SETTLEMENTS

Weary as he was from his own journey, Stevenson could not help but marvel at the previous generations of settlers who had traveled west by wagon through the Great Plains: "He may walk five miles and see nothing; ten, and it is as though he had not moved; twenty, and still he is in the midst of the same great level, and has approached no nearer to the one object within view, the flat horizon which keeps pace with his advance."[1]

Stevenson's train rolled through the Nebraska plains, a landscape "almost without a feature; an empty sky, an empty earth."[2] Railroad tracks stretched from horizon to horizon, surrounded by green prairie, and the immigrant train "toiled over this infinity like a snail." In the summer heat, wild sunflowers bloomed and animals grazed in the distance. There was little architecture to be seen on this vast landscape, with Stevenson observing only "a few dots beside the railroad which grew more and more distinct as we drew nearer till they turned into wooden cabins, and then dwindled and dwindled in our wake until they melted into their surroundings." The roar of the train and the "incessant chirp of grasshoppers" filled his ears. "Even my own body or my own head seemed a great thing in that emptiness." He imagined it possible for the settler to make a "full and various existence" with a family and livestock, but this unmarried city dweller found it difficult to comprehend how one could live in the plains.

Stevenson came across one of these settlers firsthand at a Nebraska way station when a woman boarded the train to sell milk to the passengers. Always a keen observer of those he encountered, Stevenson found she had an air of "entire contentment with her life," which was shocking to him, since "the place where she lived was to me almost ghastly."[3] Alongside the tracks were less than a dozen wooden houses, all similar in their modest size and simple plan, spread out on individual lots that appeared to him as "models that had been set down upon it ready-made." The woman's own house appeared tidy but to Stevenson there was nothing welcoming about it except a burning fire. He could not comprehend this "extreme newness" that, "above all in so naked and flat a country, gives a strong impression of artificiality." To a European citizen accustomed to villages and cities established over hundreds of years, the vastness of the American West was astonishing, as was the newly built vernacular architecture.

Railroads in the western United States, as opposed to the rest of the world, were unique in that their construction actually preceded non-Native settlement of the land. Taking advantage of this, railroad companies worked to relocate entire European communities to settle their land holdings as quickly as possible. In August 1874, the Krimmer Mennonite Brethren Church, comprising thirty-four families from the village of Annefeld outside Simferopol in Crimea, arrived to the twelve sections of land (approximately eight thousand acres) they had purchased from the Santa Fe Railroad near present-day Hillsboro, Kansas.[4] That year, Kansas suffered from a grasshopper plague—the land was dry and dusty and any crops they passed on their journey had been decimated by the insects. Jacob Wiebe and his wife, Maria, were some of the first of their group to arrive to the territory. Years later, Wiebe recalled: "We rode in a deep grass to the stake that marked the spot I had chosen. When we reached the spot, I stopped. My wife asked me, 'Why do you stop?' I said, 'We are to live here.' Then she began to weep."[5] Surrounding them was barren prairie as far as the eye could see—its three-foot-tall grasses scorched in the summer sun and waving in the hot, dry wind. There were no trees, houses, roads, or towns in sight. Although they had arrived with their community members, the Mennonites would need to start their lives nearly from scratch, building everything from the ground up with their limited resources. The anguish of Weibe's wife must have been felt by the many others who had relocated only to begin their lives completely anew. Their transportation journey had finally come to an end but a new endeavor was about to begin. For many, their hope for the future carried them through these challenging times. Stevenson, who was traveling through the territory five years later, found the barrenness to be shocking and, for him at least, uninhabitable. Not surprisingly, he was content to continue traveling west toward San Francisco and the life that awaited him there.

"That Train Was the One Piece of Life in All the Deadly Land"

When the federal government began granting lands to the railroads in the mid-nineteenth century, it initiated a new era in which railroad companies served as land agents. The purpose of the railways was no longer just to transport goods and people but also to actively promote and sell land along their lines, a process railway officials called colonization. Railroad companies determined the placement, layout, and architecture of many towns along their routes, platting acres of land on their sections along the tracks, anticipating settlement by individuals, families, and entire communities. They also began a series of advertisements and promotional campaigns to entice settlers to the vast tracts of land now in their possession.

Railway officials believed that their colonizing enterprise was the solution to creating a civilized and prosperous nation. To them, the removal of the Indigenous population from the vast tracts of land west of the Mississippi River provided a blank canvas on which to imprint their own Eurocentric notions of civility and morality. George S. Harris, land commissioner of the Burlington & Missouri River Railroad (hereafter referred to as the Burlington Railroad), wrote in a letter to the company's president that he felt inducing European immigration would serve a higher cause "by transplanting modern civilization and Christianity into these new Western states."[6] It is important to note, as historian Manu Karuka has demonstrated, that the railroad did not impact Native peoples in a uniform manner, but it was undeniably a core infrastructure of imperialism in North America, with the Plains Indians disproportionately affected by railroad development.[7] In promotional literature for the Burlington Railroad, the company referred to the rapid changes brought on by westward migration—the construction of permanent buildings, the establishment of commerce and agricultural production, and significantly, the relegation of the Native American population to that of a vanishing race:

> One of the wonders we live is the rapidity with which the various Western States have been occupied and their lands brought under cultivation. Less than a generation ago the Indian pitched his tepee where magnificent public buildings now uprear themselves, or electric street-cars carry thousands of people daily through the busy avenues of trade and commerce, and vast herds of buffalo roamed where an unbroken succession of corn fields and orchards now annually yields its enormous wealth. The buffalo is gone—practically exterminated. The Indian is gone, likewise, and is now [. . .] an object of curiosity in Nebraska or Colorado [. . .]."[8]

The railroad company presents the drastic changes to the landscape and culture as a natural progression of time, as if the changes were inevitable, without referencing the actual physical and cultural work done to institute the removal of Indigenous peoples and native wildlife to construct towns, roads, and buildings in their stead. The myth of Native Americans as a vanishing race, which posits that Indigenous peoples would eventually become extinct through contact with white civilization, was used to justify the government's actions of forced assimilation and genocide, all in the name of Manifest Destiny.[9] The perpetuation of this myth allowed American society to picture Native Americans solely in the context of a split-off historical past.[10]

Those changes were obviously not a natural progression of time but intentionally brought on largely by the railroad companies themselves, who had a vested interest in the towns and farms they intended to locate on lands west of the Mississippi. In railroad parlance, settling the "Wild West" actually entailed removing Indigenous peoples to make way for white settlers—displacing one population in favor of another. The railroads even exploited certain Native nations to maximize their own profits. In 1866, the Union Pacific Railroad hired Pawnee men to perform a war dance for the first train of excursionists traveling west from their Columbus, Nebraska, station.[11] The next day, to the delight of the upper-class guests, the Pawnees staged a mock battle. This spectacle of ethnic entertainment succeeded in demonstrating, so the railroad officials hoped, how the West had finally been tamed and made safe for white tourists and, more importantly, for settlers. Stevenson himself was grateful for the speed of the train that "conducts us swiftly" through the plains, keeping the passengers physically distant from the "thirst, hunger, the sleight and ferocity of Indians" experienced firsthand by a previous generation of settlers.[12] In reality, the Indigenous population had decreased astonishingly over the nineteenth century due to war, famine, and disease, and those who had survived were forced to live on reservations, which allowed the federal government and the railroads to forge ahead in modeling their vision of a new American West, one built on white settler culture.

Recalling again the hardships of the previous generation of westward migrants, who traveled by foot and wagon, Stevenson acknowledged the descriptions of his "trifling discomforts" were nothing in comparison to what they faced. To further emphasize his point, Stevenson transcribed a letter from an eleven-year-old unnamed boy written in 1859 to his sister, Mary, in which he recalls his wagon journey with his two brothers to California. He and his eldest brother narrowly escaped an attack by Native

Americans, who had killed many others on their journey, including their fifteen-year-old brother, Thomas.[13] While Stevenson was grateful for the train to protect them from encountering Native peoples and the landscape directly, this privileged passenger nevertheless found the journey uncomfortable and dehumanizing. True dramatist that he was, however, Stevenson included this letter to entice readers with the dangers of the American West, and, like many others in his milieu, to romanticize the "savage Indian" who threatened the white settlers, when in reality it was the other way around.

"Impromptu Cities, Full of Gold and Lust and Death, Sprang Up"

In the 1860s, substantial federal land grants to build the Transcontinental Railroad allowed the rails to eventually traverse the entire country. Using mostly immigrant laborers (a large number of whom were Chinese and Irish), railroad companies completed millions of miles of tracks, conquering the land by leveling the earth, constructing bridges and tunnels, and building stations, signal towers, and freight and powerhouses. As his train rolled through the landscape, Stevenson fantasized about those laborers who toiled away on the tracks, resorting to sensational depictions: "In these uncouth places pig-tailed Chinese pirates worked side by side with border ruffians and broken men from Europe, talking together in mixed dialect, mostly oaths, gambling, drinking, quarrelling and murdering like wolves."[14] Yet he goes on to state that it was the "gentlemen in frock coats" who were actually the true architects of this system, which was built on their capitalistic ambitions (figure 4.1). That, in fact, the railway was "the one typical achievement of the age in which we live, as if it brought together into one plot all the ends of the world and all the degrees of social rank." While his depictions of the laborers are derogatory, Stevenson does succeed in succinctly describing the cultural significance of the railroad in American history and its lasting impact on the nation.

The establishment of the railroad and the land grant system completely transformed the country's physical landscape. The federal government surveyed millions of acres and divided the land into one-mile square sections, making way for the railroad and the white settlers it would ultimately bring along its lines.[15] In exchange for building tracks in specific regions, the railroad companies received alternating sections of land while the government kept the title to the lands in between, thus establishing a checkerboard pattern of land distribution. Government lands were either used for homesteading or sold for a profit. In 1850, the Illinois Central Railroad Company became the first federal land grant railroad

Figure 4.1. A white railroad official, with his suit and top hat, gold watch, and relaxed pose, stands in sharp contrast to the Chinese laborers actually working on the Central Pacific Railroad line between Bakersfield and Los Angeles. Photograph by Andrew J. Russell, 1876. Courtesy Oakland Museum of California

in the United States, receiving over two million acres under the Fillmore administration. The railroads received alternate sections of land on either side of their proposed tracks, with each section defined as one square mile or 640 acres, for distances ranging between six and twenty miles on either side of the track. Between 1850 and 1871, the federal and state governments granted over 180 million acres of land to the railroads.[16] Once the railroads began constructing their lines, the newly formed land departments in each company worked to establish towns in the railroad's wake.

The Illinois Central Railroad was one of the first to participate in townsite development and promotion. According to an amendment in the company's charter, however, the railroad itself was forbidden to establish

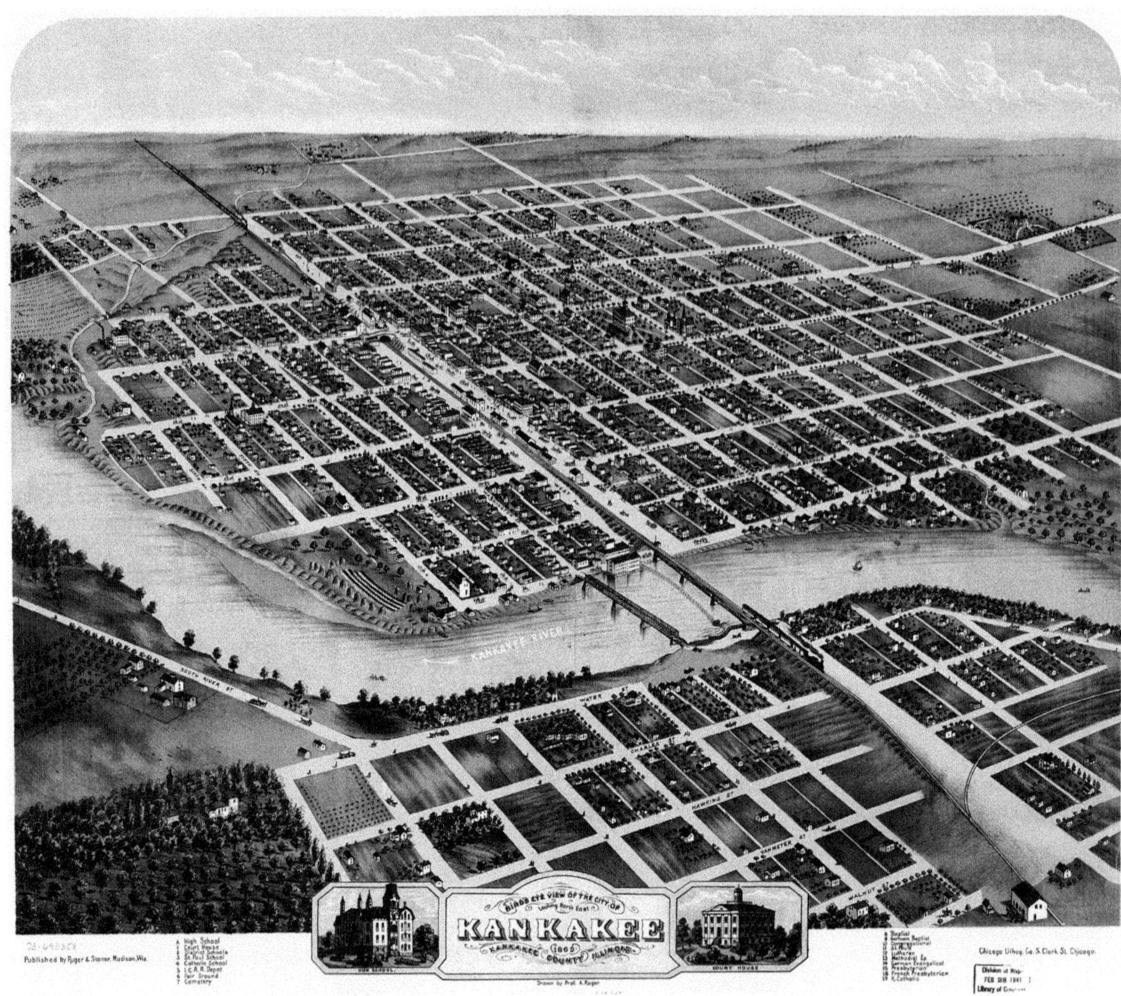

Figure 4.2. Bird's-eye view of the city of Kankakee, Kankakee County, Illinois, 1869. Courtesy of the Library of Congress, Geography and Map Division

towns on or near its line in order to promote more equitable development.[17] To circumvent this limitation and maximize capital gains, several of the company's directors banded together to form an independent group called the Associates Land Company, which would purchase the government's alternate parcels of land in areas where the Illinois Central planned to establish stops along its line. The directors of the Illinois Central then located stations on or near the Associates' land holdings, thus increasing the return profit when they eventually sold the land.[18] Many other companies operated similarly, contracting with individuals or groups with financial ties to those same railroad companies—a system akin to insider trading in today's economy.[19] Directing town growth and development allowed railroad companies and officials to capitalize their investment in the long term by providing continuous traffic along their lines. Railroad officials thus profited from towns in which they were not legally supposed to have a hand in establishing.

The Illinois Central, and other railroad companies, platted towns every seven to ten miles along the tracks (figure 4.2). Regular intervals discouraged independent promoters from starting towns and it also promoted business growth, since those towns served as trade centers along a specific route. Of course, this is not to say that railway towns were the only ones to develop in the West. There were cities and towns in place before the railroad arrived, and many other independent towns (not necessarily the product of corporations) also sprang up throughout the country.[20] But other railroad companies followed more or less the same model set forth by the Illinois Central: railroad survey engineers first determined suitable town locations, then turned their data over to private townsite agents who hired surveyors to stake out the town lots.

Drawings of the town plan supplied visual cues as to how the railroad and land companies planned for them to develop. Although just a series of wooden stakes to begin with, the size of the building lots indicated where commercial and residential areas would develop. Despite any differences in organization, each of the railway towns featured a grid of streets with building lots of varying sizes indicating the intended purpose (business or residential) that were located on or near the rail lines. Residential streets and lots were typically wider than those of the commercial district. Many railroads imposed restrictions on the size of business lots, typically limiting its width to around twenty-four feet, ensuring that the businesses themselves remained small. That way, if a business failed, a smaller building would allow for quicker turnover; it would be more difficult to find purchasers for a larger structure in the developing towns where there was less demand for such a sizeable business. Railroad companies such as the Union Pacific and the Northern Pacific actually prohibited the sale of adjacent lots to the same purchaser, discouraging the development of larger businesses. Across the prairie, grids of wooden stakes formed the footprint of the towns that would soon come to life.

Some land companies, such as the Associates working for the Illinois Central, developed a standard town plat to be utilized in their settlements: east–west streets were named after trees, north–south streets were numbered, and the train tracks ran east–west through the center of the grid.[21] To hasten development of the town, the Associates donated lots to Christian organizations to secure the construction of churches. These lots were in the vicinity of the Associates' land holdings in order to increase their own property values. In Kankakee, Illinois, the Illinois Central donated a lot for the city courthouse as well as $5,000 toward its construction. Other railroad companies did the same, offering lands for schools, churches, courthouses, and other public buildings—the cornerstones of the civilization they hoped to bring to the American West. Geographer John C. Hudson notes that while the townsite proprietors recognized the need for public buildings, they "had a blind spot when it came to improvements that might make their towns more livable"—for example, they usually overlooked any requests for parks, tree planting, or street maintenance.[22] Those responsibilities, the proprietors felt, would be tended to by the local government after the town was formally incorporated. Meanwhile, the railroad land departments actively sought businessmen and merchants to purchase business lots near the railroad tracks.

By focusing on the sale of business lots and donating property for religious and civic purposes, land companies provided the institutions necessary to entice settlers. The Northern Pacific assured potential settlers that "the needs of all members of the community" would be met, since wherever a town was established "there will be found near its center the blacksmith, shoemaker, carpenter, mason, storekeeper, the Post-Office, the schoolhouse, the Sunday-school, the church [. . .] and the farmers will find a market for their grain at the railroad station."[23] One English immigrant, searching for lands in Iowa or Nebraska along the Burlington Railroad, wrote a letter to the editor of London's *American Settler*, explaining how "towns had sprung up like mushrooms in the night."[24] The towns along the railways were certainly forming quickly and the brochures published by the railroad companies were part of what drew people to these settlements.

The hastened development received negative attention from contemporary architecture critics, who rejected the towns' unimaginative design and predicted them to be failures.[25] Like Stevenson's dismay at the small Nebraska settlement he observed from the train window, one anonymous critic from *American Architect and Building News* felt that these towns were "dropped at random upon the flat and featureless prairies along our western railroads," indicating his proclivity toward a picturesque landscape or perhaps a preference for towns that evolved more organically, not the forced development by railroad officials.[26] The critic went on to state, "In the ordinary course of civilization, such characterless sites are not the ones in which populations cleave." For railroad officials, however, these towns were symbols of the westward movement of white civilization. In platting towns, these companies provided a tangible aspect of that intended progress and offered the promise of civilization to the millions of white settlers who eventually traveled west to obtain their share of the prosperity that had been marketed to them.

Grid plans were undeniably the most practical solution for division of property into saleable lots, and while railroad companies did little to vary town plans, they did attempt to alter the landscape of the "flat and featureless prairie" so abhorred by the *American Architect and Building News* critic. Predominantly covered with a variety of grasses and shrubs, the prairie contained few trees. This, along with the relatively flat lands, contributed to high wind speeds. Furthermore, without access to woodlands the settlers would have to pay high prices to purchase their timber elsewhere, ultimately increasing the railroad companies' revenues. Even though wood was necessary to build houses and barns and provide fuel for heat and cooking, some of the railroads used the lack of trees to their advantage, reminding settlers that they would not have to clear the land of trees to plant crops and erect dwellings. Rather, they could establish farms immediately on arrival and order the lumber as needed, while planting hedges for fences instead of using wood to build them.[27] John Waugh, a Nebraska settler, affirmed the benefits of the prairie lands: "I found that in Nebraska there are no forest trees to be felled, no stumps to dig up, no rocks to be moved, [and] no deep ploughing to be done [. . .]."[28] While the lack of trees made things easier for planting crops, it was, in fact, an impediment to construction.

Many of the railroad companies took action to make the prairie more appealing to potential settlers. The first division of the St. Paul & Pacific Railroad began a tree-planting campaign in 1872, which lowered the land price to six dollars an acre, free of interest and with no payments to be made for three and a half years, for those wishing to buy a section or more, on the condition that they break, cultivate, and fence the land, in addition to planting forty acres of trees with the seeds and seedlings furnished by the railroads.[29] The Illinois Central also realized early on that it would need trees to entice settlers. In the 1850s, the company contracted Chester B. Rushmore to cultivate locust trees on several sections of their Illinois lands. Illinois Central also contracted Rushmore and another arborist, James Sumpter, to plant Osage orange hedges along the Illinois Central tracks to serve as natural fences for the cattle that the railroad hoped would soon be grazing nearby.[30] The Burlington Railroad corresponded with Royal Danish Forester F. C. Stannis about a possible project "to undertake the most desirable improvement on [the company's] Nebraska lands," including the planting of forests, "which in different ways may have a beneficial influence in the whole State of Nebraska."[31] By altering the prairie environment, the railroad companies sought to make it more habitable for white settlers and to continue directing the flow of migration westward, shaping the land along with the population.

"We Continued to Steam Westward Toward the Land of Gold"

As architects, engineers, and horticulturists designed the built and natural environment along the tracks, railroad officials began advertising the lands to potential settlers. Particularly from the late 1860s through the 1890s, railroad advertisements appeared in newspapers and other periodicals in the United States and abroad, with railroad land departments creating pamphlets and circulars for distribution. Interested settlers were instructed to contact land department agents for further information on the lands available, on prices and credit terms, and on statistics of the average rainfall, climate, and other data. Early promotional campaigns were directed at those residing in the eastern states. The advertisements were effective: in 1857, historian Fred Gerhard stated that "in the morning, long before the hour of opening, the doors of the Illinois Central Railroad Company's Land Office at Chicago are thronged with people; and when opened the office is soon densely filled with eager purchasers. [. . .] Hundreds of people are weekly coming from the East to Chicago" (figure 4.3).[32] In response to the heavy advertising, land department agents were flooded with requests from both individual settlers and also from those hoping to sponsor colonies.

Despite successful campaigns in the 1850s, the flow of migration from the eastern states was not sufficient enough to sell the vast tracts of the railroad's lands or to establish a substantial agricultural base west of the Mississippi.[33] This was especially true during the Civil War, when the flow of migrants from the East slowed drastically. In order to encourage migration to their lands, railroad officials increasingly focused their attentions on Europe, where economic and social instability due to rapid growth in population, industrialization, and urbanization in the mid-to-late nineteenth century left many unemployed, landless, and struggling to feed their families. Illinois Central's vice president David Neal believed foreign immigration would provide a boost to settlement. He sent Swedish immigrant Oscar Malmborg (who was fluent in French, German, and the Scandinavian languages) to Norway, Sweden, and Germany to work as a foreign agent promoting Illinois Central lands. Malmborg translated promotional literature and visited rural communities throughout Scandinavia, persuading people to emigrate to the United States, particularly to the Illinois Central's land holdings.[34]

The efforts of the various land companies, which established businesses and religious and civic organizations, were used to the advantage of

Figure 4.3. "In Line at the Land Office, Perry, Sept. 23, 1893. 9 o'clock A.M. waiting to file." A crowd of men wait to file their claim on land on the Cherokee Strip in Oklahoma Territory. Courtesy National Archives, photo no. 516458

railroad officials, who hoped to bring more settlers west along their lines. American railroad companies offered cheap transportation, reduced cost of freight, temporary lodging, affordable land, and above all, the promise of prosperity to the struggling masses in Europe. Promotional material in the form of pamphlets, circulars, and advertisements in periodicals pervaded the European press. The potential benefits available on American soil, along with the declining opportunities in Europe, were compelling incentives for the hundreds of thousands of people who immigrated to the United States.

Given that the railroad companies were profit-seeking, officials knew they would not always secure the trust of potential settlers. Some companies addressed this issue directly in advertisements. The Santa Fe Railroad, for example, published a statement assuring settlers: "It is as much *for our interest to tell you the truth* as it is for you to know the truth [. . .] we have the largest and keenest interest in your welfare both present and future, for upon your success, year by year depends our own prosperity. If we deceive you we injure ourselves, for it is largely to your efforts in the future that we look for aid and cooperation in building up the country and the business of our road [emphasis in original]."[35]

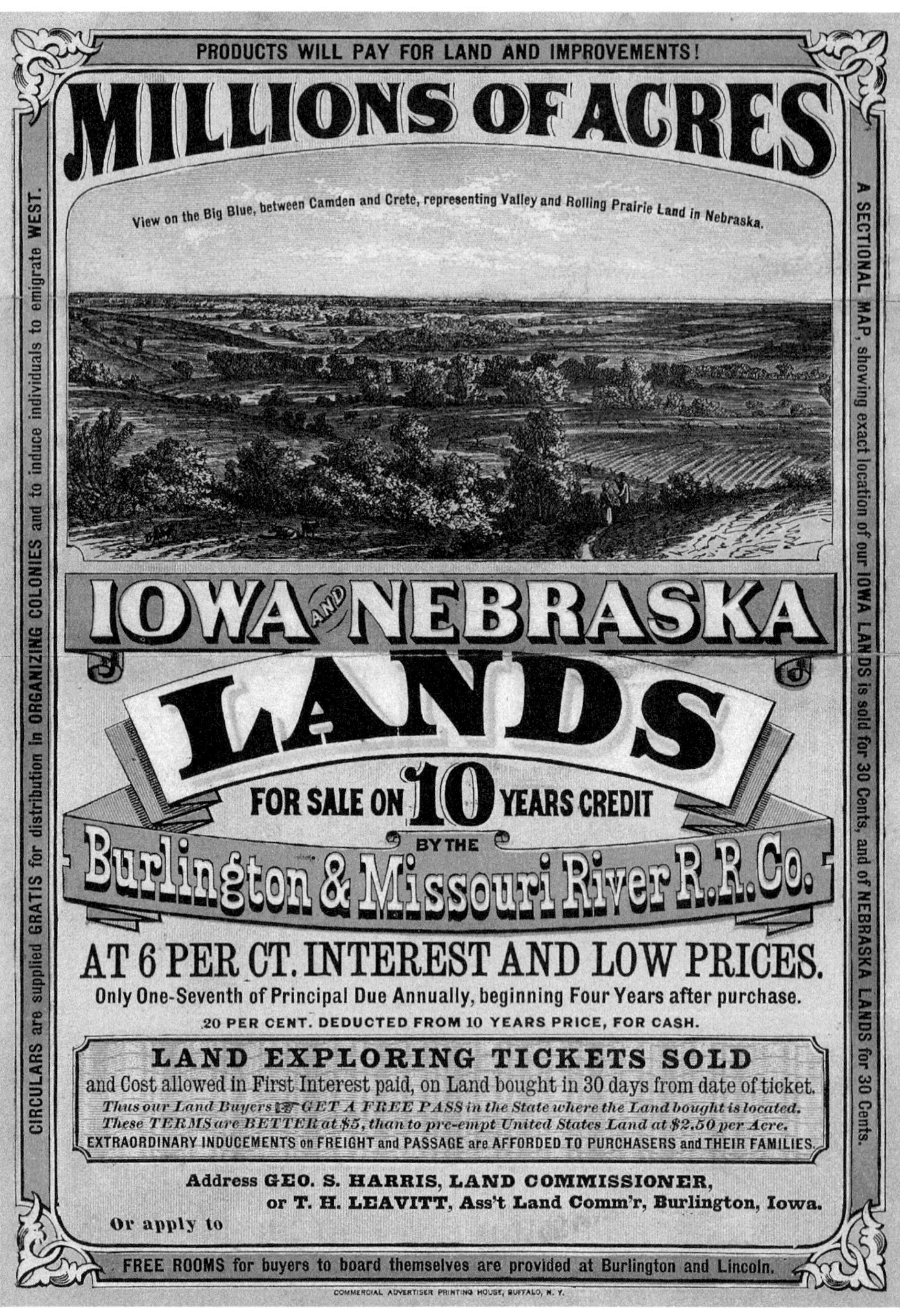

Figure 4.4. Circular from the Burlington & Missouri River Railroad Company (1872) advertising low land prices, free passes for those purchasing land from the railroad, and the free rooms available to potential settlers. Courtesy of the Library of Congress, Rare Book and Special Collections Division, Printed Ephemera Collection

Railroad officials did not stop at assuring settlers of their well-intentioned motives; they also formed partnerships with religious and missionary figures whom they knew potential settlers would trust. The Burlington Railroad hired a British clergyman, Reverend King, to encourage immigration by publishing letters in periodicals, giving lectures, and even organizing several colonies of his own. King took his position seriously and was a persistent letter-writer to Burlington land commissioner George Harris, recounting his work in the colonization efforts and frequently asking for an increase in salary. In one letter, he was so bold as to ask for the elk horns that adorned Harris's office in Lincoln, Nebraska—no doubt to entice potential settlers with the American curio.[36] Railway companies hired men like King in the hope that those who were skeptical of a railroad company's motives would, perhaps, trust the good and faithful reverend to be sincere in his discussions of immigration and colonization. Railroad officials also formed agreements with missionary groups in the United States to support the immigrants' best interests in return for promotion of their railroad company. In 1887, for example, the Burlington Railroad formed an agreement with the Board of the Emigrant Mission of the City of New York. In exchange for reduced transportation rates, temporary housing, and land donation for religious and educational purposes, the board would promote the Burlington's lands from its New York office.[37]

The Burlington Railroad also offered land explorer's tickets as another incentive to purchase company lands (figure 4.4). With these tickets, potential settlers could alight at multiple stations along the route, deciding which lands were most suitable. When the settler purchased a section of land owned by the Burlington, the cost of the land explorer's ticket was deducted from the sale price, so that, as the company advertised, land seekers rode the rails for free. The provision of free land seeker's tickets, however, was not a welcome strategy for competing railroad companies. The general passenger agent for the New York, Lake Erie & Western Railroad wrote a personal letter to the Burlington's general passenger agent, A. E. Touzalin, beseeching him to stop providing free tickets from Chicago westward, since other land departments had begun to complain that they would have to do the same.[38] In the 1870s, the Burlington Railroad was thus well ahead of its competition in offering incentives to the passengers riding its rails and purchasing its lands.

The Burlington Railroad also became one of the first companies to provide free temporary lodging for settlers. Much like the inn at which Stevenson's fellow travelers spent the night in Council Bluffs, the Burlington's temporary "emigrant homes," as they called them, were in the cities of Burlington and Lincoln in Kansas—major stops along the route.

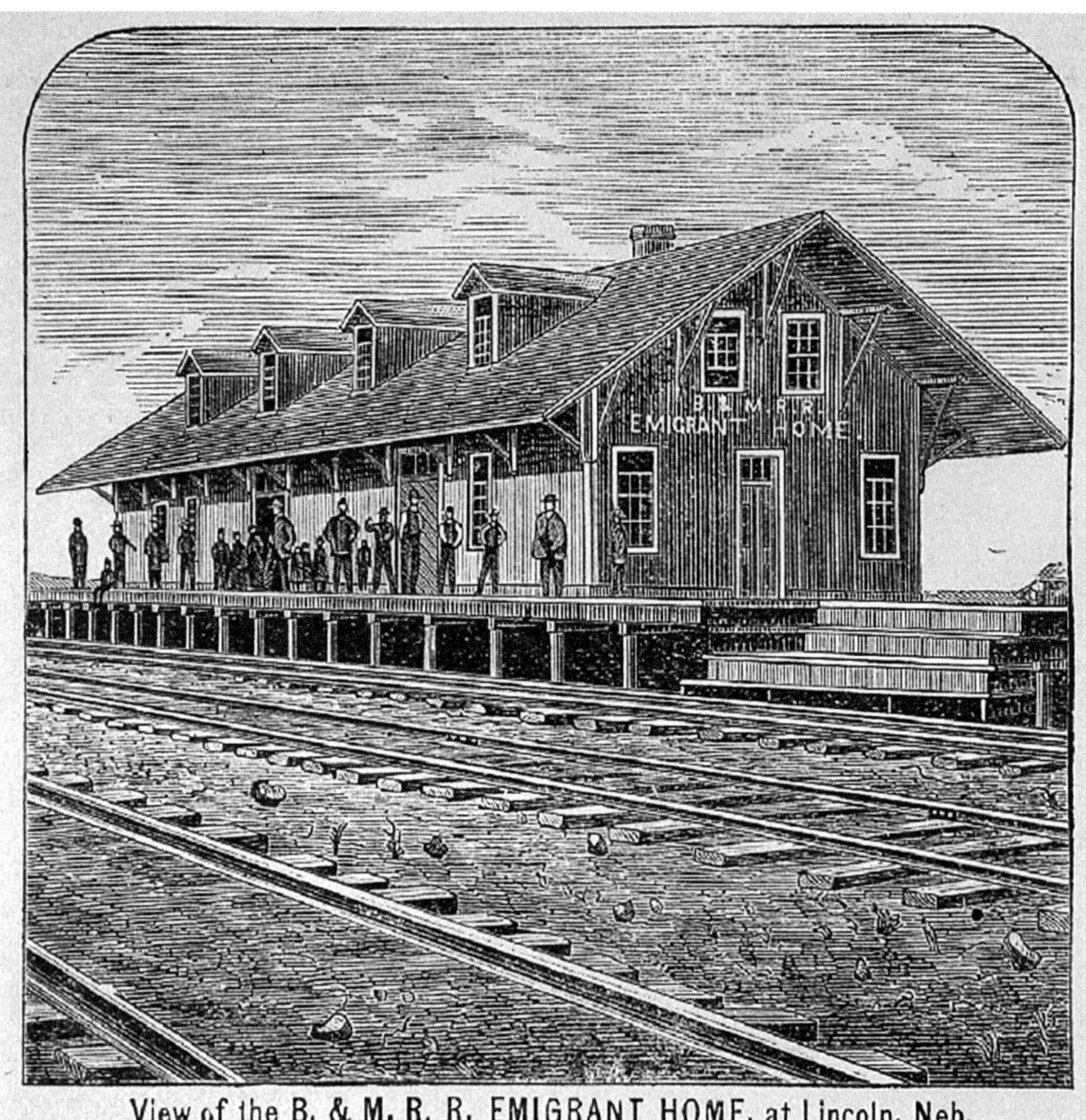

Figure 4.5. Burlington Railroad's Emigrant Home at Lincoln, Kansas, 1883. Courtesy of the Library of Congress, Rare Book and Special Collections Division, Printed Ephemera Collection

Managing the residences were multilingual caretakers, fluent in English, German, and the Scandinavian languages. At Burlington, the temporary lodging shared the space of the train station and land department offices. The boarding rooms were on the lower level of the wood-framed, one-and-a-half-story structure. Similar to the Union Pacific Transfer Station in Council Bluffs, the land department offices were located within the

Emigrant Home, on the upper level beneath a steeply pitched roof. In contrast, the temporary lodging at Lincoln was located in a purpose-built structure, separate from the railroad's land offices (figure 4.5). Located next to the train station, the 100-by-24-foot wooden building contained a washroom with running water, a dining room, kitchen, communal room, and a baggage room on the first floor. The upper level featured two rooms meant to house either ten families or women and men in separate quarters. The building's proximity to the railroad station allowed travelers to unload their belongings directly from the train to their respective rooms.

The temporary lodging at Lincoln was completed in 1871 and in its first year of operation, it housed more than six hundred land seekers who received free lodging.[39] At its opening, the local newspapers remarked that the new building was "very clean and orderly," although one English visitor commented that those staying at the Lincoln building "are of course expected to rough it; for no railway, however opulent, would find it politic or profitable to provide luxurious quarters under such circumstances."[40] The accommodations were undoubtedly minimal and most of the furnishings, with the exception of the ovens, were provided by the immigrants themselves. However, the space afforded shelter to the newly arrived settlers and was a welcome amenity to those who would otherwise have to pay for lodging (if they could find a reputable place) or camp outdoors.

Frederick Hedde, a foreign agent stationed in Hamburg and working for the State of Nebraska, believed the Burlington to be the only railroad to establish these shelters and urged other states and railways to follow their example, which they did.[41] Only two years after the completion of the houses at Burlington and Lincoln, the Northern Pacific Railroad had begun to advertise its own "colonists' reception homes" in Minnesota. Located in Duluth, Brainerd, and Glyndon, these houses could accommodate several hundred people, were under "the charge of competent superintendents," and were outfitted with cooking stoves, washing conveniences, and beds.[42] Furthermore, each establishment had an adjacent hospital, although the extent of the hospital facility is unknown (it was likely a doctor's office with a few patient rooms). Just as the railroad companies had advertised their superior immigrant trains in order to gain more passengers, companies also offered lodging and other amenities along their lines to remain competitive in the endeavor to secure immigrant patronage.

For some lands that were situated further from the railroad, land department officials devised ways to make the distance from the station appear less to the prospective settlers, thus making the location more attractive to buyers. In June 1887, the Nebraska Land Department of the

Burlington Railroad worked with one of its foreign agents to arrange for a group of Scandinavian immigrants to purchase land in Boone County. Once the group arrived in Columbus, Nebraska, there were two options to reach their destination: they could either travel to their lots by wagon from the Columbus stop or transfer trains to Albion and then travel by wagon to their destined locations. Perceval Lowell, a Burlington land agent, suggested the latter option because the former gave the "impression that they were settling a long distance from the railroad, whereas, if they were taken by rail to Albion and thence by wagon they would form a more favorable impression of the region of country in which they locate."[43] Every effort to entice settlers was part of the railroads' larger strategy to establish settlements along their lines and ensure continuous profits for the future. Officials did whatever they could to impart a favorable impression of the area on prospective settlers.

In reality, however, the land along the railroads in the Midwestern states was flat prairie punctured with wooden stakes, with houses infrequently dotting the landscape and a train station often serving as the only indication of a town—with perhaps a row of buildings near it that indicated a more prosperous railway town. Railroad officials designed a wide-scale proselytization of the American Midwest to the settlers, relying on promotional literature, art, and the media to build a vision of America as a land of plenty—where rich, fertile soil yielded an abundance of bounty, and financial gain awaited any person courageous enough to relocate to this Promised Land (figure 4.6). The companies' exploitation of the white settlers' Christian beliefs, by employing clergy and missionary groups to carry out their promotional efforts, ensured that the railways remained in control of populating the nation. Once the lands were occupied and cultivated by industrious Christian settlers, the railroad companies' goal of civilizing, or taming, the American frontier would be complete, resulting, of course, in exponential profits for those very companies.

The land departments of various railroad companies hawked their lands as a veritable Garden of Eden, forming relationships with the media in an effort to validate their claims, particularly after periods of unfavorable weather or blights on the land. The 1874 drought and grasshopper plague in Kansas, for example, made the Kansas railroads a subject of ridicule for railway companies operating in other states. In response, A. S. Johnson of the Santa Fe Railroad's land department organized a delegation of 225 journalists who ultimately proclaimed Kansas the "Garden of the West" and put to rest the claims that nothing could grow in the state.[44] In another instance, an English journalist traveled to the United States in 1872 to visit the lands of Nebraska at the expense of the Burlington

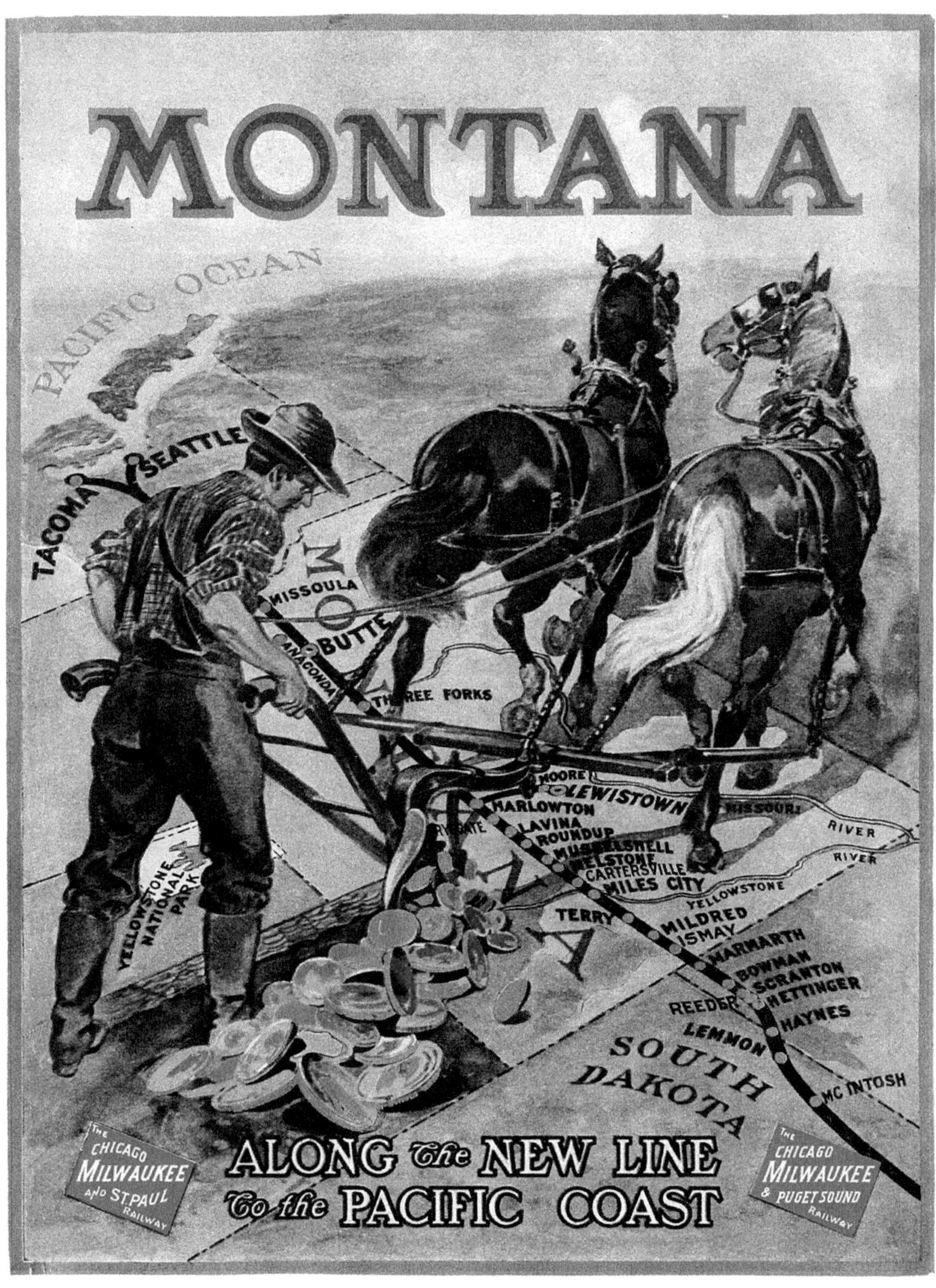

Figure 4.6. "Montana; along the new line to the Pacific Coast," 1910, pamphlet published by the Chicago, Milwaukee and St. Paul Railway, c. 1912. Courtesy of Archives and Special Collections, Maureen and Mike Mansfield Library, University of Montana-Missoula

Railroad. Upon his return to London, he wrote favorably of the state, declaring it a land where "all the cereals [. . .] are grown with ease, certainty, and success, [. . .] every species of berry will ripen lusciously [and] sheep are never diseased there." [45] This journalist, echoing the sentiments of others on the journey, described the land of Nebraska as a "fragment of Heaven let loose upon the earth." The journalists assuaged the railroad companies' and state government's concerns over negative press by providing potential settlers with the reassurance that the lands to which they would potentially relocate were of the finest quality. Many immigrants, however, were disappointed with the lands that had been advertised to them by railroad companies. One settler complained, "No wonder they give this land away to the settlers for surely no one would ever buy it."[46] The advertisements often did not feature accurate depictions of the land available to settlers. One North Dakota advertisement, for example, illustrated the more fertile eastern part of the state, not the arid western lands that were actually for sale.[47]

State governments also produced promotional literature extolling the virtues of their lands and, just like the railroads, often exaggerated those features. In 1871, under the direction of Governor Horace Austin, the State of Minnesota published a pamphlet with the lengthy title *Minnesota: Its Resources and Progress; Its Beauty, Healthfulness and Fertility; and its Attractions and Advantages as a Home for Immigrants*. In it, the author describes the varied benefits of the land, including the soil, minerals, rivers, lakes, agriculture, and even the state's climate. While it listed average winter temperatures ranging from ten to thirty degrees below zero, sometimes even lower, the author claimed that "the severity of these days is much softened by the brilliancy of the sun and the stillness of the air."[48] To confirm the healthfulness of the climate, testimonials from various reverends, doctors, and professors are also included in the text, thus supporting claims that the Minnesota climate is home to "joyous, healthy, prosperous people, strong in physical, intellectual, and moral capabilities."

Pamphlets such as these also served as guides to potential settlers, offering information on obtaining lands and starting farms, in addition to population statistics. The 1871 Minnesota pamphlet noted that the highest percentage of settlers relocated from the eastern states (although no mention is made of when those settlers arrived in the United States), and the next largest groups arrived from the Scandinavian countries and Germany. Listing the nationalities of the settlers would encourage their countrymen to immigrate to Minnesota, or so the state government hoped. At the same time, however, listing only the nationalities of the majority and acknowledging others merely by stating that there are also "a smaller amount from elsewhere" would perhaps discourage so-called undesirable immigrants, such as Eastern Europeans, from settling there, where they would be isolated from their countrymen.[49]

Some railroad companies, while they also published vast amounts of printed matter promoting individual companies and their lands, found more creative ways in the 1870s to secure passengers by reaching beyond print advertisement. Railroad officials and their foreign agents began lecture tours throughout the British Isles, in which they described the benefits of immigration. Land department officials answered audience questions regarding specific lands, credit terms, agricultural opportunities, and so forth. On a lecture circuit in England, Burlington agent Henry Wilson spoke of the enormous wealth available in America. One of the attending journalists reported on Wilson's lecture: "Speaking of American wealth, the lecturer said there was an old saying that no man ever saw a dead ass, [and] would ask how many present ever saw or heard of a poor American. This was the thing that always struck an English traveler, accustomed as he was to workhouses, soup kitchens, poor rates, and people dying of starvation. The reason was that the people of the United States were rich as a whole. America with all her resources would be little without immigration. This was the secret of her immense property."[50] By drawing attention to the poor living conditions then experienced in England, and juxtaposing those conditions with the resources available in America, Wilson hoped to increase immigration to the United States and secure the sale of Burlington lands. These lectures were often well attended and the land department usually received several inquiries, if not complete applications for land, in the days following the event.[51]

The railroads also employed large-scale visual media to advertise their lands. One of the most successful of these promotional campaigns was Hardy Gillard's moving panorama entitled *Over the Continent from New York to San Francisco*, which first exhibited at Queen's Hall in Liverpool in October 1871 (figure 4.7). The panorama opened with a bird's-eye view of the entire railroad route on a canvas measuring forty by eight feet, in front of which Gillard lectured for a half hour describing the route and extolling the engineering feats of building such a railway. Gillard then unveiled the rest of the thirty-six paintings, unrolled as if the viewers were experiencing them through the window of a moving train. The paintings depicted scenes such as the Hudson River, the Niagara Falls Suspension Bridge, the city of Chicago, Midwestern prairies, and the trees of California. The panorama was highly popular from the start and received much media attention, particularly because the Great Chicago Fire occurred nearly a week after the panorama's debut, and the public

Figure 4.7. Advertisement for Hardy Gillard's panorama, "Over the Continent from New York to San Francisco," c. 1880. Together with lecture tours, the railroads commissioned large-scale media presentations to entice settlers to the American West. From the New York Public Library

expressed interest in seeing a representation of how the city once looked. The press praised what they believed to be the authenticity of the work, stating that "intending travelers and emigrants ought to see the pictures and hear [. . .] a lecturer who has seen the districts he describes." Not only do these "artistic gems" (as one critic called the paintings) depict the scenery along the route, but they also conveyed the impressive feat of constructing the railroad over such vast territory, making it "one of the most gigantic undertakings which has ever been successfully accomplished in the annals of the human race." The panorama, seen by the upper and lower classes alike, incited the interest of many of the attendees. For the upper-class viewers, the panorama opened up to them possibilities for tourism; however, for the lower classes, the rolling prairies depicted in the panorama offered up agricultural opportunities that were unavailable to them in their own country. The English press described the panorama as "highly instructive" to emigrants seeking to try their luck in America.[52]

C. S. Dawson's *Sylphorama of America by Sea, River and Railroad: The Great Overland Route to California* was another example of a large-scale visual work meant to promote American railroads, specifically the Burlington Railroad, along which the scenes took place. Consisting of eighty-five colored views, the moving panorama filled 250 square feet of canvas and, like Gillard's panorama, was unrolled onstage to simulate viewing the landscape through a train window. Touring exhibits like Dawson's and Gillard's were instrumental in capturing the interests of potential settlers and ultimately contributed to the railroad's land sales. Dawson, for example, was actually employed by the Burlington Railroad to establish relationships with local religious and civic organizations in order to form colonies to emigrate to the American Midwest.[53] Given the crucial need for settlers along their lines, using varied forms of promotional campaigns allowed the railway companies to cast a wider net in their attempt to secure immigration to their lands.

While easterners and the merchant classes had mostly been the target for sale of town lots, the railroads turned to foreign immigration to populate the rural lands surrounding those towns. Advertisements largely targeted northern Europeans, whom railroad officials credited with better agricultural skills. George Harris, land commissioner for the Burlington Railroad, wrote, "I have so poor an opinion of the French & Italian immigrants for agriculturists that I shall not issue any circulars in their languages. My efforts will be most confined to Germans, Scandinavians, English, Welsh, and Scotch, as they make good farmers [. . .]."[54] Other railroad companies followed a similar advertising program, limiting their foreign efforts to the British Isles, Germany, and the Scandinavian countries.

Eastern and southern Europeans, in the eyes of railroad officials, did not have the qualities necessary to thrive in the United States—that is, neither the agricultural and industrial skills nor the moral qualities. Due to discriminatory nineteenth-century laws, Asian immigrants were not allowed to purchase land, and although eastern and southern Europeans were legally allowed to obtain land, the railroads instead ran targeted promotional campaigns to those whom they wished to immigrate.

"It Is the Settlers, After All, at Whom We Have Right to Marvel"

Those foreigners who read promotional advertisements and heard success stories from their fellow countrymen who had migrated before them were encouraged by the prospect of building a secure future for themselves. Yet immigration brought with it many challenges, physically and emotionally, particularly for those who intended to pursue agriculture. The long and often arduous journey by sea, rail, and wagon was exhausting, to say the least, and once the immigrants purchased land, they set to the hard task of constructing shelter and establishing farms. There were also emotional trials stemming from not knowing the English language and feelings of isolation that arose from living in a foreign land. For those traveling alone to the United States, the difficulty of leaving behind one's family and friends proved almost too much to bear. Henrietta Jessen, a Norwegian immigrant who came to the United States in 1850 with her husband, wrote home to her family: "It was a bitter cup for me to drink, to leave a dear mother and sisters and to part forever in this life, though living. Only the thought of the coming world . . . [is] my consolation; there I shall see you all. . . . I hope that time will heal the wound, but up to the present I cannot deny that homesickness gnaws at me hard."[55] For Jessen, life in America was a kind of death—of her old life, of her culture, of her family. She knew that the chance of seeing her family and homeland again was unlikely.

Traveling with extended family and community members, however, had the potential to lessen the difficulties of immigration, or at least make them somewhat more bearable. The railroads capitalized on this notion by printing circulars and newspaper advertisements that described the advantages of organized colonization:

> Nearly all privations and discomforts complained of by settlers in a new country have arisen from the fact that they have emigrated as individuals, or as isolated families, instead of organized bodies. Let a small community, embracing as many families and individuals previously acquainted as possible, of various trades and professions, and intending to follow various pursuits,

> emigrate and settle together, then society, mutual help, comfort, security, and economy will be at once secured, the anticipated hardships and trials of an emigrant's life will vanish away, and the whole colony, bound together by a community of interest, will rapidly grow in strength and prosperity.[56]

Several other railroad companies also stressed the point that immigrating in a large group was surely the most sensible course of action. In one of its pamphlets, the Northern Pacific proposed that if a large group of fifty to one hundred people purchased all the land held by the railroad in a particular town, they could establish a community with employment in various industries and all that is needed to "make up the sum of civilization at once: good government, good neighbors, morality, security to property, comfort and prosperity."[57] Surrounded by their own countrymen, the foreigners arrived with towns already in place, one that was bound by their own established standards and interests, and one that could use their cohesiveness to secure success. With these colonization efforts, the railroads effectively transported entire communities from Europe to the American Midwest.

Yet railroad companies did not want large numbers of just *any* immigrant; rather, they sought a specific type of person—a white person, to be sure—but also one possessing a strong moral character, a resilient work ethic, and knowledge of agriculture. For the first of those reasons, the railroad companies often targeted religious groups in their colonization efforts. D. E. Jones of the Burlington Railroad believed that the company had previously "greatly erred [. . .] in not having a well-understood and well-established *system of Christian immigration*" since "the *benefits* of such a method of immigration would not only have appeared in the concentration of moral power, by the saving of funds, and in the manifold blessings that come to any community where there is general co-operation in erecting and maintaining the institutions of the Gospel [emphasis in original]."[58] Better still, some immigrant groups met all the railroad officials' criteria—good morals, hard workers, and expert farmers. The Burlington Railroad received a letter from an agent ranking Christian sects "in point of agricultural worth as well as wealth, in the following order: Mennonites, Lutherans, Baptists, Catholics. The first two classes are especially a people possessing in a high degree the characteristics of industry, frugality, and temperance, and rank among the best farmers in the world."[59] Mennonites ranked high on the list of those who fulfilled the railroad's desired qualities, and in the 1870s, when Mennonites sought to flee Russia, they became the subject of an intense competition between the American and Canadian railways, as well as among the American railroad companies themselves.

"And It Was Still Westward That They Ran"

The relocation of German-speaking Mennonites from Russia on the Santa Fe Railroad Company lands in Kansas formed one of the largest colonization efforts in American railway history. The Mennonites were no strangers to migration. Originally from Dutch- and German-speaking lands, when Mennonites began experiencing religious persecution they relocated to what was then southeastern Russia (now Ukraine) at the invitation of Catherine II (commonly known as Catherine the Great), who issued a manifesto in 1763 inviting Europeans to settle there.[60] Like the nineteenth-century efforts by the United States government to populate the lands taken from Native American nations, the attempts of the Russian Empire to colonize the land seized from the Turkish Army in the eighteenth century during the Russo-Turkish War led to increased immigration to the empire. Beginning in 1789, Mennonite communities who had been living in the Netherlands relocated to Russia. Under their agreement with the Russian Empire, they eventually occupied several million acres of farming lands, with each family receiving 175 acres, and were able to act as a state within a state, speaking their own language of Plattdeutsch (Low German), establishing their own German-speaking churches and schools, and forming their own elected board of administrators.[61]

After several years of adjusting to the arid climate, the Mennonite community thrived. Their land was prone to drought and grasshopper plagues—plights that also affected the settlers in the American Midwest. The colonies followed an agricultural village model, with fifteen to thirty families sharing large open fields and a communal pasture. The farming lands were divided into long, narrow strips and distributed equally to each family in the settlement, which meant they shared the benefits or drawbacks of the soil quality—a system they would ultimately bring with them to the United States. In the 1830s, the work of agriculturalist Johann Cornies, himself a part of the Mennonite colony, established the Mennonite farms as models for all agriculture in southern Russia. Due to Cornies's innovative methods of increasing the supply of soil moisture, the Mennonites were able to yield fertile crops in an area prone to drought.[62] He also encouraged farmers to plant orchards around their houses and promoted forestation programs throughout the settlements to serve as windbreaks.[63] The Mennonites' experience with drought would ultimately help them thrive in Kansas, an area with a similar climate, and aid in establishing the state as one of the United States' key agricultural producers.

In 1871, the Russian government established new regulations that forced many Mennonite colonies to emigrate. Emperor Alexander II abolished Catherine the Great's agreement with the Mennonites, which had granted them freedom from military service due to their religious beliefs. Furthermore, under the czar's new Russianization program, the Mennonites would no longer be able to run German schools or have their own administration. The Russian government also imposed certain ownership laws on the Mennonite villages that would no longer allow farmers to sell, mortgage, or subdivide their lots.[64] When efforts to contest these changes were unsuccessful, the Mennonites turned their sights to other countries where they might be able to carry on their way of life.

Cornelius Jansen, a merchant in the Mennonite colony of Berdiansk, wrote to the British consul about availability of land in Canada as well as to John F. Funk, editor of a Mennonite newspaper in Elkhart, Indiana, about settlement in the American Midwest.[65] To both the United States and Canadian governments, the Mennonites relayed their request to be free from military service, to live in closed settlements with autonomous local administration, and to allow German to remain their primary language. To retain their way of life, the Mennonites required vast amounts of unoccupied land—space that, conveniently, the American and Canadian governments, as well as their respective railroad companies, were eager to have occupied. The Canadian government ceded to the Mennonites on all requests; however, the Mennonites sent to scout the land found the region of Manitoba, which the government had offered to them, to be isolated and not well served by the railroads. While some of the group did eventually establish colonies there, others turned to the United States. The US federal government was not as immediately accommodating as Canada, although the individual states of Minnesota, Kansas, and Nebraska worked quickly to pass laws in 1873 and 1874 allowing freedom from military conscription as a means to attract the Mennonite farmers.

Congress was generally opposed to the creation of settlements that would allow immigrants to retain their European ways.[66] Senator Matthew H. Carpenter of Wisconsin vehemently opposed the bill, arguing: "We do not desire to have a town or a county settled by any foreign nationality, speaking their own language, having their natural amusements, and in all things separated and different from Americans."[67] Those resisting the settlement were not necessarily opposed to the Mennonites themselves. Many of the senators recognized the potential contributions to the country if the Mennonites did in fact immigrate to the United States. Some congressmen, however, such as Senator Allen G. Thurman of Ohio, recognized that "if we pass this bill because they are worthy people, can we refuse to pass similar bills whenever other people ask us to do so? [. . .] Are you going to refuse them on the ground that their sect of religion is not as good as the Mennonites or that you do not quite agree with their sentiments in morals or politics or something else?"[68] The federal government ultimately refused to pass a bill that would allow tracts of land to be set aside for the promotion and establishment of ethnic enclaves.

Since the Mennonites were known to be expert agriculturists, they did indeed receive their fair share of supporters. In a letter to the superintendent of the Burlington Railroad, one land agent wrote of the Mennonites that "no better people in the world could be found to *utilizing* [*sic*] *every acre of land* in the various districts where they may settle, and wherever they may go, a *dense population, producing a large export surplus* will be the result of their location [emphasis in original]."[69] Certain members of Congress recognized the contribution the group could make to American agriculture. Senator William Windom of Minnesota (the same senator who would later serve as treasury secretary during the establishment of Ellis Island) argued that turning away "forty thousand of the very best farmers of Russia who are now competing with us in the markets of the world with some ten million bushels of their wheat" would be giving Russia, or Canada if they chose to settle there, the advantage.[70] Windom was in the minority of those who wanted to induce immigration of the Mennonites, and furthermore, the United States government was largely reluctant to interfere with Russian internal affairs.[71] In fact, the Russian government was trying to prevent mass migration by raising the cost of passports, intercepting foreign mail, and making it difficult to sell property, among other actions.

Despite the government's opposition, American railroad companies began aggressive competition with one another, as well as with the Canadian railroads, to secure the sale of their lands to the Mennonite immigrants. The competition began in earnest, with each company trying to meet the needs of the Mennonites and offer additional enticements. In fact, railroad agents went so far as to steal Mennonite passengers from competing lines. Carl Ernst, land agent for the Burlington Railroad, went to Castle Garden and, as he later recalled, "swiped a whole trainload [of Mennonites] from the two Kansas [rail]roads, each of which had a special train awaiting their arrival in Atchison, but I stole the whole bunch, except less than a dozen unmarried young men, and carried them all by special train, free, to Lincoln, Nebraska."[72] Given the large quantities of time and money the railroads had dedicated to promotional campaigns and the organization of colonies, the mass migration of Mennonites proved to be an immediate, and easier, solution to settling the railroad's lands. Ernst later recalled, "Those were certainly strenuous days for settling up our prairie states."[73]

Of the American companies, the Northern Pacific Railroad, the Burlington Railroad, and the Santa Fe Railroad were the likely sources from

Figure 4.8. Temporary immigrant home for the Alexanderwohl community provided by the Santa Fe Railroad. Once the immigrants built their homes, the temporary lodging house served as the location for civic and religious meetings. From Frank Leslie's *Illustrierte Zeitung*, September 6, 1873. Courtesy of the Mennonite Library and Archives, Bethel College, North Newton, Kansas

which the Mennonites could purchase property, since their lines traversed vast tracts of open land. A Mennonite delegation of five traveled to the United States to scout possible locations. They considered the Northern Pacific lands in Dakota to be too stony and they feared its proximity to a federal Native American reservation, thus putting the Northern Pacific out of the running. The Mennonite delegation ultimately selected the Santa Fe's lands in Kansas, where water was more readily available, over the Burlington's lands in Nebraska, where deep wells would be needed. The Kansas lands were also covered with a fine grass to make hay for the winter. When the delegation's spokesman, Rev. H. Richert, stated that the availability of hay was one of the reasons for selecting the Kansas lands, Burlington agent A. E. Touzalin promptly replied to the translator, "You tell Mr. Reichert that the [Burlington] Railway will furnish all hay needed for the winter free of charge."[74] Thus began a bidding war between the two railroads, whatever Touzalin offered on the part of the Burlington Railroad, the Santa Fe land agent, Carl Bernhard Schmidt, also met. When Touzalin offered the lands for free to the Mennonites, Schmidt remained silent. Schmidt later stated that he realized the Mennonites would come to the Kansas lands and thus did not need to meet Touzalin's offer of free land, although he had been told by his superiors to "bring those Mennonites at any cost." Touzalin undoubtedly received similar instructions.[75]

The mass exodus of approximately 45,000 Mennonites from Russia began in 1873 and within five years, more than 10,000 Mennonites had come to the United States, with over half settling in Kansas.[76] To them, the Santa Fe Railroad offered reduced freight rates (on which they claimed to receive no profit), land prices at $2.50 per acre (the going rate at the time was $5.00 per acre), and lots donated by the railroad for church and school

Figure 4.9. Interior of the Alexanderwohl temporary lodging. From Frank Leslie's *Illustrierte Zeitung*, September 6, 1873. Courtesy of the Mennonite Library and Archives, Bethel College, North Newton, Kansas

purposes.[77] With the 1874 arrival of several hundred Mennonites to Marion and McPherson counties in eastern Kansas, the railroad constructed temporary lodging for the settlers. In modern-day Goessel, Kansas, the Alexanderwohl community, most of whom arrived in September 1874, lived in five separate single-story wooden buildings measuring 200 feet long by 18 feet wide (figure 4.8). The Santa Fe provided the materials and workers necessary to erect the buildings and the Mennonites furnished additional workers to complete construction. Each building featured six windows along each side and entrances at either end. A kitchen shed projected out of the center of the structure and stoves for heating and cooking lined the interior. Once completed, these long houses were the site for all household activities: baking, sewing, washing, and so on. The settlers lived communally in a space that often grew crowded, given the dozens of families residing in each building (figure 4.9). The settlers quickly busied themselves with building houses, digging wells, making hay, and completing other preparations for the upcoming winter. With all of the work to be done, for both individual family dwellings and community structures, most of the families lived in the temporary lodging throughout the winter. Once their houses were completed and occupied, the temporary shelters served as the location for religious and civic meetings until the Mennonites could erect separate buildings for those purposes. Many of the families that arrived were poor, despite erroneous reports by American journalists that they arrived with millions of dollars. American Mennonites organized funds to help these families get established. The approximate amount of funds raised was around $150,000 in the form of transportation fees, direct aid, or loans.[78] The group purchased the railroad lands and was able to form homogenous communities that reestablished, for the most part, the agricultural villages they had left behind in Russia.

"This Was 'the Good Country' We Had Been Going To So Long"

When the Mennonites settled in Kansas, they brought their established land-use patterns and architectural styles. In the village of Gnadenau, for example, located on twelve sections of railroad land near present-day Hillsboro, the first farms of the settlement were cultivated on five sections that formed a checkerboard pattern. The settlers built their houses on the north side of a road that traversed east–west along the center of the settlement. The settlers divided the center section into long, narrow strips on which they built their houses, which numbered about two dozen. The other sections of land were also divided into long, narrow strips, with each homeowner receiving an allotment in each section; thus, the land was equally distributed so that they shared any variations in soil (figure 4.10). In this way, they continued the cooperative way of living they had established in Russia.[79]

While most prairie settlers constructed sod houses, and occasionally wood-frame houses if, and when, they had the funds and access to lumber, many of the Mennonites constructed their dwellings from adobe brick. On the prairie, wood was scarce, and with the cost of traveling and setting up farms most settlers did not immediately have the financial means to order lumber from other regions. Mennonite settlers first cleared their land of prairie sod, digging down a layer of earth or clay to loosen it and then wetting it with water to create mud. They mixed straw in the mud and used their horses to tamp down the mixture. Using what wood they had to make a frame for the bricks—eighteen inches deep and several feet high—the Mennonite settlers formed their houses, cutting window and door openings once the mud walls dried. Wood was only needed for the frame, gables, and ceiling, thus minimizing the settlers' reliance on the scarce building material.

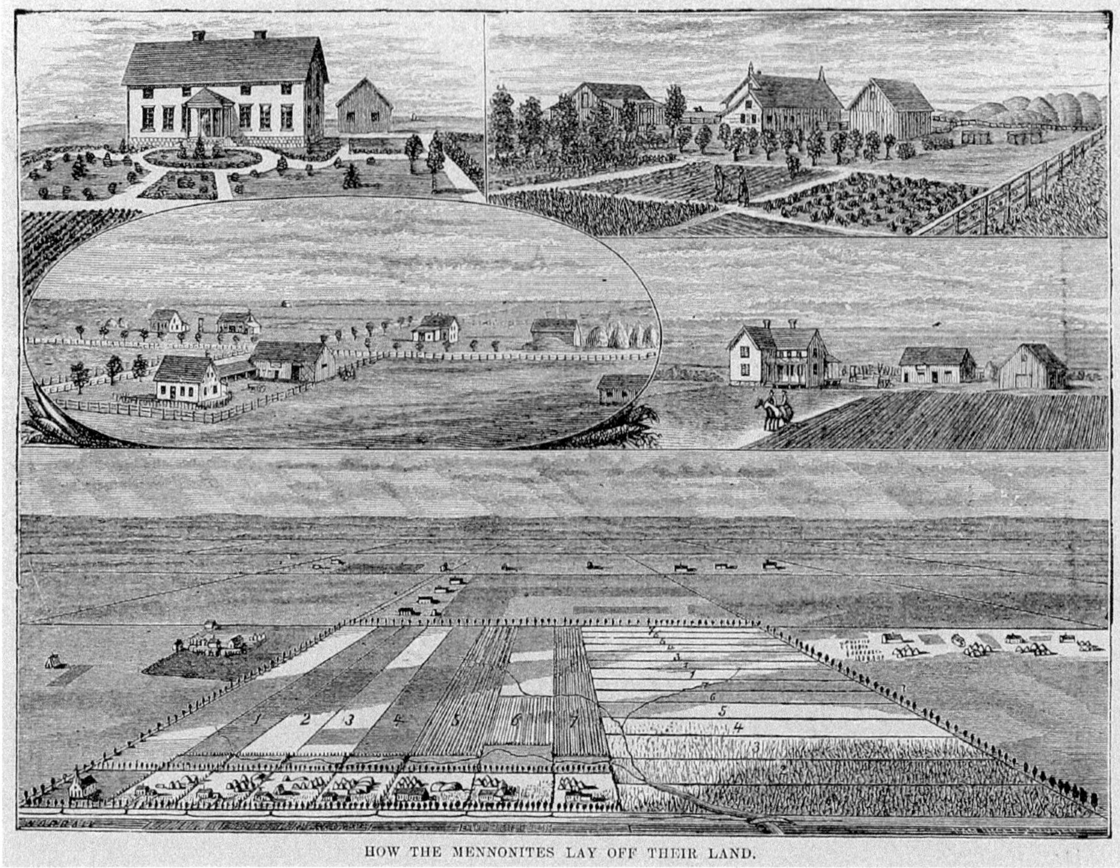

Figure 4.10. In the agricultural village of Hochfeld, in Marion County, Kansas, Mennonite settlers owned long, narrow strips of land in order to share any soil variations. In the bottom illustration, the numbers indicate to whom the land belongs. Courtesy of the Library of Congress, Rare Book and Special Collections Division, Printed Ephemera Collection

A quicker type of construction, often temporary as opposed to the longer-lasting adobe homes, was a building called a *saraj* or *burdei*—an A-frame structure that used cottonwood poles to form the frame and sod, adobe, and thatch made of prairie grass as infill (figure 4.11).[80] One end of the structure served as the family's house and the other, a barn. This type of construction, called byre-dwelling, was somewhat of a shock to Americans. W. J. Groat, upon a visit to Gnadenau only five months after its settlement, printed his observations in the *Marion County Record*:

> The majority of these "fix-ups" have no side walls whatsoever, the roof starting from the ground, and only gables are laid up with these [adobe] brick. The roof is simply composed of poles thatched, or shingled, with prairie

Figure 4.11. In Gnadenau, Kansas, Mennonite settlers combined the family's living quarters and barn in a single, A-framed byre-dwelling called a saraj or burdei, which minimized building materials. Courtesy of the Mennonite Library and Archives, Bethel College, North Newton, Kansas

> grass; with an adobe chimney, projecting twelve or sixteen inches only above the dry hay. We were not in the fire insurance business or we would not have halted. We were met at the door and invited in, and following, we were in the rear, and closing the door behind us, which darkened the room, we started in their wake; but what was our astonishment to find ourself [*sic*] plank upon the heels of a horse, but we were soon relieved by our hostess throwing open another door on the opposite side of the stable (for such it proved to be) revealing a small passage between a horse and a cow leading into the presence of the family; each one coming forward and saying "welcome," at the same time giving us a hearty shake of the hand.[81]

Although not common in the United States, byre-dwelling was a practical construction for the Mennonites in Russia, where the harsh conditions allowed farmers to tend to their animals during winter without venturing out into the bitter cold.[82]

The settlement at Gnadenau became a curiosity for the other white settlers already in the region. Visitors first encountered the Mennonites at the temporary lodging house in Topeka, where the Santa Fe Railroad housed them in a brick warehouse that had originally been built to service the railroad cars. Constructed around the same time that the Mennonites arrived, the warehouse had not yet been outfitted with machinery and was thus a large empty space suitable to house the dozens of families heading to Gnadenau. A few months after the construction of the houses at Gnadenau, the journalist W. J. Groat marveled at the "strange village" he encountered. He noted that the triangular structure of the saraj gave the appearance of a haystack from a distance and only upon getting closer and seeing people bustling about tending to their chores did he realize they were houses. Just as Stevenson observed the individual dwellings that appeared as "a few dots" from a passing train, from afar the structures seemed insignificant in the landscape until a closer view revealed their true purpose.

In addition to their architecture, the Mennonite settlers brought with them their knowledge of agriculture, which ultimately proved to be one of their greatest contributions to the United States. When Noble L. Prentis visited the Kansas settlements for the second time in 1882, he observed that when he had last visited in 1875, he left bare prairie but "returned to find a score of miniature forests in sight from any point of view. [. . .] Several acres around every house were set in hedges, orchards, lanes, and alleys of trees; trees in lines, trees in groups, and trees all along."[83] The Mennonite settlers continued the practices they had started under Johann Cornies in Russia: they planted orchards around their houses; they established lines of trees to serve as windbreaks; and they even grew mulberry trees to harvest silkworms.[84] Like the railroad companies, the Mennonites had also transformed the barren prairie on which their settlements were located.

The Mennonites became known for a type of wheat they had grown in Russia—Turkey red wheat. A winter wheat, this variety was hardier and able to withstand the arid climate of Kansas. Many of the settlers arriving to the Midwest from the eastern United States and from northern European countries had little experience with the climate and soil of the Great Plains. The Mennonites emigrating from Russia, however, were accustomed to drought and their winter wheat thrived. Mark Alfred Carleton, a historian writing in 1914, noted the similarities between the Kansas lands and southeastern Russia: "A traveler on the Plains of Kansas, if suddenly transported while asleep to Southern Russia, and deposited in the Crimea, would discover very little difference in his surroundings except as to the people and the character of farm improvements and live stock [*sic*]. Even the last would be of the same kind, if he were transported from certain localities in Kansas where Russian immigrants now live."[85] The Russian climate, however, was somewhat harsher than that of Kansas, meaning that the winter wheat had the potential to fare even better in the American Midwest. It is highly likely this variety of wheat existed in the United States prior to the Mennonites' arrival; their success with it, however, led historians to credit the Mennonites with its introduction.[86] Turkey red wheat did not become widely distributed until the late 1870s, after the development of mill equipment able to process the hard winter wheat, and after the Santa Fe Railroad constructed a branch from Marion to McPherson counties in Kansas.[87] As the railroad began servicing the very settlements they had established, the Mennonites began to conduct business with towns outside of their own, spreading their agricultural endeavors to the non-Mennonite community.

The continued success of the Mennonites was precisely what the railroads had hoped for in establishing colonies in the Midwest. Along the rails, many other towns thrived as well—communities that had also been started by foreigners. One Danish immigrant, Hans Jacobsen (who had Americanized his surname from Jørgensen), arrived in the United States in 1892 and worked hard for three years until he could build a house and afford the overseas passage for his wife and six children. Jacobsen tried for years to also encourage his other family members to emigrate from Denmark; he wrote home that "there are much better conditions here and much more freedom. If it wasn't for the fact that I don't have a single relative here, I wouldn't miss Europe for a moment."[88] In an effort to encourage family members and friends to emigrate, however, many immigrants spoke only of the riches they encountered in this new land. Dan Perekrestenko, whose brother had emigrated to the United States from Ukraine, stated that settlers "never mentioned the hardships they endured . . . they did not want to admit what a hard time they were really having in this new country."[89] Migration certainly brought with it many challenges, and many struggled in this foreign land with its unfamiliar language, climate, and customs.

In their continued promotion of lands along their lines, railroad companies focused on the progress achieved by their towns' citizens to encourage continued migration. Advertising went on into the 1920s, when the state governments and the railroad companies worked together to boast of the booming agricultural and industrial production in various regions. In a booklet highlighting the prosperity of northwestern Nebraska, published by the Burlington Railroad in conjunction with the chambers of commerce of several counties, one image depicts the great success of a pioneer family: a white-washed, one-and-a-half-story, bungalow-style house, complete with veranda, stands next to the family's original sod house, a simple structure built by the settlers when they first arrived, most likely in the 1880s (figure 4.12).[90] The deteriorating sod house next to the pristine white permanent structure tells the tale of the settlers' struggles upon first arriving to Nebraska and the prosperous life they built for themselves, ultimately encouraging readers that they, too, could achieve such prosperity.

Colonization served the immediate purpose of settling the lands and establishing agricultural and other business endeavors, thus ensuring continuous profit for the railroads, but it also had a measured effect on the culture of the American Midwest. Since most of these groups settled

Figure 4.12. The sod house at right was the family's initial dwelling until they could build the more substantial and permanent residence seen on the left. The barn roof is visible behind the sod house. Photo from *Northwestern Nebraska*, a booklet published jointly by the Burlington Railroad and the Chambers of Commerce of several counties, c. 1920s–early 1930s.

in the United States alongside members of their own ethnicity, these groups influenced the architecture and planning of their towns and thus developed a local cultural heritage. Where the Mennonite communities originally settled in Marion and McPherson counties in Kansas, for example, today there remains a large Mennonite population. One of the local Kansas history museums, the Mennonite Heritage and Agricultural Museum in Goessel, was established in 1974 to commemorate the centennial of the Alexanderwohl colony. The site of the museum is in fact a replica of the temporary lodging erected by the Santa Fe Railroad for the first settlers of the colony. The Mennonite colonization of the area remains a vital part of the town's cultural heritage.

The railroads reshaped the West according to their own terms, deciding which white ethnic groups would be most suited for the towns along the rail lines. Even though the United States government balked at setting aside land specifically for the purpose of establishing ethnic enclaves in the Midwest, they enabled the railroad companies to do so by granting them the land on which they worked so fervently to occupy. The railroad companies built the tracks that determined settlement locations and designed those towns rapidly and economically. Once the foundations were laid, the targeted promotional campaigns and colonization schemes directed by railroad officials brought the settlers who would breathe life into those railway towns and ultimately mold each according to their own style, values, and beliefs. In this way, as the railways physically altered the country's landscape, they were integral in shaping the nation's cultural landscape as well.

Figure 5.1. “The Great Fear of the Period: That Uncle Sam May Be Swallowed By Foreigners,” 1860s lithograph. Highly stereotyped Irish and Chinese males devour Uncle Sam until eventually the Chinese immigrant also devours the Irishman. The background landscape features several trains as a direct commentary on the fact that countless Irish and Chinese found work on the railroads. Courtesy of the Library of Congress, Prints & Photographs Division, Reproduction Number LC-DIG-pga-03047

SAN FRANCISCO

In a chapter entitled "Despised Races," Stevenson documents his fellow white passengers' prejudices toward nonwhite people, particularly the Chinese train passengers and the Native American families selling their wares at station stops. He observes that his fellow passengers "seemed never to have looked at them, or thought of them, but hated them *a priori*."[1] He also criticizes the American government's large-scale injustices toward Indigenous peoples, such as the eviction of the Cherokee, among many others, from their ancestral lands, their forced relocation onto reservations in "the hideous mountain deserts," and subsequent mistreatment by government agents. He observes such despicable behavior toward Indigenous peoples firsthand when, at a way station, some white passengers "danced and jested round [a Native family] with a truly Cockney baseness." Rather than the "wild or independent Indian" typically depicted in the American West (whom Stevenson himself sensationalizes earlier in his memoir with the inclusion of an 1850s letter by a young boy attacked by Native Americans), here the family is dressed in "the sweepings of civilization"—that is, European-American dress—and Stevenson remarks on the "silent stoicism of their conduct."[2] He pities them inasmuch as a privileged white man can, feeling moved by their plight and yet continuing unencumbered onto his next encounter as the train lumbers away from the station.

The further west Stevenson traveled, the more he encountered nonwhite people. In the railway space, Stevenson observed that "hungry Europe and hungry China, each pouring from their gates in search of provender, had here come face-to-face."[3] He and other westward European travelers eagerly seeking "the land of gold" soon discovered that Chinese immigrants had traveled east for the same reason. To Stevenson's disappointment, "the whole round world had been prospected and condemned; there was no El Dorado anywhere."[4] As Stevenson's train rolled further west toward California, he was shocked to see crowded immigrant trains returning east, loaded with disenchanted passengers crying out the windows "in a kind of wailing chorus, to 'Come back.'"[5] For the Chinese in particular, several thousand miles from home, the myth of easily attainable wealth and prosperity in America was realized for what it was—a painful lie. Instead, what awaited them on American shores was humiliation, oppression, and overt racism that was used to justify their imprisonment.

Stevenson often sympathizes with the Chinese and their treatment at the hands of their fellow travelers, albeit at several points in the text he gives in to the impulse of exoticizing them. At one point, Stevenson marvels at Chinese civilization's advancements: "I could not look but with wonder and respect on the Chinese. Their forefathers watched the stars before mine had begun to keep pigs."[6] And yet on immigrant trains, he witnesses the Chinese treated no better than pigs. On his journey, he states that white travelers frequently claimed that the Chinese were the filthiest and most foul-smelling of the passengers. Stevenson is quick to point out that the Chinese car was, in fact, the tidiest of all the immigrant cars and that the Chinese travelers' "efforts at cleanliness put us all to shame."[7] Indeed, "these very foul and malodorous Caucasians entertained the surprising illusion that it was the Chinese waggon [*sic*], and that alone, which stank."[8] After being cooped up in a train car for ninety hours, Stevenson stated the obvious, that their own cars "had begun to stink abominably."[9] In railway space, contemporary prejudice toward the Chinese was reproduced and reinforced; not only were they segregated from other immigrant passengers but the Chinese car was also, notably, the passenger car closest to the engine—the most dangerous location on the train. The railway's segregated spaces both expressed American prejudices toward newly arrived foreigners and also revealed a racial hierarchy present among the immigrants themselves, with the Chinese relegated to the lowest class.

Stevenson was well aware of the changing attitudes toward immigration in the United States: "A while ago it was the Irish, now it is the Chinese that must go" (figure 5.1).[10] In the eastern states in particular, white citizens felt threatened by the influx of Irish immigrants who were escaping famine in the mid-nineteenth century, whom they believed would become a public burden and take jobs away from those already in the country. On the West Coast, also in the mid-nineteenth century, tens of thousands of Chinese sailed across the Pacific to what they called *Gam*

Saan—Gold Mountain. The discovery of gold in California had sparked the hopes of many emigrants, including the Chinese, who were suffering from political and economic instability in China as a result of the Opium Wars and the Taiping Civil War.[11] Word first spread to China of the discovery of gold in California in 1848. In 1852, more than twenty thousand Chinese left their war-torn and famished country and sailed to San Francisco with the hope of earning enough to make a living and to send money to their struggling families who remained in China. The Chinese were not the only ones traveling to California in search of gold, though. Most gold-seekers, called "forty-niners" in reference to 1849, the year in which they arrived, came from throughout the United States, but many also arrived from Europe, Latin America, and Australia. After gold rush fervor subsided in the 1860s (when many of the gold fields and mines had been exhausted), Chinese miners found work with the railroads, particularly with the Central Pacific Railroad Company in the Transcontinental Railroad's construction, which was begun in 1863 and completed in 1869. The Central Pacific faced a shortage of laborers in the West and subsequently relied mainly on Chinese immigrant laborers, who were willing to do the difficult and dangerous work required of them. Central Pacific's president, Leland Stanford, stated that "a large majority of the white laboring class on the Pacific Coast find more profitable and congenial employment in mining and agricultural pursuits, than in railroad work. The greater portion of the laborers employed by us are Chinese, who constitute a large element in the population of California."[12] The Union Pacific, which built the Transcontinental Railroad's eastern line, employed mostly Civil War army veterans and Irish immigrants. By 1880, more than three hundred thousand Chinese were living in California, amounting to approximately one-tenth of the state's population. With the increasing population of California came further development of towns and railways—and the continued need for workers to build them.

The Transcontinental Railroad joined east and west in more ways than one. It geographically united the country and its construction also brought Chinese immigrant laborers to the Western world. Yet the hiring of Chinese laborers increasingly escalated racial tensions. The Chinese labor surplus contributed greatly to mounting anti-Chinese sentiment and fear that white laborers would be out of work—a fact not lost on Stevenson: "The Mongols were their enemies in that cruel and treacherous battle-field of money."[13] Railroad officials exploited the Chinese laborers, who typically performed the more strenuous and oftentimes more dangerous work required to build the railroads, including tunneling and the use of explosives, all for lower wages than white laborers (figure 5.2).[14] Not

Figure 5.2. Construction of the Summit Tunnel through the Sierra Nevada mountain range was one of the most difficult and dangerous tasks completed by Chinese workers for the Central Pacific Railroad. In this photograph, workers stand amid the granite rocks they excavated to form the tunnel. They dug 1,659 feet through solid granite in sixteen months, although the project was planned to take three years. Photograph by Alfred A. Hart, c. 1865–1869. Courtesy of the Library of Congress, Prints & Photographs Division, Reproduction Number LC-DIG-stereo-1s00510

only did the white lower class view the Chinese as an existential threat, taking their jobs and livelihood, but their fears were also xenophobic—they often viewed the Chinese laborer's appearance, language, and manner as inferior and even offensive. To placate public outcry, the legislature seriously considered exclusionary laws as early as the beginning of the

Chinese migration to the United States but there was significant opposition among mining representatives and certain legislators. Historian Mark Kanazawa proposes one explanation for this opposition, asserting that Chinese miners contributed significantly to state and local tax revenues yet required relatively few public services such as schools, since most Chinese immigrants were adult males.[15] This additional revenue was particularly welcome after statehood, when the state and localities were in dire need of money. Kanazawa notes that by 1858, when California's finances improved, the state first enacted exclusionary legislation.

From the moment Chinese immigrants set foot on American shores, cartoonists expressed the nation's xenophobic fears by producing racialized portrayals published in periodicals. Images of Chinese people as subhuman and animalistic, unaware of basic hygiene, living in squalor, and high on opium pervaded the popular press. Chinese women were categorized as prostitutes and the nature of Chinese dress and style, for example, the fact that men wore their hair in a queue (long hair worn in a single braid down the back), suggested an androgynous appearance in the eyes of white Euro-Americans. Stevenson himself at times confused young Chinese men for European women when seen from a distance: "Now, as a matter of fact, the young Chinese man is so like a large class of European women, that on raising my head and suddenly catching sight of one at a considerable distance, I have for an instant been deceived by the resemblance."[16] The fact that many Chinese men lived as bachelors instead of with their families (wives and children usually remained in China) also challenged gender roles that frightened the white Euro-American population.[17] Racist political cartoons perpetuated xenophobic attitudes and depicted the social hierarchies of the time. Where Americans once believed the Irish to be the least desirable sort of immigrant, now the Chinese had that dubious distinction. Chinese labor threatened whites, among whom the Irish counted themselves, and thus the Chinese were perceived as a threat to their very existence.[18]

"There Was Not One Good Circumstance in That God-Forsaken Land"

The extreme discrimination toward Chinese immigrants on the part of American citizens, European immigrants, the media, and government officials eventually resulted in strict legislation against entry of Chinese into the United States, ushering in a new era in which the United States became a gatekeeping nation.[19] The anti-Chinese agitation that had begun in the 1840s culminated in the Chinese Exclusion Act of 1882, signed by

President Chester A. Arthur, and its subsequent renewal in 1892 and 1902. The law restricted entry for all Chinese laborers for a period of ten years and prohibited Chinese immigrants already in the country from becoming naturalized citizens. The extension of the 1882 law, the Geary Act of 1892, stated that "if a Chinese resident were found without a certificate, he would be subject to immediate and summary deportation unless he could find one white witness to confirm that he had resided in the United States before November 17, 1880."[20] The fact that the government's strict law required the word of a white person to testify to the immigrant's claim to have resided in the United States not only demonstrated the blatant racism evident in immigration policy in the late nineteenth and early twentieth centuries but also pointed to the many ways in which the Chinese community was dehumanized at the western port of entry to the United States. Even if the individual had been born in the country or had arrived legally, every Chinese person was considered suspect by inspection officers; it was only through the testimony of a white witness that the Chinese individual's claims could be validated.

Prior to the 1910 establishment of a government-owned immigration facility in San Francisco Bay, inspection of arriving foreigners occurred in a two-story shed owned and operated by the Pacific Mail Steamship Company at San Francisco's Pier 40 (figure 5.3). Like the port of Baltimore in the mid-nineteenth century, San Francisco was served primarily by one railroad company, the Central Pacific, which was acquired by the Southern Pacific Railroad Company in 1885. The Southern Pacific also acquired the Pacific Mail Steamship Company in 1893, developing freight and passenger service from Asia to San Francisco and on to New York via rail or to Central America via Pacific Mail steamships. This merger was thus instrumental in opening up the Pacific for passenger travel between Asia and the United States. Yet as Asian immigrants arrived in San Francisco, they did not board waiting immigrant trains or enter the city, as was the case for European immigrants arriving on the East Coast; rather, they were detained for days and even weeks in the Pacific Mail Steamship Company detention sheds for inspection by immigration officers. Conditions were not any better at other West Coast ports, such as Seattle or San Diego, but San Francisco received the greatest number of arrivals.

The Chinese immigrants referred to the detention shed as *muk uk* or "wooden barracks," but also as the "iron cage" or "Chinese jail."[21] Measuring 100 feet by 50 feet, the wooden structure with pitched roof contained only six windows on each of the two floors and had a single exit. The wooden building was "a veritable fire trap," according to one immigrant

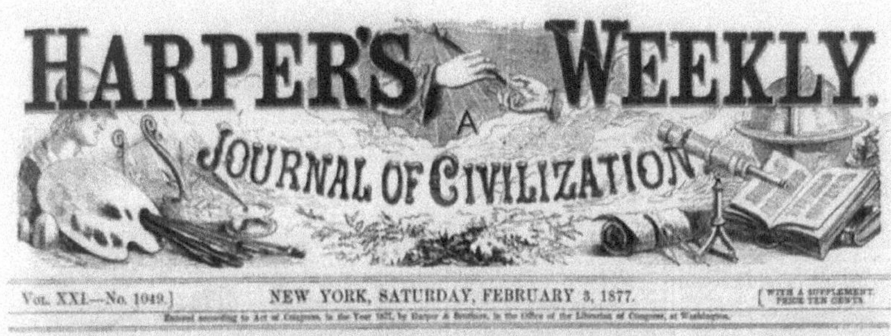

Figure 5.3. Before Angel Island Immigration Station was built, Chinese immigrants disembarked at the Pacific Mail Steamship Company piers in San Francisco. This dark and crowded space is depicted on the cover of Harper's Weekly, February 3, 1877. Courtesy of the Library of Congress, Prints & Photographs Division, Reproduction Number LC-USZ62–93673

inspector.[22] As many as five hundred people occupied it at once, although it had been built to house only two hundred. To accommodate the extra detainees, additional bunks were placed in the aisles, which further contributed to overcrowding, not to mention increased fire hazard. With poor ventilation, many detainees fell sick and there were even some cases of death.[23] *Chinese World* editors wrote that "the mistreatment of us Chinese there was worse than for jailed prisoners."[24]

The unsanitary and dangerous conditions under which these detainees were held became the focus of Chinese community leaders in San Francisco's Chinatown. In one case, the Chinese daily *Chung Sai Yat Po* reprinted a petition signed on behalf of the Chinese community in California by the Officers and Mercantile Members of the Chinese Six Companies.[25] In the petition, the authors described the "harsh treatment accorded the Chinese by the United States Immigration Officials" and expressed that the Chinese were "habitually subjected to delay and embarrassment."[26] In creating and publishing this petition, the authors hoped to secure the American government's attention. Merchants in China also protested US discriminatory policies by staging a boycott of American goods beginning in May 1905, which continued for several months. The boycott started in Shanghai and then spread to other Chinese cities and overseas Chinese communities. The solidarity of this action, between individuals in China and the United States, was indicative of a newfound transpacific Chinese nationalism.[27] Groups such as the Chinese Chamber of Commerce and the Chinese-American League of Justice of Los Angeles sent complaints about the harsh treatment and discrimination during inspection and registration of Chinese travelers at the immigration station. Chinese leaders such as Wu Tingfang, the Chinese minister of foreign affairs, sent petitions and letters to American presidents Theodore Roosevelt, William Howard Taft, and Woodrow Wilson, complaining of the harsh treatment and discriminatory procedures of exclusion enforcement.[28]

The government finally responded to the objections although never fully addressed the physical environment in which the detainees were held. President Theodore Roosevelt instituted several changes to immigration practices after acknowledging that "in the effort to carry out the policy of excluding Chinese laborers [. . .] grave injustices and wrongs have been done to this nation and to the people of China."[29] Several of the changes affected interrogation proceedings: Chinese detainees could now have their attorneys and interpreters present at the hearings, although they themselves could not actively participate; attorneys could now examine testimonies and make copies of it in preparation for their cases; and attorneys were allowed to lengthen the time given to make an appeal.[30] Finally, one of the most significant changes was the end of the Bertillon system of identification, an anthropometric system of physical measurements of body parts that was utilized in the field of criminology in the late nineteenth and early twentieth centuries.[31] The process, which had been used for immigrant inspection since 1903, was time-consuming, and its adoption at immigration stations inherently linked arriving immigrants with criminals. Even with the system's eradication, Asian immigrants would still unfortunately be treated with suspicion by government officials and the public-at-large. In fact, one of the immigration officials' concerns regarding the existing facility was the Chinese detainees' attempts to escape from the Pacific Mail shed—thirty-two Chinese detainees had escaped between September and November 1908 and only three had been caught.[32]

When the commissioner-general of immigration, Frank P. Sargent, finally inspected the Pacific Mail Steamship Company detention shed on November 2, 1902, he found that conditions were "disgraceful—cramped in dimensions [and] lacking in every facility for cleanliness and decency," yet no efforts were made by the steamship company or the government to improve conditions.[33] Only after the secretary of commerce and labor, Victor H. Metcalf, recognized the facility as endangering government employees, in addition to the Chinese, did the Immigration Bureau take action to construct a new station. Metcalf felt that "the sanitary conditions are so poor that not only is the health and physical welfare of the detained persons constantly subjected to serious menace, but the danger to the government employees and others who are compelled to transact official business at the detention quarters is a matter of grave consequence."[34] Until this point, conditions for the detainees were abominable but excused or ignored by the government because it was mainly Chinese travelers held there. Yet once the government discovered that its own employees—white American citizens—were affected, officials finally took action to build a new facility.

"I Was Ashamed for the Thing We Call Civilization"

While the European immigrants entering through New York's Ellis Island formed a part of a larger network, one in which the railways and the government worked together to transport foreigners into the country and settle the nation's lands, for Asian immigrants on the West Coast the entry procedures were quite different. Not only did new arrivals have incredible difficulty entering the country, but even those who had been born in the country or entered legally were considered foreign to many Americans, and therefore inferior, because of their race. The racial, economic, and political forces that supported restrictive immigration legislation resulted in a particular architectural design for Angel Island Immigration Station, one in which detainees were segregated by race and constantly monitored. Opened in 1910 and shuttered in 1940 after a fire destroyed the administration building, the physical environment of Angel Island—its secluded location, segregated facilities, furnishings, constant surveillance, and oppressive atmosphere—served as the embodiment of the discrimination inherent in the Chinese Exclusion Act. In fact, immigration officials working at Angel Island referred to it as the "Guardian of the Western Gate." Although Angel Island did receive immigrants from many nationalities, including Japanese, Korean, Indian, Russian, Mexican, and Italian, among others, the majority of immigrants detained there were Chinese.[35]

For the facility's design and location, Commissioner-General Sargent recommended an island location to prevent escape and the spread of communicable disease, as well as inhibit communication between detainees and any friends or relatives who might coach them on how to pass interrogations.[36] Congress approved the use of the federally owned Angel Island, the largest island in San Francisco Bay, to be the site of the new immigration station. Named Isla de Los Angeles by Spanish explorer Juan Manuel de Ayala in 1775, the island was home to the Coast Miwok's Hookooeko tribe, whose population was all but destroyed by the contagious diseases spread by European settlers.[37] In 1858, the United States government took control of the island and established Camp Reynolds, later renamed Fort McDowell. The military constructed three artillery batteries to protect the bay against the Confederate army—an attack that never happened. At the outbreak of the Spanish–American War in 1898, the island housed its first detention center, where the US government held captured soldiers and Native Americans who had been taken prisoner during campaigns in Arizona. The federal government also built a quarantine station on Angel Island in 1892 to prevent entrance of "loathsome or dangerously contagious" diseases.[38] The staff employed at the quarantine station was responsible for inspection of incoming ships' passengers and crew, the fumigation of ships arriving from ports with epidemics present, and quarantine or deportation of any individuals with contagious diseases. The facility consisted of forty buildings including a detention barracks with four hundred beds, a disinfecting plant, laboratories, and housing for employees. Given that it was already the location of a quarantine station, government officials knew the 740-acre island could readily accommodate the proposed immigration station (figure 5.4).

Architect Walter J. Mathews received the contract to design the new immigration facility at Angel Island. There was no architectural

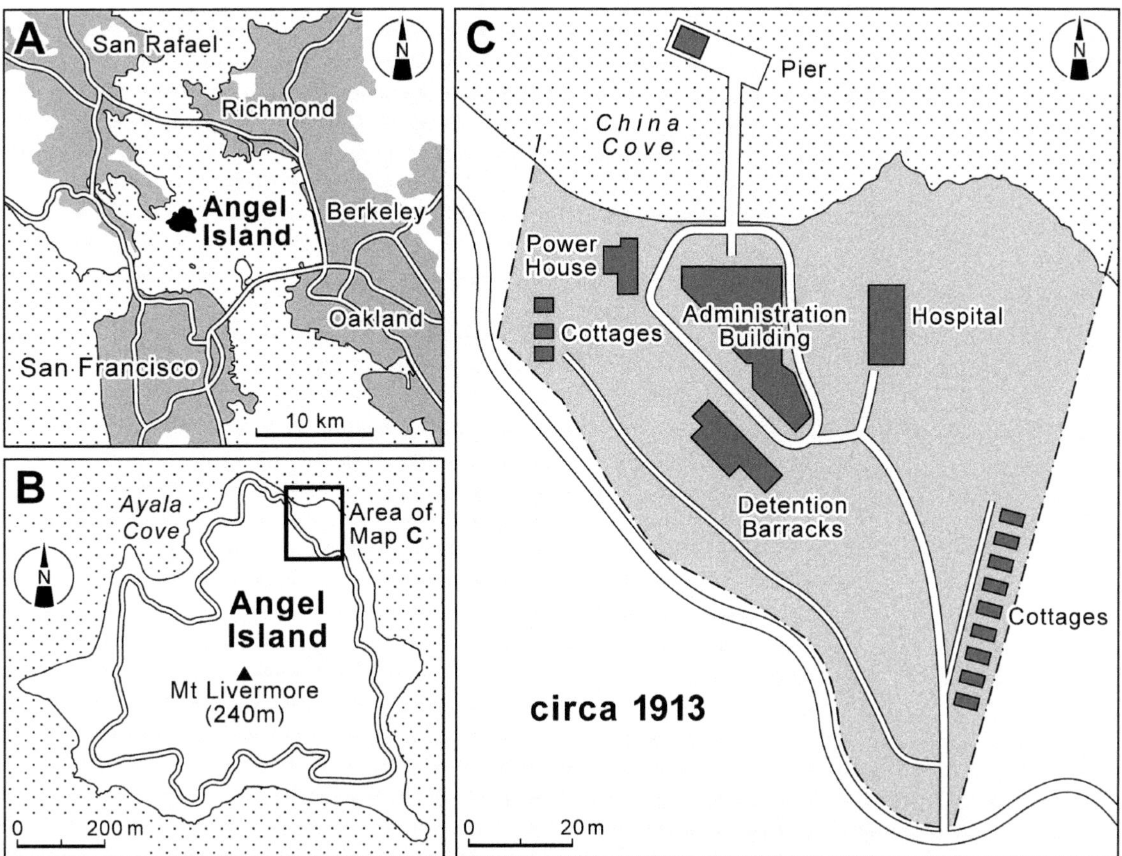

Figure 5.4. Map indicating the location of Angel Island in San Francisco Bay (a), the location of the immigration station on the island (b), and the layout of the facility c. 1913 (c). The quarantine station was located in Ayala Cove, west of the immigration station. Courtesy of Gareth Hoskins

competition under the Tarsney Act, as had been the case in the design for Ellis Island, a facility that was more prominently located and subject to intense scrutiny by the New York media. The Oakland architect had met with Commissioner Sargent in Washington, DC, in March 1905, just as the commissioner was charged with opening up the San Francisco facility.[39] Mathews assured Sargent that "if I should be appointed the architect and carry out the construction of this station, I would come to Washington and while there would make the sketches for the station under your personal supervision, which, in my judgment, is the only method to get complete and satisfactory results to all parties concerned."[40] Sargent then wrote to the secretary of commerce and labor asking whether he would like to open up a competition for architects or if Sargent should secure the services of Mathews.[41] Mathews, who served as Oakland's city architect in the 1890s, was offered the job and signed his contract by September, indicating that the federal government preferred to secure the services of this willing architect rather than potentially spending a larger sum of money on a more prestigious firm selected through competition. Construction on the facility began immediately but was interrupted by the 1906 San Francisco earthquake, which damaged the Angel Island wharf and made it nearly impossible to transport machinery and supplies to the island from the city. Work resumed the following year.

When the planning for an immigration station at Angel Island began, Senator George C. Perkins of California recommended that the facility model Ellis Island's cottage system.[42] The cottage plan, as it was begun to be used by hospitals and asylums in the second half of the nineteenth century, consisted of a series of smaller structures housing separate functions rather than one large institutional building. Although the hospital of Ellis Island did employ the cottage plan on the second and third islands, the majority of immigrants only passed through the massive main building on the first island. Mathews traveled to Ellis Island to study its layout before planning Angel Island. The cottage plan appealed to the architect and his superiors for several reasons: first, the hilly island could accommodate smaller, separate structures more readily than one monolithic building; second, separate structures could enforce segregation of Asians from Europeans as well as the healthy from the sick; and finally, smaller structures would cost significantly less. Mathews's final design consisted of an administration building with adjacent dining hall, detention barracks, a hospital, staff housing, water supply and powerhouse, and a pier with boat service to the mainland (figure 5.5). The facility was largely completed by 1908. Commissioner of Immigration Hart Hyatt North abruptly fired Mathews in July 1909, since government inspections revealed a number of deficiencies, including lack of fire protection, shoddy construction, and limited water supply. He then hired his sister-in-law, architect Julia Morgan, who had recently become the first woman licensed to practice architecture in California, to design twelve employee cottages to house staff members and their families. The cottages were constructed in 1910, the facility's opening year.[43]

The immigration station was situated on fifteen acres on the island's northeastern coast. Former assistant secretary of commerce and labor William R. Wheeler inquired into the expense involved in opening the facility and believed its remote location would result in an additional $50,000 per annum, with a major additional cost being the transportation of food to the island.[44] Furthermore, while "the station is delightfully located, so far as scenic, climatic, and health conditions are concerned," Wheeler believed "[it] is rather too remote from San Francisco, the trip from wharf

Figure 5.5. US Immigration Station, Angel Island, San Francisco Bay, 1910. Courtesy National Archives, photo no. 6402792

to wharf consuming approximately forty-five minutes."[45] Although the remote location would require additional expense, immigration officials believed the protection of American citizens and the isolation of Chinese immigrants were well worth the cost.

Angel Island Immigration Station officially opened on January 21, 1910. Chinese community leaders feared the treatment of detainees would not improve at the new site. San Francisco's Chinese-language newspaper, the *Chinese World*, printed an editorial reflecting on the past and anticipating the future: "Ever since the establishment of this wooden shed at the wharf, the mistreatment of us Chinese confined there was worse than for jailed prisoners. The walls were covered with poems; traces of tears soaked the floor. There were even some who could not endure the cruel abuse and took their own lives. The ropes they used to hang themselves are still visible. Those seeing this cannot help but feel aggrieved and gnash their teeth in anger. Now the Chinese had been moved from this wooden shed. From now on we will be confined on a barren offshore island."[46] For immigration officials, seclusion was a positive attribute of the new facility. For detainees and the Chinese community in San Francisco, the remote location of Angel Island only reinforced the isolation felt by detainees as they waited, full of fear and anguish, for officials to determine their future. The Downtown Association of San Francisco petitioned the commissioner of immigration not to remove the facility from the city, claiming that the establishment of a station on the island "will not only work a hardship on the incoming Orientals themselves" but would also inhibit the ability of their witnesses to submit their testimony.[47] The Chinese community, despite efforts to convince the government to build on the mainland, feared the new facility would instill the same oppression on its inmates, yet this time, beyond their reach.

When immigrants sailed into San Francisco Bay, their race, nationality, and economic status determined whether they would enter the country immediately or remain out to sea, so to speak, awaiting their fate at Angel Island. The primary medical and immigration inspections took place on board the steamship. Immigrant inspectors, interpreters, doctors, and nurses boarded the ship to examine passengers, conducting cursory health examinations and asking identifying questions such as name, age, marital status, and occupation. First-class passengers, the majority of whom were wealthy white American citizens or European travelers, were typically examined by medical officers in the privacy of their own rooms aboard the steamships and thus spared the humiliation of public exams and lengthy interrogations at the immigration station. Public health officers believed that wealthier passengers were less susceptible to disease since they could afford better conditions and nourishment during transit.[48] Those with satisfactory papers were allowed to go ashore in San Francisco. Many second-class passengers and all third-class or steerage passengers boarded the ferry for further inspection at the immigration station and to await hearings to determine whether they would be allowed entry. The ferry contained segregated cabins for its passengers; officials directed Asians to the main deck and Europeans to the upper deck. When they arrived at Angel Island, officials segregated white passengers from Asians, and among the latter, Chinese from the Japanese, Korean, and South Asian passengers, before they headed onto the island.

The ferry service, which completed four round trips daily between the mainland and the island, was the only transportation contracted with the Bureau of Immigration. There was no extensive transportation system that developed to move mass quantities of people between sea and rail, as was the case on the East Coast. The immigrants detained at Angel Island were suspect according to immigration officials, and there was no need on the government's part to form an agreement with railroad companies to transport them outside of San Francisco, since the chance of deportation was high. The rail system was also much more extensive on the East Coast. For European immigrants arriving at eastern ports, the inspection and registration process was a relatively brief interruption to their travels. For many Asians, however, the Angel Island Immigration Station was not a transitory experience; it was a place where they remained for days, weeks, or months before learning where their travels would ultimately take them—into the United States or back to Asia. The government extended their time in this highly regulated space in-between.

After landing at Angel Island, guards led passengers to the administration building located at the foot of the wharf. This two-story, Italian

Figure 5.6. US Immigration Station, Angel Island, San Francisco Bay, Examination Room–Main Building, 1910. Courtesy National Archives, photo no. 19086636

Renaissance Revival wooden structure formed the focal point and station's administrative center; it was the site of inspection, registration, the administrative offices, and the dining hall. The building's classical design featured a symmetrical facade with colonnaded porch, a low-pitched roof, and shallow projecting pavilions with hip roofs at either end. One detainee noted the simple wooden construction of Angel Island's buildings in contrast to the grander structures he had heard of that existed in the United States: "The Western styled buildings are lofty; but I have not the luck to live in them. How was anyone to know that my dwelling place would be a prison?"[49] Angel Island Immigration Station was nowhere near as complex—in scale, material, or program—as Boring & Tilton's Beaux-Arts building on Ellis Island. While Ellis Island stood as an architectural monument in New York Harbor and was visible from all surrounding shores, Angel Island's buildings were on its northeastern coast, visually

Figure 5.7. Women and children are detained in caged waiting areas at Angel Island Immigration Station, c. 1910–1919. An American charity worker (*right*) looks at the camera. Courtesy of the National Library of Medicine, Images from the History of Medicine, 101547036

tucked behind the island's natural hills, facing away from the city of San Francisco to the south. The station's imposing nature lay not in its grand architecture but rather in its secluded location and spare buildings.

Stepping onto the raised porch and passing through the colonnade, guards led the new arrivals into the main examination room, which constituted the majority of the ground floor. Three entrances marked the building: the large central staircase was used by those proceeding into the building for inspection; the left entrance led to the inspectors' rooms, dining rooms, detention quarters, and the stenographers' pool; the right entrance to the commissioner's office. Individuals were segregated by race and gender in the waiting areas. The largest room, on the first floor, was filled with rows of wooden benches (figure 5.6). Here, immigrants were segregated according to race, with the room's largest section reserved for the Chinese, who comprised the majority of travelers. Men and women, including husbands and wives, were also separated at this point and not allowed to communicate with each other until they were either admitted to the country or deported; children under the age of twelve remained with their mothers. After preliminary inspection of papers and receiving their identification numbers, the immigrants ascended a half flight of stairs to the registry division room, where four large, caged areas with benches lined the room's sides and the processing desk; in them, individuals were again grouped according to race and gender. These caged areas were frightening; a twenty-three-year-old Chinese detainee, Mrs. Woo, later recalled that the Angel Island inspectors "locked us up like criminals in compartments like cages at a zoo" (figure 5.7).[50]

Once the inspections were completed, guards led detainees to their dormitories. European quarters were located on the administration building's second floor, while the Asian dormitory was in a separate building on the hillside above the administration building. The two-story, wood-framed dormitory was even more subdued in its exterior design than the administration building. It was a boxy structure with balanced facades and a shingled hipped roof. The exterior was painted in a three-color scheme: gray at the base, yellow at the first floor, and white at the second floor and trim. Barbed-wire fencing surrounded the building's rear and sides and extended around the immigrant station's entire perimeter.

The dormitory, or detention barracks, housed the Chinese and Japanese separately (figure 5.8). The first floor was reserved for the Japanese, with men in the east wing and women and children in the west. Chinese detainees were on the second floor, with the same division of men and women. Each floor contained washrooms, lavatories, sitting and recreation areas, and storage closets. This was the intended plan for the building; however, during the facility's history, the structure often served as an all-male dormitory since men were much more numerous than women.[51] Chinese men occupied rooms on the first and second floors and Japanese, Korean, and South Asian men were in a room on the second floor. Russian men were also housed there during periods of high immigration. The women, who had been moved from the detention barracks, stayed in the administration building's second-floor rooms after its 1911 renovation, although racial segregation was reinforced there as well. All dormitory windows were secured with thick wire screens to prevent escape.

Detainees spent the majority of their time in the cramped barracks, which were demoralizing and unsanitary, given the facility's limited janitorial services.[52] The men's and women's rooms each contained four rows of bunk beds, three high and two across. These metal bunks folded up to allow more space in the aisles when unoccupied. Contemporary images

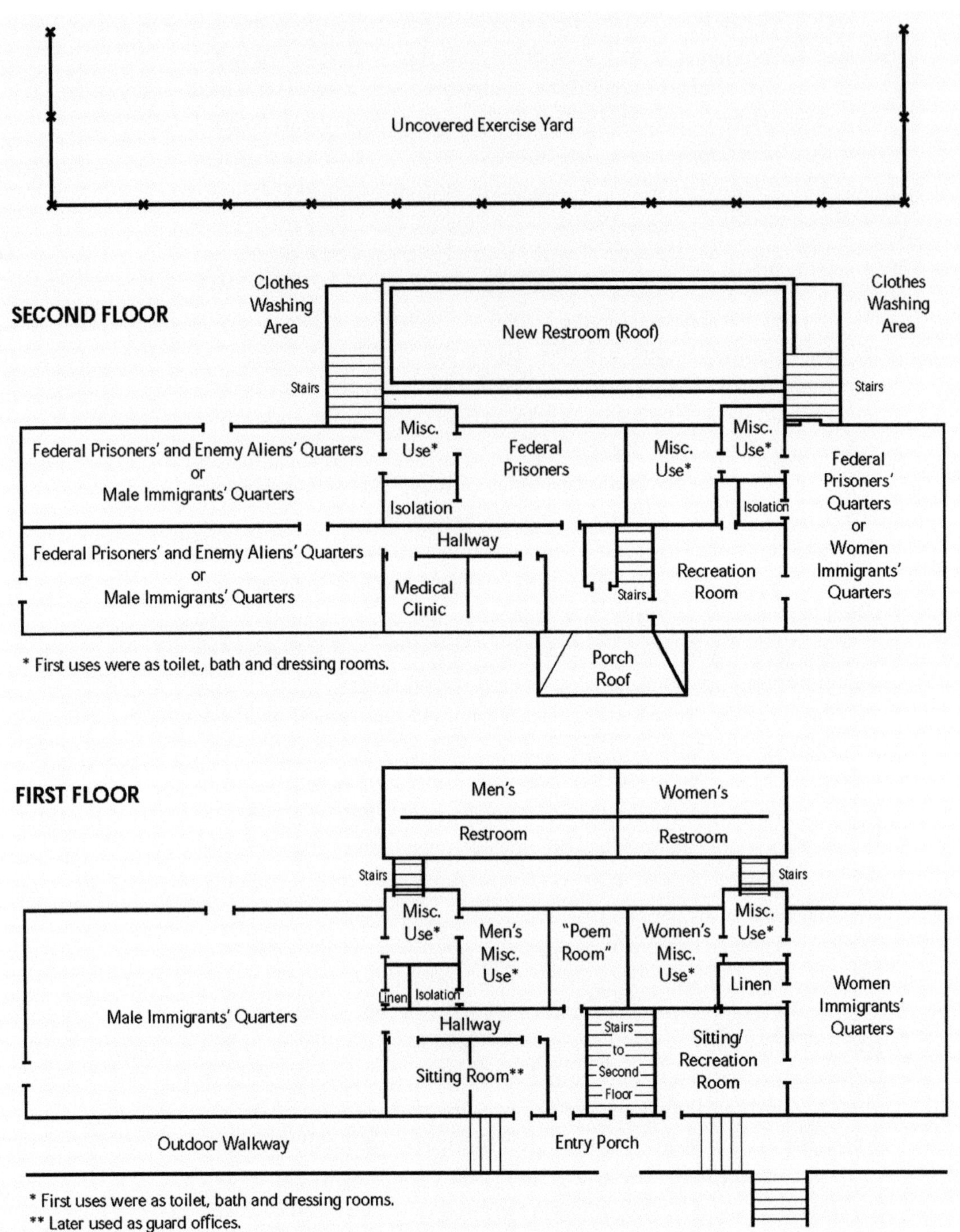

Figure 5.8. Floor plan of the Asian detention barracks at Angel Island. This plan also shows how the immigrant quarters were used to house federal prisoners and enemy aliens during the first and second World Wars. Courtesy Americans All

from the barracks show that any free space in the dormitories was covered with the detainee's belongings, with clothes hanging from bunks and ceilings. In the women's dormitory, this arrangement provided room for between seventy and one hundred detainees; the larger men's dormitory fit between two hundred and three hundred. The large, open rooms allowed for minimal privacy and optimal surveillance. Yet the architecture did not serve as the only means of control—guards stationed themselves at the door of each dormitory to enforce gender separation and to ensure no one escaped.

Race defined the treatment and accommodations received by the detainees. Not only were European immigrants passed through inspection at a faster rate than their Asian counterparts, but they also received preferential living quarters. Assistant surgeon M. W. Glover of the Public Health and Marine Hospital Service observed that the Europeans' quarters were "in better condition than any other."[53] Before the immigration station opened in 1910, the local press was already praising the European immigrants' quarters, which they claimed were "excellent accommodations" that had "most of the conveniences of a first-class hotel."[54] The "Oriental quarters" were described as "the perfect scheme of sanitation" and references to the modern hospital facility addressed the supposed dangers to public health posed by the Asian population.[55]

Race also played a factor in the barracks' furnishing. In 1908, as construction of Angel Island was underway, the Bureau of Immigration requested a proposal from the Standard Wire Mattress Company of Boston for their Patented Folding Bunk Bed #118, a similar model to the bunks that furnished the federal immigration station in Boston (figure 5.9). E. S. Fuller of Standard Wire submitted the proposal and suggested "that a thin, compact, extra-close tufted mattress [. . .] be used, filled with cotton of a good staple and color. As these mattresses are likely to receive hard usage and become soiled in a short time we have submitted for your consideration a bid for furnishing loose covers made of Khaki Drill. [. . .] These covers could be easily removed and washed."[56] Standard Wire expected to furnish each bed they provided; however, Commissioner North advised the Immigration Bureau to order only half of the mattresses and khaki covers for the Asian quarters.[57] He sent a detailed list of how many beds to furnish: all 120 beds in the European men's dormitory; all 54 beds in the European women's dormitory; and in the Asian men's and women's dormitories, North eliminated more than 300 mattresses from the nearly 700 beds in those quarters.

Commissioner North based his decision on his own knowledge of Chinese and Japanese culture. Explaining his position, he argued that

Figure 5.9. Standard Wire Mattress Company patented this bunk bed design in 1904. The bunks are shown open (*left*) and closed (*right*). Courtesy National Archives

this practice would be both culturally sensitive and save the government money: "It is customary for Chinese and Japanese both in their own country and here to sleep on wooden beds without mattresses, and I therefore think that when provided with blankets and a wire spring bed they will, not only require, but probably would not wish mattresses of any kind, and I certainly am of the opinion that if 350 mattresses are furnished with the appropriate covers, they will be all that is necessary, and these changes would reduce the cost of furnishing a very considerable amount."[58] North believed that since the detainees traditionally slept on wooden beds, bare wire mattresses would be similar and thus preferred by the Chinese and Japanese. Yet this decision was made by North himself, with no input from the Asian community. In fact, when Commissioner-General Frank H. Larned contacted Standard Wire to order mattresses for only half the beds, he provided the explanation "that Chinese immigrants are not accustomed to the use of mattresses, and prefer to use blankets on woven wire springs."[59] The Immigration Bureau gave the impression this decision was made in conference with Chinese and Japanese representatives; however, it was the white American government officials who ultimately decided, claiming to act in the detainees' best interests while in reality catering to their own budgetary concerns.

The racial segregation that defined the administration building and the barracks continued at the hospital, where individuals were brought for medical inspection. The structure, like the administration building, was a two-story, wood-framed building in a restrained classical style and featured a raised porch with colonnade. It consisted of four wings symmetrically laid out and connected by a large central wing, with a fifth wing projecting perpendicular from the central wing. The administrative rooms and communal spaces, surgery facility, mortuary, kitchen and dining rooms, employee quarters, and a disinfector room were located on the first floor. This disinfector room, which was added at the request of Dr. Glover during the first operating year at the station, was intended for fumigation of the patients' clothes and any additional items that required further disinfection (figure 5.10).[60] (Initial fumigation of luggage occurred at the quarantine station at Ayala Cove upon their arrival to Angel Island.) Patient wards were on the second floor, with each wing corresponding to the segregated wards. The Chinese and Japanese men's wards were at the building's south end; the shared Chinese and Japanese women's ward occupied the center; and the European men's and women's wards were located at the north end—as far as possible from the Asian men. Stairwells and smaller rooms such as the nurses' rooms, the doctor's office, dressing rooms, and bathrooms separated each ward, thus preventing interaction between the white and Asian patients.

To limit the spread of germs, the rooms contained large windows for light and ventilation, a design based on the miasma theory of contagion, the medical assumption that noxious air caused disease. This theory was discredited, of course, with the rise of germ theory in the late nineteenth century, although architectural historian Annmarie Adams has shown that it took time for hospital architecture to respond to germ theory.[61] Early-twentieth-century doctors also believed coved ceilings, seen at both Angel Island and Ellis Island, limited the number of corners in a room that could potentially harbor germs. The obsession with disease went beyond the architecture. Medical inspections at Angel Island were more thorough than the majority of those at Ellis Island. American citizens feared the spread of foreign-borne illness, to be sure, but foreign-borne *Asian* illnesses were believed to be even more loathsome.[62] Public health

Figure 5.10. Disinfecting clothing at Angel Island Immigration Station, 1931. Courtesy of the National Library of Medicine, Images from the History of Medicine, 101447225

officers first performed a line inspection, as was also the custom at Ellis Island, searching for visible symptoms of excludable diseases, such as trachoma, and any medical defects. Yet at Angel Island, the medical examinations also included inspection of the undressed body, searching for abnormalities and symptoms of disease (figure 5.11). Doctors also took blood and stool samples in order to detect parasitic diseases such as uncinariasis (hookworm), filariasis (threadworm), and clonorchiasis (liver

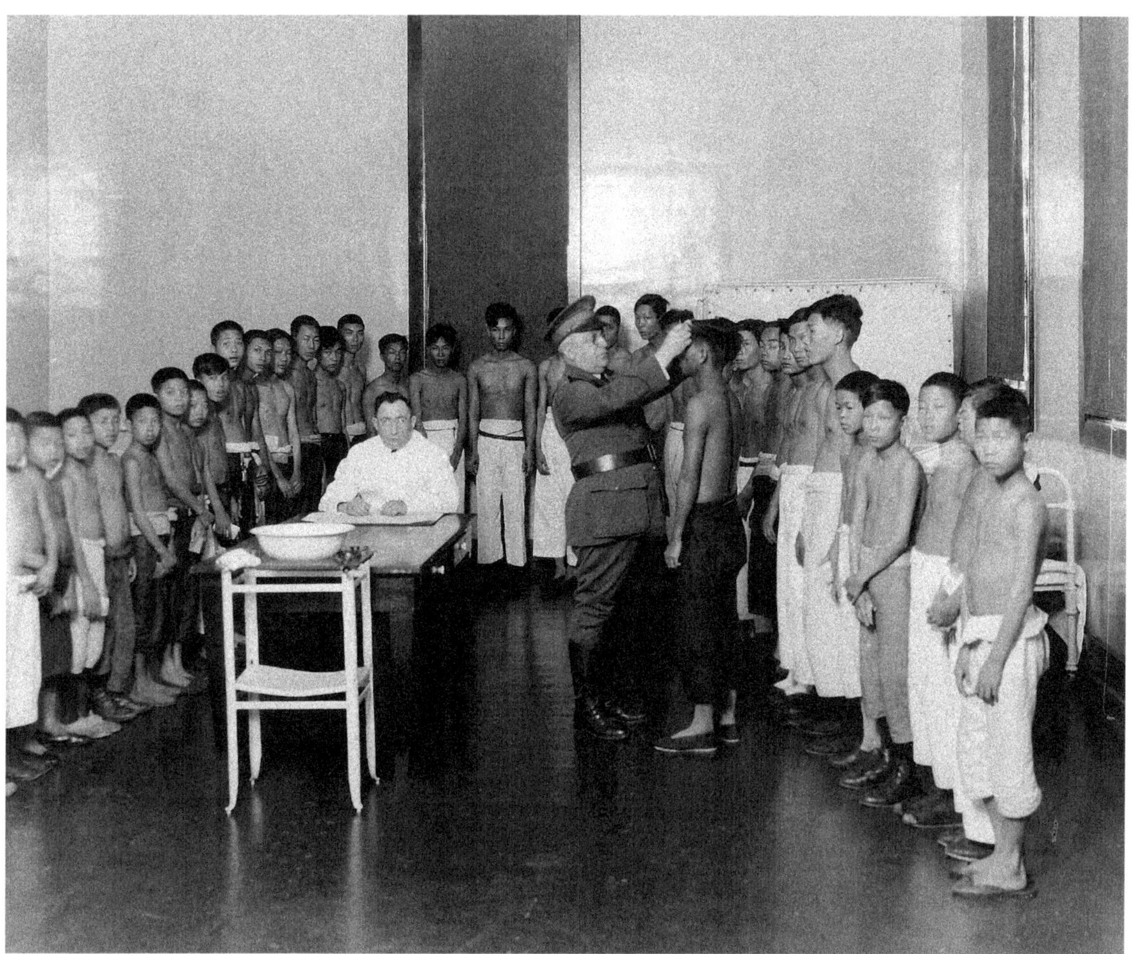

Figure 5.11. Medical inspections were more extensive for Asians than Europeans at Angel Island Immigration Station. Courtesy National Archives, photo no. 176251228

fluke). The list of excludable diseases changed over time; diseases were added as outbreaks occurred and they were omitted from the list once doctors established treatments that eradicated them.[63]

The hospital at Angel Island contained an advanced bacteriological laboratory in order to examine the blood and stool samples. The US Board of Public Health labeled these parasitic diseases as dangerously contagious. However, because these diseases primarily afflicted the Chinese, particularly those from rural China, leaders in San Francisco's Chinatown felt these regulations to be further barriers to grant entry to the United States.[64] Hookworm, for example, was a disease transmitted through exposed skin on the foot or ingestion of contaminated soil, thus making this disease more common among farm laborers working in the rice fields. Some of these parasitic diseases, such as threadworm and liver fluke, were not actually contagious in the United States and were in fact treatable, yet since they were borne by Asian people, government officials determined them excludable. In 1922, San Francisco's Chinese community sent Dr. King H. Kwan (Guan Qiangting) of China to Washington, DC, to convince the Department of Commerce and Labor that filariasis was not a dangerous contagious disease, and in 1927, the Chinese Chambers of Commerce of Honolulu and San Francisco sent Dr. Fred Lam (Lin Ronggui) of Honolulu to Washington, DC, to prove that clonorchiasis was not contagious in the United States. Both doctors were successful.[65] Due to testimonies by these and other Chinese and American doctors, public health officials eventually amended their regulations in the 1920s, allowing those afflicted with threadworm and liver fluke to remain in the United States. Even with these changes, however, immigration officials remained diligent in medically inspecting the Asian population entering through San Francisco.

Each of the buildings at Angel Island Immigration Station was intentionally designed to enforce a racially segregated system and the Bureau of Immigration wholeheartedly approved of its design. In a letter to Commissioner Sargent, architect Mathews explained his design:

> I also wish to call your attention to the Hospital Building and the principle upon which I have arranged it, which is that the Japanese and Chinese wards are *entirely separate and distinct*, with the rooms connected herewith. The entrance for the Chinese and Japanese to their quarters is *entirely separate and distinct* from the Europeans' entrance to the Hospital and their wards, *practically making it two distinct buildings*. The plan for the Chinese and Japanese Detention Quarters will explain itself, and I will call your attention to one point, that is, that after the Chinese and Japanese leave the detention room they pass under a covered way leading up to the covered bridge over road. This covered bridge extends up to their quarters, and the covered way and covered bridge over road is enclosed on the side with heavy wire screens. At the foot of the covered bridge over road is a gate separating the Chinese and Japanese in going to and from their dining room to their quarters from the Europeans' dining room, and practically makes the dining room and their quarters *one enclosed space to which they can be confined* [emphasis added].[66]

Sargent replied to Mathews that "you have submitted a most complete, comprehensive and well-arranged plan. It gives further evidence that you fully understand what is needed for the service at San Francisco. [. . .] The entire arrangement, as explained by you, meets with my hearty

Figure 5.12. The covered walkway connects the detention barracks (*above*) to the rear of the administration building (*below right*). Note the fencing at the far left of the photograph. Courtesy National Archives, photo no. 19086633

approval [. . .]."[67] Mathews's design ensured complete segregation and containment of Asian immigrants on the island, thus protecting the white population from the perceived threat of Asian immigrants. Furthermore, Mathews included certain security measures to prevent escape, such as the covered walkway enclosed with wire screens that connected the dormitory and administration building (figure 5.12). Government approval of the design, however, did not guarantee that the facility would be satisfactorily built, nor did the Immigration Bureau anticipate the influx of immigrants.

Although the immigration station was intended to be a state-of-the-art facility, its design and construction proved highly inadequate, even during its earliest years. Faulty structural design, poor maintenance, shortage of fresh water, and chronic overcrowding were some of the most pressing issues facing immigration officials.[68] The wood-framed buildings also posed a serious threat. Considering that Ellis Island's main building burned in 1897, and that the government required it to be rebuilt using fireproof materials, the choice of wood for Angel Island seems especially ill-conceived. Commissioner-general of immigration W. W. Husband declared in 1922 that the facility "has practically nothing to commend it. It is made of a conglomeration of ramshackle buildings which are nothing but firetraps. They are illy [*sic*] arranged and inconvenient. The sanitary arrangements are awful. If a private individual had such an establishment he would be arrested by the local health authorities."[69] Like the rest of the immigration station, the hospital also suffered from overcrowding, unsanitary conditions, water shortage, poor ventilation, and lack of proper toilet facilities. In its first year of operation, Dr. Glover of the Public Health and Marine Hospital Service criticized the facility, stating that "in no way does the hospital meet the requirements for this station. At best it is and always will remain a makeshift."[70] It is therefore not surprising that Mathews, the architect of the facility, was fired in 1909 over the constant problems encountered from the engineering and design of the station's buildings, piers, and auxiliary structures.

Just three years after its opening, the inadequacy of Angel Island prompted government officials to look elsewhere for possible locations to house a new immigration station, including Alcatraz Island. In 1913, the Bureau of Immigration submitted a memorandum to the Department of Labor that suggested the immigration station be transferred to the military prison on Alcatraz Island, which had recently been renovated.[71] The island had been used for incarceration since the mid-nineteenth century. In 1858, the government erected the prison, which subsequently housed inmates during the Civil War and the Spanish–American War, as well as convicts from the city prison after the 1906 San Francisco earthquake. Several additions had been made to the original structure throughout the building's history, and between 1910 and 1912 the prison was entirely rebuilt in stone, brick, and concrete. By 1915, the Bureau of Immigration was seriously considering this transfer to the Alcatraz prison, for several reasons: the buildings were fireproof; the island was significantly closer to the mainland, allowing for reduced travel time on the ferries; and the prison was secure enough to prevent escape, a concern officials had in mind when selecting the site of Angel Island in the first place.

The choice of an existing penitentiary as the potential site for a new immigration station is significant. The design of Angel Island Immigration Station enforced Asian incarceration from its inception. The proposal to transfer the immigration station to Alcatraz would only serve to reinforce the practices that prompted the Chinese detainees to refer to Angel

Island as a prison. A couple decades after the initial proposal, in 1934, the prison at Alcatraz became a maximum-security federal penitentiary under the US Department of Justice. The site that had once been considered as a potential location for the immigration station would now house high-risk inmates. Certainly there were architectural differences between the immigration station and the prison, the most important being that the prison housed inmates in small cells as opposed to the dormitory's open floor plan at Angel Island. The constant surveillance, barbed-wire fencing, and barred windows, however, paralleled the prison environment of Alcatraz. The immigration station's transfer from Angel Island to Alcatraz never occurred, since the war's progression limited government resources for such an undertaking, yet even without the official designation of a prison building, Angel Island Immigration Station largely remained a barrier for Asian immigrants trying to enter the country.

"Oppression Drives a Wise Man Mad"

Detainees suffered the effects of the facility's enforced segregation and constant surveillance. Sam Hubert Huey, detained in 1923, felt that Angel Island was "terrible, [. . .] there were people there for years, months. It was like a prison."[72] Some immigrants were forced to remain on the island while their family members passed inspection and went on to San Francisco. One detainee, Dong Kingman, later recalled in his autobiography the distress of being left behind in what he felt was a prison: "Watching my family leave with other passengers on the ferry for San Francisco while I remained behind barb-wired windows was like a stab in my heart. [. . .] So unfair to treat me like an outcast or criminal."[73] The island location and the buildings effectively enforced the Chinese Exclusion Act. The Immigration Bureau intended its West Coast immigration facility to be a detention center, whereas Ellis Island was purposefully built to process as many new arrivals as quickly and efficiently as possible. The government's regulation of movement and the architecture itself reveals the opposing immigration policies on the East and West Coasts.

Life at Angel Island was difficult, not only because of exhaustive interrogation sessions and poor living conditions but also because of the detainees' lack of freedom. Detainees were allowed to leave their quarters only once or twice a week for one half hour, to exercise and breathe fresh air in small fenced outdoor recreation areas adjacent to the barracks (see figure 5.8).[74] Women and children, who numbered far less than Chinese males, were given somewhat more freedom and were allowed to walk the grounds in a supervised group. But for the majority of the day, with the

Figure 5.13. Interior, washroom and lavatory, Angel Island Immigration Station, 1910. Note that the stalls at right do not have doors. Courtesy National Archives, photo no. 19086632

exception of mealtimes, detainees were locked inside the barracks under the supervision of an armed guard. Languishing in the barracks, detainees found various ways to occupy their time: some found entertainment in gambling (though the stakes were typically low given their limited funds); some women sewed or knitted; the literate read the Chinese newspapers sent from San Francisco; and by the late 1920s or early 1930s the detainees had raised enough money to purchase a phonograph and Chinese opera records.[75]

Yet even with these distractions, the constant surveillance remained oppressive. Mr. Leung, a twenty-four-year-old detainee, recalled that "the windows had barbed wire. They opened the door. They watched you go into the mess hall. They locked the mess door and they watched you. No way you could get away. We played volleyball, but the courtyard was fenced all around so you couldn't run away."[76] Armed guards escorted detainees throughout the compound and were stationed at each dormitory room. There was minimal privacy, not only in the dormitories and communal rooms but also in the bathrooms, where there were no doors on bathroom and shower stalls, at least in the first decades of operation (figure 5.13). During her stay in 1940, one woman recalled that "there were two bathrooms and three or four stalls inside of each. The toilet doors were cut off at the bottom so they could see your feet. Maybe it was because they were afraid of people committing suicide."[77] Sixteen-year-old Mr. Lowe recalled, "The worst part was the toilet. It was a ditch congested with filth. It stank up the whole barracks. We slept on three tiers of canvas bunks. The blankets were so coarse that it might have been woven of wolf's hair. It was indeed a most humiliating imprisonment."[78] To the Asian detainees, this loss of privacy was altogether dehumanizing. The invasive medical examinations were also a major source of degradation. One Chinese detainee in 1930 recalled, "The doctor told us to take off everything. Really though, it was humiliating. The Chinese never expose themselves like that. They checked you and checked you. We never got used to that kind of thing—and in front of whites."[79] The Chinese, by and large, endured these oppressive practices much more than any other group detained at the immigration station.

The buildings at Angel Island stressed imprisonment with their locked doors, caged waiting areas, barbed-wire fences, and enclosed stairways. Repetitive interrogations, invasive medical examinations, and constant surveillance further enforced the confinement inherent in the architecture at Angel Island. Ellis Island, on the other hand, had been designed, architecturally and administratively, to process immigrants as quickly as possible through its massive main building. This circulation of bodies in space continued as the immigrants took ferries from the island to the railroad stations and got onto the trains—bodies in continuous migration. The majority of European immigrants entering through Ellis Island were released within a matter of hours; in contrast, the average length of detainment for a Chinese immigrant was two to three weeks.[80] Furthermore, the 18 percent deportation rate at Angel Island was significantly higher than that occurring at Ellis Island, which totaled only 1 percent.[81] The migration of Europeans into the United States largely flowed west—from Europe, to ports of entry, to settlements—motion that is expressed in the architectural plans of Ellis Island, which the government designed to expedite processing and registration. During the exclusion era, Asian migration into the United States was halted at worst, or limited at best, and the Angel Island Immigration Station externalized the racist policy and attitudes of the time.

"No Country Is Bound to Submit to Immigration Any More Than to Invasion"

In many ways, officials at Angel Island did everything in their power to find evidence to deny Asians entry to the United States. Commissioner North estimated that "nearly ninety percent" of Chinese people who gained entry into the country did so fraudulently, a highly speculative estimate that indicated the government's inherent distrust of the Chinese population.[82] However, the barring of Chinese laborers, as part of the Chinese Exclusion Act, had in fact given rise to the "paper son" system, where many immigrants falsely claimed status in one of the classes exempt from the exclusion laws—Chinese merchants and native-born American citizens.[83] The practice of selling illegal documentation became even more prevalent after 1906, when the San Francisco earthquake and fire destroyed the city's birth records. Mr. Chan, a former detainee of Angel Island, explained that "we didn't want to come in illegally, but we were forced to because of the immigration laws. They particularly picked on the Chinese. If we told the truth, it didn't work. So we had to take the crooked path."[84] Whereas officials at Ellis Island sought to verify a foreigner's right to entry through a series of questions lasting approximately two minutes—questions such as name, place of birth, occupation, monetary means, and criminal status—interrogations at Angel Island were far more probing and exhaustive. Inspectors conducted questioning over several days and weeks with the assistance of interpreters, comparing answers from previous transcripts in order to catch any discrepancies that would indicate false identities. Since a stenographer transcribed every single interrogation session (which totaled several hours per individual), Samuel Backus, Hart's replacement as commissioner at Angel Island, stated in 1911 that "the proper disposition of one Chinese case may require stenographic work equal to that required in the handling of several hundred aliens of other races."[85] The sheer amount of paperwork involved in the processing of one immigrant was astounding. Commissioner-General Sargent defended his employees' practices, arguing that any cruel treatment in their enforcement of the Chinese exclusion laws was not because of "the injustice or inhumanity of the officers, but of the failure of the Chinese themselves to comply with the provisions of the law."[86] Detainees were only able to visit the storehouse to collect personal belongings once a week, and authorities routinely inspected letters and gift packages for possible coaching messages that would assist the detainee in passing interrogations.[87]

The interrogation procedures and the architecture at Angel Island were meant to intimidate, and to control, those detained there; however,

Figure 5.14. Poetic verse carved into the walls of the detention barracks express the immigrants' feelings about their unjust detainment at Angel Island. Photograph by Carol M. Highsmith, 2013. Courtesy of The Jon B. Lovelace Collection of California Photographs in Carol M. Highsmith's America Project, Prints & Photographs Division, Library of Congress, LC-DIG-highsm-25218

those individuals found a way to resist the architecture that contained them. Locked in their barracks, unsure of the fate that awaited them, detainees expressed their feelings of disillusion, resentment, and bitterness about their treatment at Angel Island by inscribing poems on the barracks' walls (figure 5.14).[88] Many poems were written in pencil and ink, while others were carved into the walls made of Douglas fir, a softwood suitable for carving. The majority were undated and unsigned, although a large number were written before 1930, a fact known because two detainees, Smiley Jann and Tet Yee (detained in 1931 and 1932, respectively), copied most of these poems.[89] Nearly half of the poems express the authors' resentment of their confinement, while others dreamed of the home and families they had left behind.[90] One detainee, who only identified himself as an old man from Taishan, carved:

> Imprisoned in this wooden building, I am always sad and bored.
> I remember since I left my native village, it has been several full moons. [. . .]
> Prisoners in this wooden building constantly suffer sadness and boredom.
> I remember the hardships I had to endure when I was coming here.
> I cannot prophesy which day I will cross the barrier.
> The years and months are easily spent in vain.[91]

An immigrant's state of flux during migration was compounded at Angel Island, where the outcome and length of detainment were indeterminate. While this particular detainee had endured many hardships to finally arrive on American shores, he remained an outsider, unsure of when, or if, he would be able to enter.

Like the previous poem, several others referenced the wooden building in which they were imprisoned. One anonymous poem illustrates both the physical and emotional effects of detainment:

> I, a seven foot man, am ashamed I cannot extend myself.
> Curled up in an enclosure, my movements are dictated by others.
> Enduring a hundred humiliations, I can only cry in vain.
> This person's tears fall, but what can the blue heavens do?[92]

For the immigrants at Angel Island, the emotional anguish experienced during their imprisonment was inextricably linked to their physical confinement. Kept from family members and effectually locked behind bars, the detainees found emotional release by imprinting their feelings on the very building that confined them. Although the poems were written by people of varying education (some are written by those familiar with classical poetry, while others employ incorrect characters and usages), the raw emotion that compelled them to be written in the first place remained constant. To modern readers, the poems' poignant nature is all too evident, yet immigration officials viewed these inscriptions as graffiti. Angel Island employees covered up the poems by plastering over the carvings and painting over the written lines, methods that ironically served the purpose of preserving them.

Prisoners of war and non-Chinese immigrants also inscribed their frustration onto the walls of Angel Island's barracks. Historians have focused on the Chinese poems, however, not only because they are more visible and numerous but also because they contained a sustained poetic form not present in the inscriptions written in other languages.[93] World War I had brought greater numbers of white immigrants to the United States; a large percentage of them were Russian, as well as European relatives of American residents arriving on the West Coast by means of Siberia, Manchuria, and Japan.[94] In the 1930s, immigration officials also detained and interrogated those whom the American government considered alien enemies—namely, citizens of Germany and the Austro-Hungarian Empire—as well as resident immigrants under arrest for purported radical political activity.[95] These federal prisoners shared the facilities with the detained immigrants. During this time, immigration officials added a guard tower near the recreation yard for increased surveillance. Like the Chinese, the detainees described as alien enemies also complained about the immigration station's conditions. In a letter to San Francisco's district director of immigration, German prisoners of war detained at Angel Island complained of the unsanitary conditions there, particularly the inadequate toilet and bathing facilities, unclean kitchen and dining areas, poor ventilation in overcrowded rooms, and lack of drinking water.[96]

In addition to the sanitary concerns, throughout the station's history immigration officials noted the lack of fireproofing in the wooden buildings, concerns that were finally realized on the evening of August 12, 1940, when a fire, caused by an overloaded circuit in the basement, burned down the administration building and the covered staircase behind it that led to the detention barracks.[97] Reports in both 1915 and 1923 had indicated that the administration and detention buildings lacked "any fire protection at all," and furthermore, if fire broke out at the hospital building, "there would be a serious loss of life."[98] Even still, the Angel Island facility had a much smaller construction budget than the fireproof facility at Ellis Island, and some immigration officials felt that the Angel Island facility, though certainly lacking, was suitable for the Asian population it served. Special Immigrant Inspector A. Warner Parker opined in 1915 that the hospital was "fairly well adapted to the *present* needs of the Station [emphasis added]," referencing the Asian detainees that occupied it; however, should European immigration increase, Parker stated that improved facilities would be necessary.[99] Even during the fire's extreme circumstances, guards maintained the segregation that defined the buildings of Angel Island as they evacuated the detainees: women stayed at the hospital; Chinese men in the army stables; European men in the guardhouse; and the German sailors who had been at Angel Island waiting to return home via the Pacific were held at the quarantine station.[100]

Given all the complaints and structural problems posed by the facility since its construction, the government shuttered the station and turned the location over to the US Army on February 4, 1941. The army renamed the facility North Garrison and used it to process and house American troops during World War II. They also held Japanese and German prisoners of war and enemy aliens in the former immigration station's barracks. The US Military changed little, if anything, in the existing detention barracks—they were already suited to house prisoners. Unlike the thousands of Chinese detainees who remained there for long periods of time, however, the facility served as a temporary holding place for prisoners of war before they were transferred to various places throughout the American West.

The war's arrival also brought about the long-overdue repeal of the Chinese Exclusion Act. The Magnuson Act, or the Chinese Exclusion Repeal Act as it is also known, was passed on December 17, 1943, in the same year the United States and China became allies in World War II.[101] Even with the act's repeal, however, the Chinese were only allowed to enter the country at a rate of just 105 people per year, a quota that had been set by the Immigration Act of 1924. This law set quotas based on national origin, numbers that were derived from the percentages of the current population already in the United States, which meant that the residents whom immigration officials considered undesirable faced highly restrictive quotas. Additionally, the act allowed for some Chinese already in the country to become naturalized citizens, yet property ownership rights remained banned until the Magnuson Act itself was fully repealed in 1965. Prior to the act's repeal, the Chinese remained outsiders in a country that had closed its doors to them. After struggling to enter the country, they experienced further hurdles as they applied for naturalization. The discrimination experienced by the Chinese thus continued in the United States for over a century, from their arrival in the 1840s until the full repeal of the Chinese exclusion in 1965.

"Everyone Was Waiting, Breathless, for the Sun"

As Stevenson's train entered California, the excitement among the passengers was palpable. "Not I only, but all the passengers on board, threw off their sense of dirt and heat and weariness, and bawled like schoolboys, and thronged with shining eyes upon the platform and became new creatures within and without."[102] By afternoon they reached Sacramento, and on the following morning, Saturday, August 30, 1879, Stevenson first saw San Francisco Bay. The three-thousand-mile train journey had taken eleven and a half days, and now he could leave behind the immigrant train and purchase a ticket to continue on the Southern Pacific to Salinas, and then another train ride on the Monterey & Salinas Valley Railroad to Monterey, where his future wife, Fanny Osbourne (née Van de Grift), was distancing herself from her estranged husband, who was living in

Oakland at the time. For Stevenson, the six-thousand-mile journey from Scotland led him to a new life, one full of promise. Fanny filed for divorce in mid-October 1879, and she and Stevenson married the following year. The journey was but a brief adventure among many others he would have in his life. San Francisco was a starting point for him, a new beginning. He disembarked from the immigrant train and went off into the city toward his intended destination. Even in New York, because he had a second-class steamship ticket, he was able to bypass the inspections at Castle Garden and proceed unimpeded into the city.

For the Chinese immigrants arriving in San Francisco, however, their travels were suspended in a sort of purgatory—the space in-between—where their fate was unknown and their movement into the country halted by racist laws and practices. Angel Island, in particular, emphasized the fact that spaces of immigration within the United States were not experienced by all travelers in the same way. Largely dependent on race and class, these tangible spaces were symbolic of the immigrant's status in American society at the time. Immigration stations, whether federally or privately owned, theoretically shared the same purpose—determining an immigrant's eligibility to enter the country. In practice, however, the facilities reveal vastly different agendas. On the East Coast, European immigrants became part of a network; the railroad and steamship companies worked together to encourage emigration from Europe and once the foreigners arrived in America, they traveled inland by train to vast tracts of land sold to them by government and railroad land agents. In Baltimore, the Baltimore & Ohio Railroad Company worked with the North German Lloyd Steamship Company to direct immigrant traffic to its port, and in New York, the railways and the government worked together at the Ellis Island immigration station. On the West Coast, however, immigration officials succeeded in building a physical barrier to the country in addition to the intangible barrier of lengthy detainments, exhaustive interrogations, and exclusionary legislation. In this way, Angel Island Immigration Station did indeed fulfill its intended role as guardian of the Western Gate, literally keeping Asian immigrants out of the mainland, a gulf between them and American citizenship.

EPILOGUE

The Journey Today

Stevenson's personal account is an important glimpse into the arduous journey undertaken by millions of people throughout the nineteenth and early twentieth centuries, with his travel memoir providing crucial insight into the physical spaces through which immigrants traveled. These physical spaces reveal aspects of a migrant's psychological journey as well, wherein foreign passengers are segregated in accordance with racist and discriminatory practices and legislation on the part of the United States government and private industry. While historians have frequently heralded the United States as a "nation of immigrants," this phrase is entirely problematic, not taking into account settler colonialism, slavery, and the deliberate attempts (both historically and today) to limit or cease immigration from certain nations. As scholars undertake the important work of critiquing and challenging the historiographies and methodologies that have reified systemic oppression and biased hierarchies, the built environment must be reexamined from a new perspective, one that takes into account the *experiences* of physical spaces, not just the design of them.[1] In the context of immigration, how did these physical spaces embody the cultural and political influences of the time? This book demonstrates that the space in-between is not exclusive to physical distance or place but is a cultural exchange, one in which society's complexities, particularly the biases of a white population, are revealed and indeed reinforced. The built environment of the country's immigrant transportation network can thus be read as a physical manifestation of the foreigner's role in American politics, capitalism, and culture.

This is true even today, when considering the historiography of immigration in the United States. While Ellis Island's immigration station was written into the country's historical narrative early on in the station's history, perpetuating the myth of the United States as open for all, Angel Island exemplified the exclusionary nature of American immigration policy. The juxtaposition of Ellis Island and Angel Island, and the subsequent attention (or lack of attention) paid to each of these facilities in American historiography, indicates a conscious shaping of the historical narrative. Although Americans may have once tried to forget or deny this part of the nation's history, those detained at the immigration station could never forget. Carved into the barracks' walls by a poet identifying himself only as "one from Xiangshan," the author powerfully declares this sentiment:

> There are tens of thousands of poems composed on these walls.
> They are all cries of complaint and sadness.
> The day I am rid of this prison and attain success,
> I must remember that this chapter once existed.[2]

This individual is but one of many who endured hardships while attempting to enter the United States, and the immigration station stands as a physical reminder of this unfair treatment based on race and class. This is not to say that Europeans entering the country were spared the stresses of immigration procedures. On the contrary, they were just as frightened by the threat of deportation, the inspection procedures, and medical examinations. Yet when we examine the built environment and how immigrants were allowed—or not allowed—to move through space, the disparities become evident.

While this book is by no means a comprehensive study of migration to and within the United States, its methodologies and various source materials are founded on an interdisciplinary model that employs various historical sources—oral, literary, and archival, as well as the absences and silences in the historical record—to understand the role of everyday spatial practices in the formation of cultural and political spheres. How can these methods be applied to other spaces of immigration in the United States? During the period covered in this book, the late nineteenth and early twentieth centuries, the land borders of Mexico and Canada were relatively unrestricted until the establishment of the US Border Patrol in 1924. Not only were there new "official" spaces of immigration established along these borders (in the form of government entry points) but the borderlands themselves, particularly along the US–Mexico border where immigration became increasingly restrictive into the twenty-first century, developed into a distinct cultural landscape. In terms of the built environment, this region now comprises walls and fences, guard towers and gates, tents and other enclosures, and Border Patrol regional facility offices, which are mainly low-budget structures and mobile trailers—a network of spaces that have effectively transformed the border into a militarized zone in which those who attempt to enter the country do so by dangerous, and sometimes deadly, pathways.[3] According to the Global Detention Project, a human rights nonprofit organization based in Geneva, Switzerland, the United States currently operates the world's largest immigrant detention system, holding approximately thirty thousand people daily in its two hundred facilities, which include privately operated detention facilities and family centers, local jails, juvenile detention centers, and field offices.[4] Like at Angel Island Immigration Station, the architectural design of contemporary detention facilities reinforces xenophobic views of migrants as criminals and has profound psychological effects on those detained within.[5] The US Immigration and Customs Enforcement noted that the majority of its facilities were "largely designed for penal, not civil, detention," in which migrants are housed in single or double cells or dormitories in which detainees spend the majority of their time.[6]

Anti-immigrant rhetoric has persisted throughout the history of the country, despite the celebrated belief of the United States as a nation of immigrants. It can be difficult to reconcile the two versions of the same country. As Erika Lee notes, while the United States "has welcomed millions from around the world, it has also deported more immigrants than any other nation—over fifty-five million since 1882."[7] The built environment, as a manifestation of cultural and societal values, serves as a lens through which to view this aspect of American culture. The way stations along an immigrant's path—ports, government and railroad stations, and trains—were intentionally designed by public and private entities in response to the racism and xenophobia prevalent in the American cultural fabric. However, because *white* immigrants were customers and potential citizens, both private and public forces strove to maintain a balance between profit and ideology, inviting some white ethnic groups while excluding others. Immigrant travelers were propelled westward by rail cheaply and efficiently, and settled into the American heartland at alarming speeds, all the while carefully contained and segregated from American citizens. In this way, private enterprise and national policy were intimately connected, in effect determining who was considered "American" and who was not, based on a variety of factors such as class, proximity to the frontier, and notions of whiteness. Here, the space in-between played a major role in exemplifying national attitudes as physically manifested through separate quarters, waiting rooms, and train cars. Simultaneously, an immigrant's journey through these spaces was largely predetermined by social class and skin color, and on a larger scale foreshadowed their path to citizenship and assimilation.

Sadly, many of the prejudices and phobias Stevenson observed over one hundred years ago remain largely unchanged, and are issues the United States continues to grapple with as it reconciles with race and citizenship, what ultimately defines an "American," and the country's relationship to its borders and immigrants. We are living in an era of unprecedented global migration, and as such, the intersection of transportation, capitalism, politics, and race is especially relevant today. These spaces of immigration allow us to understand the built environment's role in the construction of modern, capitalist American culture. The space in-between—between borders and between cultures, historically and today—impacts and is, in turn, shaped by these broader cultural processes.

NOTES

Introduction: The Journey Begins

1. Robert Louis Stevenson, *The Amateur Emigrant* (1896; reis., New York: Carroll and Graf, 2002), 113–17. All subsequent citations are from this copy.

2. Originally, Stevenson's journey was written in various parts: *The Amateur Emigrant from the Clyde to Sandy Hook* (ready for publication in 1880 but withdrawn); *Across the Plains* (1892); and *The Silverado Squatters* (1883). The 1895 publication was the first to pair Stevenson's account of his sea and rail travels into one book.

3. On cultural landscape, see Barbara Bender, ed., *Landscape: Politics and Perspectives* (Providence, RI: Berg, 1993); Michael P. Conzen, ed., *The Making of the American Landscape* (Boston: Unwin Hyman, 1990); Paul Groth and Todd W. Bressi, eds., *Understanding Ordinary Landscapes* (New Haven, CT: Yale University Press, 1997); Paul Groth and Chris Wilson, eds., *Everyday America: Cultural Landscape Studies after J. B. Jackson* (Berkeley: University of California Press, 2003).

4. Paul Groth and Chris Wilson, "The Polyphony of Cultural Landscape Study: An Introduction," in *Everyday America*, 1–2.

5. See Paul Groth, *Living Downtown: A History of Residential Hotels in the United States* (Berkeley: University of California Press, 1999); Jessica Ellen Sewell, *Women and the Everyday City: Public Space in San Francisco, 1890–1915* (Minneapolis: University of Minnesota Press, 2011); and John Michael Vlach, *Back of the Big House: The Architecture of Plantation Slavery* (Chapel Hill: University of North Carolina Press, 1993).

6. Robert Louis Stevenson to Thomas and Margaret Stevenson, April 1, 1881, in *The Letters of Robert Louis Stevenson*, edited by Bradford A. Booth and Ernest Mehew (New Haven, CT: Yale University Press, 1994), 3:167.

7. On the waves of migration throughout American history, see Roger Daniels, *Coming to America: A History of Immigration and Ethnicity in American Life*, 2nd ed. (New York: Harper Collins, 2002).

8. Charles L. Davis II, "Henry Van Brunt and White Settler Colonialism in the Midwest," in *Race and Modern Architecture: A Critical History from the Enlightenment to the Present*, edited by Irene Chang, Charles L. Davis II, and Mabel O. Wilson (Pittsburgh, PA: University of Pittsburgh Press, 2020), 100.

9. See Paul Spickard, Francisco Beltrán, and Laura Hooton, *Almost All Aliens: Immigration, Race and Colonialism in American History and Identity*, 2nd ed. (New York: Routledge, 2022).

10. Israel Zangwill, *The Melting-Pot* (New York: Macmillan, 1921).

11. Timothy Greenfield-Sanders, dir., *Toni Morrison: The Pieces I Am* (New York: Magnolia Pictures, 2019), DVD.

12. See Grace Elizabeth Hale, *Making Whiteness: The Culture of Segregation in the South, 1890–1940* (New York: Vintage Books, 1999); Matthew Frye Jacobson, *Whiteness of a Different Color: European Immigrants and the Alchemy of Race* (Cambridge, MA: Harvard University Press, 1998); and David R. Roediger, *The Wages of Whiteness: Race and the Making of the American Working Class*, 4th ed. (New York: Verso, 2022) and *Working Toward Whiteness: How America's Immigrants Became White*, updated ed. (New York: Basic Books, 2018). For a study on how race and ethnicity shape American places and landscapes, see John W. Frazier, Eugene L. Tettey-Fio, and Norah F. Henry, eds., *Race, Ethnicity, and Place in a Changing America*, 3rd ed. (Binghamton: State University of New York Press, 2016).

13. Alan Kraut, *Silent Travelers: Germs, Genes, and the Immigrant Menace* (Baltimore: Johns Hopkins University Press, 1995); Amy Fairchild, *Science at the Borders: Immigrant Medical Inspection and the Shaping of the Modern Industrial Labor Force* (Baltimore: Johns Hopkins University Press, 2003).

14. Amy Richter, *Home on the Rails: Women, the Railroad, and the Rise of Public Domesticity* (Chapel Hill: University of North Carolina Press, 2005), 5.

15. See Catherine Boland Erkkila, "American Railways and the Cultural Landscape of Immigration," *Buildings and Landscapes: Journal of the Vernacular Architecture Forum* 22, no. 1 (Spring 2015): 36–62.

16. Wolfgang Schivelbusch, "Railroad Space and Railroad Time," *New German Critique* 14 (Spring 1978): 34–35.

17. In addition to Schivelbusch's work, see also Daniel Walker Howe, ed., *Victorian America* (Philadelphia: University of Pennsylvania Press, 1976), and Richter, *Home on the Rails*.

18. Alan Trachtenberg, foreword to *The Railway Journey: The Industrialization of Time and Space in the Nineteenth Century* by Wolfgang Schivelbusch (Berkeley: University of California Press, 1986), xv.

19. Hale, *Making Whiteness*, xi.

20. Historian Mia Bay examines how Black mobility and travel segregation have always been a focal point of struggles over equality and difference. See Mia Bay, *Traveling Black: A Story of Race and Resistance* (Cambridge, MA: Belknap Press of Harvard University Press, 2021).

21. Jacobson, *Whiteness of a Different Color*, 13–136. For further discussion of the influence of race on American immigration policy during the Progressive Era, see Jeanne D. Petit, *The Men and Women We Want: Gender, Race, and the Progressive Era Literacy Test* (Rochester, NY: University of Rochester Press, 2010), 31–58.

22. Richter, *Home on the Rails*, 5.

23. Robert Weyeneth, "The Architecture of Racial Segregation: The Challenges of Preserving the Problematical Past," *Public Historian* 27, no. 4 (Fall 2005): 11–44.

24. Boland Erkkila, "American Railways and the Cultural Landscape of Immigration," 38.

25. Stevenson, *Amateur Emigrant*, 159.

26. For further discussions of whiteness as a social construct, see Jacobson, *Whiteness of a Different Color*, and Hale, *Making Whiteness*.

27. See Kerry Abrams, "Polygamy, Prostitution, and the Federalization of Immigration Law," *Columbia Law Review* 105, no. 3 (April 2005): 641–716. For a study of the sexualized nature of border control, see Eithne Luibhéid, *Entry Denied: Controlling Sexuality at the Border* (Minneapolis: University of Minnesota Press, 2002).

28. Erika Lee, *At America's Gates: Chinese Immigration during the Exclusion Era, 1882–1943* (Chapel Hill: University of North Carolina, 2003).

29. See Katherine Benton-Cohen, *Inventing the Immigration Problem: The Dillingham Commission and Its Legacy* (Cambridge, MA: Harvard University Press, 2018).

30. William Paul Dillingham, *A Dictionary of Races or Peoples* (Washington, DC: Government Printing Office, 1911). See Jacobson, *Whiteness of a Different Color*, 78–80, for a discussion of the influence of this document on legislation.

31. Lee, *At America's Gates*, 123–26. For more on the Bertillon system, see Henry T. F. Rhodes, *Alphonse Bertillon, Father of Scientific Detection* (New York: Greenwood Press, 1968).

32. A steerage ticket at the time was six guineas, so Stevenson paid eight guineas for his second-class ticket. In 1880, the difference in cost—two guineas—would have been the equivalent of six days' work for a skilled tradesman, according to the currency converter of the UK National Archives. In 2021, this would roughly be the equivalent of £150.

33. Stevenson, *Amateur Emigrant*, 4.

34. Stevenson, *Amateur Emigrant*, 6.

35. Stevenson, *Amateur Emigrant*, 80.

36. Ian Bell, *Dreams of Exile: Robert Louis Stevenson* (New York: Henry Holt, 2015).

37. Stevenson, *Amateur Emigrant*, 15–16.

38. Stevenson, *Amateur Emigrant*, 16.

39. Claire Harman, *Myself and the Other Fellow: A Life of Robert Louis Stevenson* (New York: Harper Collins, 2005), 204–9.

40. Stevenson, *Amateur Emigrant*, 13.

41. Stevenson, *Amateur Emigrant*, 14.

42. Stevenson, *Amateur Emigrant*, 15.

43. Prior to this, American land borders were relatively unrestricted in comparison to ports of entry. There is a significant amount of literature on the US–Mexico border, with Gloria Anzaldúa's *Borderlands/La Frontera: The New Mestiza* (1987) one of the most powerful portrayals of the borderlands, not only the physical border but also the psychological, sexual, and spiritual borderlands of those occupying the territory. For a study of the built environment of the US–Mexico border, see Katherine G. Morrissey and John-Michael H. Warner, eds., *Border Spaces: Visualizing the US–Mexico Frontera* (Tucson: University of Arizona Press, 2018). David Monteyne explores the immigration facilities operated by Canada's Dominion government in *For the Temporary Accommodation of Settlers: Architecture and Immigrant Reception in Canada, 1870–1930* (Montreal: McGill-Queen's University Press, 2021).

44. Deryck W. Holdsworth, "Geography: Buildings as Settings for Seeing Systems and Networks," *Journal of the Society of Architectural Historians* 65, no. 1 (March 2006): 18–20.

45. See William Cronon, *Nature's Metropolis: Chicago and the Great West* (New York: W. W. Norton, 1991).

46. Frederick Jackson Turner, *The Frontier in American History* (New York: Henry Holt, 1921), 3–4.

47. The most complete study to date of Angel Island Immigration Station is Erika Lee and Judy Yung, *Angel Island: Immigrant Gateway to America* (New York: Oxford University Press, 2010).

48. Letter from Stevenson to Sidney Colvin, June 4, 1880. Stevenson, *Amateur Emigrant*, x.

Chapter 1: New York

Subheadings are from Stevenson, *Amateur Emigrant*, 115, 101, 114, 116, and 89, respectively.

1. Stevenson, *Amateur Emigrant*, 95.

2. Stevenson, *Amateur Emigrant*, 97.

3. For a contemporary testimony of defrauding as practiced by boardinghouse keepers and runners, see Friedrich Kapp, *Immigration and the Commissioners of Emigration of the State of New York* (New York: Nation Press, 1870), 62–67.

4. Quoted in Kerby A. Miller, *Emigrants and Exiles: Ireland and the Irish Exodus to North America* (New York: Oxford University Press, 1985), 263.

5. See Dorothee Schneider, "Leaving Home," in *Crossing Borders: Migration and Citizenship in the Twentieth-Century United States* (Cambridge, MA: Harvard University Press, 2011), 10–60.

6. The board consisted of ten members, six of whom were appointed by the governor and four of whom were ex officio, including the mayors of New York City and Brooklyn, as well as the presidents of the Irish and German emigrant societies. The board's first headquarters were located in a former almshouse building at the north end of present-day City Hall Park. George J. Svejda, *Castle Garden as Immigrant Depot* (Washington, DC: National Park Service, 1969), 21–22, and Nicole Ingrid Kvale, "Emigrant Trains: Migratory Transportation Networks through Germany and the United States, 1847–1914" (PhD diss., University of Wisconsin–Madison, 2009), 183.

7. See Kathryn Stephenson, "The Quarantine War: The Burning of the New York Marine Hospital in 1858," *Public Health Reports* 119 (January–February 2004): 79–92.

8. Cited in John Freeman Gill, "Islands Created for Quarantine," *New York Times*, May 22, 2020.

9. Stevenson, *Amateur Emigrant*, 98.

10. There was precedence for the building type elsewhere in the world. Sydney, Australia, had an immigration depot as early as 1848, located in the repurposed Hyde Park Barracks. These barracks were part of a walled compound built by convict labor in 1819 to house the working convict population sent from England. When convict emigration ceased, the building served as an immigration depot for single women seeking employment or awaiting reunion with family members. For more on this women's immigration depot, see Bridget Berry, *Female Immigration Depot: 1848–1886* (Sydney: Historic Houses Trust of New South Wales, 2005), and Jan Gothard, "Wives or Workers? Single British Female Migration to Colonial Australia," in *Women, Gender, and Labour Migration: Historical and Global Perspectives*, edited by Pamela Sharpe (New York: Routledge, 2001), 145–62.

11. Ann Novotny, *Strangers at the Door: Ellis Island, Castle Garden, and the Great Migration to America* (Riverside, CT: Chatham Press, 1971), 44.

12. Lind's performance at Castle Garden was the first of her nine-month American tour contracted under P. T. Barnum. Although five thousand patrons attended the first concert, Barnum writes that "their entrance was marked with as much order and quiet as was ever witnessed in the assembling of a congregation at church." Proceeds for the night totaled over $17,000 and Lind contributed $10,000 of her share to New

York City charities. P. T. Barnum, *The Life of P. T. Barnum* (London: Sampson Low, 1855), 314. See also W. Porter Ware and Thaddeus C. Lockard Jr., *P. T. Barnum Presents Jenny Lind* (Baton Rouge: Louisiana State University Press, 1981).

13. Vincent J. Cannato, *American Passage: The History of Ellis Island* (New York: Harper Collins, 2010), 36.

14. Board of Councilmen of New York City, *Report of the Special Committee on the Use of Castle Garden as an Emigrant Depot, March 17, 1856.* Document No. 12 (New York: McSpedon and Baker, 1856) 2, 7, 10, and 26. See also Svejda, *Castle Garden as Immigrant Depot*, 48–50.

15. "The Commissioners of Emigration and the Railroad Interest at Castle Garden," *New York Herald*, April 4, 1855, 5, and "Castle Garden as an Immigrant Depot," *Frank Leslie's Illustrated Newspaper*, December 29, 1855, 46.

16. "The Last of Castle Garden," *New York Times*, June 15, 1855, 4.

17. *New York Tribune*, August 14, 1855, 7.

18. The progress of converting Castle Garden into an immigration facility is reported in "Progress at Castle Garden," *New York Times*, July 14, 1855, 8. The *Annual Reports of the Emigration Commission* vary in listing the number of immigrants that could be accommodated in Castle Garden. The reports of 1877, 1880, and 1881 cite potential for two thousand occupants (pp. 6, 5, and 7, respectively); the reports from 1876, 1882, 1883, 1884, 1887, and 1888 go as high as three thousand occupants (pp. 10, 7, 9, 9, 12, and 13, respectively); and reports from 1873 and 1875 cite room for four thousand occupants (pp. 16 and 7, respectively). Unfortunately, architectural plans for the facility are believed to have been destroyed.

19. "Castle Garden as an Immigrant Depot," *Frank Leslie's Illustrated Newspaper*, December 29, 1855, 46, and *New York Daily Times*, June 11, 1855, 3, 8 (quote from 3).

20. "Castle Garden as an Immigrant Depot," *Frank Leslie's Illustrated Newspaper*, December 29, 1855, 46.

21. *Albany Evening Journal* quote reprinted in "Castle Garden as an Immigrant Depot," *Frank Leslie's Illustrated Newspaper*, December 29, 1855, 46.

22. Don H. Smith, "Castle Garden, the Emigrant Receiving Station in New York Harbor," *Nauvoo Journal* 10, no. 1 (Spring 1998): 44; Novotny, *Strangers at the Door*, 48; Svejda, *Castle Garden as Immigrant Depot*, 84; Leonard Dinnerstein and David M. Reimers, *Ethnic Americans: A History of Immigration*, 5th ed. (New York: Columbia University Press, 2009), 37.

23. "Commissioners of Emigration: Annual Report of the Superintendent of Castle Garden," reprinted in *New York Herald*, January 21, 1858, 5.

24. Stevenson, *Amateur Emigrant*, 98–104.

25. Stevenson, *Amateur Emigrant*, 104–6.

26. For more on the Pennsylvania Railroad's fight to enter the Castle Garden immigration pool, see "The Commissioners of Emigration and the Railroad Interest at Castle Garden," *New York Herald*, April 4, 1858, 5; State of New York, *Report of the Majority of the Committee Appointed to Investigate Certain Charges Against the Commissioners of Emigration, No. 53. In Assembly, Jan. 18, 1859* (Albany, New York: C. Van Benthuysen, 1859), 13–15, 21, 63; and Kvale, "Emigrant Trains," 194–95.

27. State of New York, *Report of the Majority of the Committee Appointed to Investigate Certain Charges Against the Commissioners of Emigration*, 175.

28. *New York Herald*, April 4, 1858, 2; State of New York, *Report of the Majority*

of the Committee Appointed to Investigate Certain Charges Against the Commissioners of Emigration, 18–19; Svejda, *Castle Garden as Immigrant Depot*, 62–64; Kvale, "Emigrant Trains," 196–97.

29. US House of Representatives, *Testimony Taken by the Select Committee of the House of Representatives to Inquire into the Alleged Violation of the Laws Prohibiting the Importation of Contract Laborers, Paupers, Convicts, and Other Classes*, 1888, 50th Cong., 1st Sess., House Report No. 572, 415.

30. *Report of John P. Cumming: In Pursuance of a Resolution of the Castle Garden Committee, of the Commissioners of Emigration, Adopted February 2, 1866, with the Answer of Christie and McDonald, and His Reply of Them* (New York: Printed at the Office of the Iron Age, 1866); State of New York, *Annual Reports of the Commissioners of Emigration, 1873*, 19–20; and Kvale, "Emigrant Trains," 202–7.

31. Agents were stationed at destinations including Poughkeepsie, Albany, Utica, Syracuse, Buffalo, Suspension Bridge (Niagara Falls), and Dunkirk. They met the trains and assisted with transfers, inquired about the treatment of immigrants by the railroad and its employees, and investigated complaints and reported them to the general superintendent at Castle Garden. When the service was discontinued in 1875, only the Albany agent was retained.

32. Damages to Castle Garden were estimated at over $40,000, not including destroyed baggage. Nearly one thousand pieces of luggage, belonging mostly to Russian Mennonites who had arrived that day, were destroyed. The commissioners of emigration used insurance money to pay nearly $9,000 to the Mennonites for their losses after they submitted their baggage checks along with a description of the luggage lost and its value. "Castle Garden Affairs," *New York Times*, July 12, 1876.

33. Novotny, *Strangers at the Door*, 51.

34. State of New York, *Annual Report of the Commissioners of Emigration, for the Year Ending December 31, 1876*, 10.

35. Montgomery Schuyler, "Castle Garden," *Harper's Weekly* 26, no. 1327 (May 27, 1882): 331.

36. These railroad companies included the New York Central, the West Shore, the Ontario & Western, the Erie, the Pennsylvania, the Baltimore & Ohio, and the Delaware, Lackawanna & Western.

37. Trunk Line Association Commission, Passenger Department, *Contract, Organization, Agreements and Rules, 1885–86* (New York: Russell Brothers, 1887), 24–25, 33–41. See Kvale, "Emigrant Trains," 208–9, for a description of the Trunk Line Association and its members.

38. "Protecting the Immigrant," *New York Times*, April 22, 1888, and Kvale, "Emigrant Trains," 211–12.

39. "An Attack on the Pool," *New York Times*, September 8, 1887.

40. "Castle Garden's Monopoly: Cogent Reasons for the Abolition of the Emigration Commission," *New York World*, July 27, 1887, 5. Among other things, the law required "just and reasonable" rate changes, prohibited pooling of traffic or markets, and established the five-member Interstate Commerce Commission (ICC).

41. "Castle Garden's Monopoly: Cogent Reasons for the Abolition of the Emigration Commission," *New York World*, July 27, 1887, 5.

42. "Commissioners of Emigration: Annual Report of the Superintendent of Castle Garden," reprinted in *New York Herald*, January 21, 1858, 5.

43. US House of Representatives, *Report of the "Ford Committee," the Select Committee to Inquire into the Importation of Contract Laborers, Convicts, Paupers, etc., January, 1889*, 50th Cong., 2nd Sess., House Report No. 3792 (Washington, DC: Government Printing Office, 1889). The report received its fair share of criticism. See, for example, Richmond Mayo Smith's review in *Political Science Quarterly* 3, no. 3 (September 1889): 529–31.

44. Ford also proposed other drastic immigration restrictions that were not carried out: prohibiting additional classes, tightening contract labor laws, severe penalties for evasion, raising the head tax to five dollars a head, and providing legal examination of prospective immigrants in overseas US consulates.

45. Stevenson, *Amateur Emigrant*, 113.

46. Stevenson, *Amateur Emigrant*, 113.

47. Stevenson, *Amateur Emigrant*, 114.

48. Stevenson, *Amateur Emigrant*, 114.

49. Stevenson, *Amateur Emigrant*, 116.

50. See John T. Cunningham, *Ellis Island: Immigration's Shining Center* (Charleston, SC: Arcadia, 2003), 56, and Thomas M. Pitkin, *Keepers of the Gate: A History of Ellis Island* (New York: New York University Press, 1975), 11–12. Although Congress believed Ellis Island to be an ideal location for the new station, Windom thought otherwise. On his initial trip to New York Harbor in 1890 to scout out potential locations, Windom dismissed Ellis Island as an impossible place on which to build anything: "the difficulty of reaching [Ellis Island] and the observations we had at that distance from us, where it seemed to be almost on a level with the water, presented so few attractions for an immigrant depot that we steamed away from it under the impression that [. . .] it was not a desirable place." US House of Representatives, *Remarks on Ellis Island Immigrant Bureau*, 51st Congress, 1st Session, October 1, 1890 (Washington: Government Printing Office, 1890), 3085–6.

51. US House of Representatives, *Report of the Select Committee on Immigration and Naturalization*, 51st Cong., 2nd Sess., No. 3472.

52. The ammunition was brought to Fort Wadsworth on Staten Island the following month. *Congressional Record*, 51st Cong., 1st Sess., vol. 3053, 638, and Novotny, *Strangers at the Door*, 69.

53. Harlan D. Unrau, *Historic Resource Study: Ellis Island Statue of Liberty National Monument, New York–New Jersey* (US Department of the Interior, National Park Service, 1984), 2:1210–11.

54. "Fire on Ellis Island: Many Buildings Burn," *New York Tribune*, June 15, 1897, 1.

55. US Department of the Interior, National Park Service, *Historic American Buildings Survey: Ellis Island* (Washington, DC: Government Printing Office, 1988), 3, and Pitkin, *Keepers of the Gate*, 19.

56. "Landed on Ellis Island," *New York Times*, January 2, 1892, 2.

57. Quoted in Pitkin, *Keepers of the Gate*, 17.

58. "Landed on Ellis Island," *New York Times*, January 2, 1892, 2.

59. US Department of the Treasury, Secretary of the Treasury, *Annual Report of the Secretary of the Treasury*, 1891, LXII–LXIII.

60. Pitkin, *Keepers of the Gate*, 26–27.

61. "Fire on Ellis Island: Many Buildings Burn," *New York Tribune*, June 15, 1897, 1, and Pitkin, *Keepers of the Gate*, 26.

62. As the New York press continuously published stories of corruption at the Barge Office, commissioner-general of immigration Terence Powderly launched an investigation in 1900, resulting in the dismissal of several employees. US Bureau of Immigration, *Annual Report of the Commissioner-General of Immigration*, 1900, 49.

63. "The Ellis Island Immigration Station Reopens," *New York Tribune*, December 17, 1900.

64. The Tarsney Act was passed in 1893 but not implemented until 1897 under the tenure of James Knox Taylor, supervising architect of the Treasury Department. The act stipulated that no less than five architects shall be invited to any competition and that any subsequent drawings and specifications would remain under the direction of the supervising architect.

65. US House of Representatives, *Letter from the Acting Secretary of the Treasury, Submitting Estimated of the Cost of Completing the Immigrant Station at Ellis Island, New York Harbor, January 21, 1898*, 55th Cong., 2nd sess., Document No. 245 (Washington, DC: Government Printing Office, 1898), 2.

66. US Department of the Treasury, Office of the Supervising Architect, *Programme of a Competition for the Selection of a Design for Buildings for the United States Immigrant Station, Ellis Island* (Washington, DC, September 9, 1897).

67. "Architecture Appreciations III: The New York Immigrant Station on Ellis Island," *Architectural Record* 12 (December 1902): 730, 732.

68. "Architecture Appreciations III," 730, 732.

69. See, for example, Raymond L. Cohn, *Mass Migration Under Sail: European Immigration to the Antebellum United States* (New York: Cambridge University Press, 2009), 125–54; and James M. Bergquist, *Daily Life in Immigrant America, 1820–1870* (Westport, CT: Greenwood Press, 2008), 59–98.

70. Commissioner-General to Williams, May 26, 1902, Bureau of Immigration, Letters Sent, 1892–1903, William Williams Papers, Manuscripts and Archives Division, New York Public Library (hereafter referred to as the William Williams Papers).

71. "New Immigrant Station," *New York Times*, December 3, 1900, 5.

72. Novotny, *Strangers at the Door*, 17–18.

73. Quoted in David M. Brownstone, Irene M. Franck, and Douglass L. Brownstone, *Island of Hope, Island of Tears* (New York: Rawson, Wade, 1979), 177.

74. Letter from Williams to Treasury Secretary Shaw, May 1, 1902, William Williams Papers.

75. Two votes out of three determined whether an immigrant was deported or not. The third inspector, or the immigrant himself, could appeal to the secretary of commerce and labor in Washington, at which time the person could hire a lawyer. Novotny, *Strangers at the Door*, 22.

76. Barry Moreno, *Ellis Island* (Charleston, SC: Arcadia, 2003), 8.

77. "Architecture Appreciations III," 729.

78. "Architecture Appreciations III," 729.

79. "New Immigrant Station," *New York Times*, December 3, 1900, 5.

80. Taylor stated: "[The federal government] cannot avoid affecting in a pronounced degree the architectural taste, knowledge, and enjoyment of the nation [. . .] The government, therefore, enjoys in its building operations a tremendous opportunity for good in the judgment of all who regard architecture as one of the important

factors of the higher civilization." US Department of the Treasury, Secretary of the Treasury, *Annual Report of the Secretary of the Treasury on the State of Finances* (Washington, DC, 1912). Cited in Anthony Robins, *Report of the Landmarks Preservation Commission: Ellis Island* (New York: Landmarks Preservation Commission, 1993), 4.

81. US Department of the Treasury, Secretary of the Treasury, *Annual Report of the Secretary of the Treasury on the State of Finances* (Washington, DC, 1912). Cited in Robins, *Report of the Landmarks Preservation Commission: Ellis Island*, 4.

82. *New York Tribune*, December 21, 1900. Cited in Pitkin, *Keepers of the Gate*, 32.

83. See Pitkin, *Keepers of the Gate*, 19–21, for a more detailed description of declining immigration in the late nineteenth century.

84. The exact number of immigrants in 1898 equaled 229,299, with 178,748 arriving in New York. See US Bureau of Immigration, *Annual Report of the Commissioner-General of Immigration*, 1898.

85. *Annual Report of the Commissioner-General of Immigration*, 1897, 5. See also Pitkin, *Keepers of the Gate*, 21.

86. Novotny, *Strangers at the Door*, 23.

87. Within the decade the dormitory required an expansion, receiving a third story in 1914.

88. US Department of the Interior, National Park Service, *Ellis Island*, 8–9.

89. Dennis Wepman, *Immigration* (New York: Facts on File, 2002), 210–11.

90. Series I, Ellis Island 1902–1914, 1939, I.A. Correspondence, 1902–1914, William Williams Papers. See also Kvale, "Emigrant Trains," 227–29, and Unrau, *Ellis Island*, 2:220–41.

91. Notice from Williams, June 12, 1902, William Williams Papers.

92. For more on Williams' antisemitic views, see Naomi W. Cohen, "Commissioner Williams and the Jews," *American Jewish Archives Journal* 61, no. 2 (2009): 99–126.

93. Williams to Treasury Secretary Shaw, November 7, 1902, William Williams Papers.

94. Notice from Williams to employees, July 16, 1903, William Williams Papers. See also Pitkin, *Keepers of the Gate*, 66.

95. Letter from Williams to Treasury Secretary Shaw, November 7, 1902, William Williams Papers.

96. Careful review and admittance of missionaries continued under Robert Watchorn's administration (1905–1909). Commissioner Watchorn required these groups not to collect any fees for their services, to submit monthly reports of their activity, and cautioned them to curb religious zeal, specifically in consideration of the Jewish population who had arrived on American shores to escape religious persecution. Watchorn spoke directly to the American Tract Society, which had been distributing Christian tracts in Yiddish and Hebrew to Jewish immigrants at Ellis Island. See Pitkin, *Keepers of the Gate*, 79–80.

97. Williams to Pastor Berkemeier, October 10, 1902, William Williams Papers.

98. Sargent to Williams, October 11, 1902, William Williams Papers.

99. "Notice from the Department of Commerce and Labor, Immigration Service, April 9, 1903," William Williams Papers.

100. Kvale, "Emigrant Trains," 230–31. In his autobiography *Memories of an American Jew* (New York: International Press, 1932), Philip Cowen wrote of his appointment at Ellis Island.

101. Williams to Supervising Inspector, Ellis Island, September 19, 1903, Ellis Island Letters Sent, William Williams Papers.

102. Willard Heaps, *The Story of Ellis Island* (New York: Seabury Press, 1967), 95.

103. "Notice Concerning Sale of First-Class Transportation to Immigrants at Ellis Island," November 24, 1911, William Williams Papers.

104. Notice from Williams, April 9, 1903, William Williams Papers.

105. Cited in Kvale, "Emigrant Trains," 221.

106. Novotny, *Strangers at the Door*, 20.

107. Victor Safford was a US Public Health Service physician at Ellis Island from 1892 to 1902 and wrote of his experiences on the island in his book *Immigration Problems: Personal Experiences of an Official* (New York: Dodd, 1925).

108. US Bureau of Immigration, *Report of the Commission of Immigration of the State of New York. Appointed Pursuant to the Provisions of Chapter 210 of the Laws of 1908. Transmitted to the Legislature April 5, 1909* (Albany: J. B. Lyons, 1909), 73. See also Kvale, "Emigrant Trains," 223.

109. Heap, *Story of Ellis Island*, 96–97, and Kvale, "Emigrant Trains," 222.

110. US Bureau of Immigration, *Annual Report of the Commissioner of Immigration for the Port of New York for the Year Ending June 30, 1903*, 9–10.

111. Interview with Ann Vida, 1986, Ellis Island Oral History Project.

112. William Williams, "Ellis Island, Its Organization and Some of Its Work; 8/9/1911"; 52516/001A; Ellis Island—Rules, Organization, Work, 1903–1913; Subject and Policy Files, 1893–1957; Records of the Immigration and Naturalization Service, Record Group 85; National Archives at Washington, DC.

Chapter 2: Port Stations

Subheadings are from Stevenson, *Amateur Emigrant*, 155, 132, 93, 126, and 113, respectively.

1. Stevenson, *Amateur Emigrant*, 116–17. The Pennsylvania Railroad Terminal was located where Jersey City's Exchange Place now stands.

2. Stevenson, *Amateur Emigrant*, 116.

3. Stevenson, *Amateur Emigrant*, 117.

4. Stevenson, *Amateur Emigrant*, 117.

5. John Droege, *Passenger Terminals and Trains* (New York: McGraw Hill, 1916), 29.

6. Charles Cooley, *Social Organization: A Study of the Larger Mind* (New York: Charles Scribner's Sons, 1909), 180, quote from 83. See also Anthony Raynsford, "Swarm of the Metropolis: Passenger Circulation at Grand Central Terminal and the Ideology of the Crowd Aesthetic," *Journal of Architectural Education* 50, no. 1 (September 1996): 12–13. Raynsford connects Cooley's arguments to his own discussion of architecture and mechanized sociability through the example of Grand Central Terminal in New York City.

7. See Raynsford, "Swarm of the Metropolis," 2.

8. Raynsford, "Swarm of the Metropolis," 12.

9. Robert Pope, "Grand Central Terminal Station, New York," *Town Planning Review* 25 (1911): 55.

10. John Henry Hepp, *The Middle-Class City: Transforming Space and Time in Philadelphia, 1876–1926* (Philadelphia: University of Pennsylvania Press, 2003), 66.

11. Weyeneth, "The Architecture of Racial Segregation," 11–44.

12. The Directors of the Port of Boston studied the operations in New York in the hopes of creating a similar policy of transportation and plan of construction for Boston Harbor. Directors of the Port of Boston, Massachusetts, *Supplementary Report to the General Court, March 31, 1915* (Cambridge, 1915), 52.

13. *Railroad Gazette* 1889: 422.

14. The ferry house was rebuilt as a two-story structure during 1914 renovations, which separated pedestrian and vehicular traffic. Its copper-sheathed steel frame was designed in a neoclassical style. For more on the building's architectural history, see Joseph Osgood, "Central Railroad Company of New Jersey" adapted from "History of the Jersey Central," *Coupler* (April 1949): Supplement; Charles Parrot, "The Central Railroad of New Jersey, Jersey City Terminal," National Register of Historic Places Inventory-Nomination Form (Washington, DC: National Park Service, 1975); and Herbert J. Githens, et al., *A Reuse Plan for the Central Railroad of New Jersey Marine Terminal* (Newton, NJ: Historic Conservation and Interpretation, 1980).

15. "A Handsome Structure: The Erie Railway's New Station at Jersey City," *New York Times*, December 4, 1887, 9. This terminal closed down in 1958 and was demolished in 1961.

16. "A Handsome Building: The Erie Railway's New Station at Jersey City," *New York Times*, December 4, 1887.

17. William H. Shaw, *History of Essex and Hudson Counties, New Jersey* (Philadelphia: Everts and Peck, 1884), 202.

18. Stevenson, *Amateur Emigrant*, 115.

19. Quoted in Citizen of Baltimore, *A History and Description of the Baltimore and Ohio Railroad* (Baltimore: John Murphy, 1853), 27.

20. H. W. Schotter, *The Growth and Development of the Pennsylvania Railroad Company* (Philadelphia: Allen, Lane and Scott, 1927). A journey on the Pennsylvania Railroad to points west, however, was longer than on the Baltimore & Ohio, since the former first traveled north into Pennsylvania. Thus, for passengers intending to travel north, it was prudent for them to sail to New York or even to Philadelphia instead of Baltimore since it minimized overland travel. The Port of Philadelphia had its disadvantages though, since travel from Europe was around 200 miles longer than that to New York, and the ice that formed on the Delaware River during winter made it difficult for ships to pass through.

21. Baltimore & Ohio Railroad Company, "Agreement with N. German Lloyd," March 13, 1867, Section 8, *Minute Book I (8/14/1861–10/14/1868)*, Baltimore & Ohio Museum, Hays T. Watkins Research Library, Baltimore.

22. "Baltimore and Ohio Railroad," *American Railroad Journal* 24, no. 7 (February 15, 1868): 177.

23. Paula Lupkin, "Mapping Macro-Circulation: Building, Banking, and Railroad Networks in the Great Southwest" (paper presented at the Annual Meeting of the Society of Architectural Historians, Buffalo, New York, April 10–14, 2013). See also Lupkin, "Rethinking Region along the Railroads: Architecture and Cultural Economy in the Industrial Southwest, 1890–1930," *Buildings and Landscapes: Journal of the Vernacular Architecture Forum* 16, no. 2 (2009): 16–47. This article, while it does not employ the term macro-circulation, provides an excellent example of the concept using the Industrial Southwest as an example.

24. Lupkin's concept of macro-circulation is informed by William Cronon's notion of Second Nature in his book *Nature's Metropolis*, in which city and country are connected together by means of a "coordinated system of raw materials, processing, manufacturing, and distributing." Lupkin, "Rethinking Region," 17.

25. Robert C. Keith, *Baltimore Harbor: A Pictorial History*, 3rd ed. (Baltimore: Johns Hopkins University Press, 2005), 94. See also Dean R. Esslinger, "Immigration through the Port of Baltimore," in *Forgotten Doors: The Other Ports of Entry to the United States*, ed. M. Mark Stolarik (Cranbury, NJ: Associated University Presses, 1988), 63–64.

26. Esslinger, "Immigration through the Port of Baltimore," 63–64.

27. For German immigration to Baltimore, see Esslinger, "Immigration through the Port of Baltimore," 66–70.

28. Harry H. Pierce, *Railroads of New York: A Study of Government Aid, 1826–1875* (Cambridge, MA: Harvard University Press, 1953), 64–65.

29. Baltimore & Ohio Railroad Company, *Annual Report for the Year 1872*, 44; *Annual Report for the Year 1880*, 54; and *Annual Report for the Year 1881*, 50.

30. "Comfort of the Immigrant," *Baltimore Sun*, February 23, 1888.

31. Anton Hagel, "When Immigrants Poured into Baltimore," *Baltimore Sun*, August 19, 1973.

32. "Comfort of the Immigrant," *Baltimore Sun*, February 23, 1888.

33. "Comfort of the Immigrant," *Baltimore Sun*, February 23, 1888.

34. Nicholas Fessenden, "Norddeutscher Lloyd and Baltimore: A Transatlantic Partnership," *The Report: A Journal of German-American History* 48 (2020): n7, 55.

35. Henry C. Raynor, "Immigrant Tide Here Is Slowly Rising Again," *Baltimore Sun*, March 8, 1925.

36. "Comfort of the Immigrant," *Baltimore Sun*, February 23, 1888.

37. "Comfort of the Immigrant," *Baltimore Sun*, February 23, 1888.

38. The German Immigrant House at 1308 Beason Street has been home to the Immigration Museum since 2016.

39. George B. Luckey, "America's Largest Immigrant Pier," *Book of the Royal Blue* VII, no. 10 (July 1904): 1.

40. Luckey, "America's Largest Immigrant Pier," 5.

41. Luckey, "America's Largest Immigrant Pier," 10.

42. Luckey, "America's Largest Immigrant Pier," 7.

43. Luckey, "America's Largest Immigrant Pier"; for a discussion of this riddle, see William J. Lampton, "The Vicissitudes of a Problem," *The Scrapbook* I (New York: Frank A. Munsey Company, 1906), 1106–1109.

44. Luckey, "America's Largest Immigrant Pier," 8.

45. Luckey, "America's Largest Immigrant Pier," 8.

46. Luckey, "America's Largest Immigrant Pier," 10.

47. "Statement of Hon. J. Charles Linthicum, of Maryland," *Hearings before the Committee on Public Buildings and Grounds, House of Representatives*, no. 40, Friday, December 6, 1912 (Washington, DC: Government Printing Office, 1912), 14.

48. "Statement of Hon. James H. Preston, Mayor of Baltimore," *Hearings before the Committee on Public Buildings and Grounds, House of Representatives*, no. 13, February 19, 1914 (Washington, DC: Government Printing Office, 1914), 3.

49. "Statement of Mr. Henry G. Hilkens, of the Schumacher Co., Representing the North German Lloyd," *Hearings before the Committee on Public Buildings and*

Grounds, House of Representatives, no. 13, February 19, 1914 (Washington, DC: Government Printing Office, 1914), 7–8.

50. See Matthew Carl Paoni, "Dixie's Arms Are Open: The Promotion of Settlement in the Postbellum-Era of the South, 1870–1920" (PhD diss., Johns Hopkins University, 2010).

51. "Statement of Mr. W. H. Manns, Vice President and General Manager of the Southern Settlement and Development Organization," *Hearings before the Committee on Public Buildings and Grounds, House of Representatives*, no. 13, February 19, 1914 (Washington, DC: Government Printing Office, 1914), 12.

52. A. C. Hubbard, "To the Editor of the American," Archives of Maryland Polonia, Series XII. Emigration/Immigration, Special Collections Langsdale Library, University of Baltimore; Adam C. Greer, "National Parishes Within Ethnic Enclaves: The Gradual Process of Americanizing Catholic Immigrants to Baltimore" (Master's thesis: Georgetown University, 2010). See also Daughters of the American Revolution, *Thirteenth Report of the National Society of the Daughters of the American Revolution, October 11, 1909 to October 11, 1910* (Washington, DC: Government Printing Office, 1911), 49.

53. Howard Markel and Alexandra Minna Stern, "The Foreignness of Germs: The Persistent Association of Immigrants and Disease in American Society," *Milbank Quarterly: A Multidisciplinary Journal of Population Health and Health Policy* 80, no. 4 (December 2002): 760.

54. "Statement of Dr. J. A. Nydegger, United States Public Health Service," *Hearings before the Committee on Public Buildings and Grounds, House of Representatives*, no. 13, February 19, 1914 (Washington, DC: Government Printing Office, 1914), 5–6.

55. "Immigration Station at Baltimore, MD," in *United States Congressional Series Set, Issue 6553*, 63rd Cong., 2nd Sess., Report No. 552, May 26, 1914, 106.

56. "Statement of Dr. J. A. Nydegger, United States Public Health Service," 14; Henry C. Haynor, "Immigrant Tide Here is Slowly Rising Again," *Baltimore Sun*, March 8, 1925.

57. US Bureau of Immigration, *Annual Report of the Commissioner General of Immigration to the Secretary of Labor for the Year Ended June 30, 1916* (Washington, DC: Government Printing Office, 1916), 187. North German Lloyd steamers ceased service to the United States, halting the flow of immigration and trade between Baltimore and Bremen until the 1920s, when the company reinstated service. The company steamships that took refuge in American ports were seized by the US government in 1917.

Chapter 3: Immigrant Trains and Waiting Rooms

Subheadings are from Stevenson, *Amateur Emigrant*, 139, 118, 126, and 132, respectively.

1. Stevenson, *Amateur Emigrant*, 106.

2. Stevenson, *Amateur Emigrant*, 117–18.

3. For the immigrant car's origin in the United States, see Kvale, "Emigrant Trains," 239–53. For a discussion of immigrant trains and stations throughout the world, see John MacKenzie and Jeffrey Richards, *The Railway Station: A Social History* (New York: Oxford University Press, 1986), 137–59.

4. See John H. White Jr., *The American Railroad Passenger Car* (Baltimore: Johns Hopkins University Press, 1978), and *A History of the American Locomotive: Its Development, 1830–1880* (New York, Dover Publications, 1979) for more on the construction and development of American train cars.

5. Norris C. Hagen, *A Life in Garnet* (unpublished manuscript, 1941), n.p. Manuscript Series, 4/23–4/25, North Dakota Institute for Regional Studies Records, University Archives, North Dakota State University, Fargo.

6. Anthony Bianculli, *Trains and Technology: The American Railroad in the Nineteenth Century*, vol. II (Newark: University of Delaware Press, 2001), 34, and Kvale, "Emigrant Trains," 242.

7. MacKenzie and Richards, *The Railway Station*, 147.

8. Stevenson, *Amateur Emigrant*, 133.

9. Thomas Curtis Clarke, et al., *The American Railway: Its Construction, Development, Management and Appliances* (New York: Charles Scribner's Sons, 1889), 251–52.

10. Stevenson, *Amateur Emigrant*, 133.

11. Stevenson, *Amateur Emigrant*, 34–135.

12. Stevenson, *Amateur Emigrant*, 136.

13. John Lukacs, "Bancroft: The Historian as Celebrity," *American Heritage* 12, no. 6 (1961): 65–68.

14. Stevenson, *Amateur Emigrant*, 133.

15. Stevenson, *Amateur Emigrant*, 37–138.

16. Stevenson, *Amateur Emigrant*, 138–39; Kenneth O. Bjork, *West of the Great Divide: Norwegian Migration to the Pacific Coast, 1847–1893* (Northfield, MN: Norwegian-American Historical Association, 1958), 412–14; Kvale, "Emigrant Trains," 243–44.

17. John Remeeus, "Journey of an Immigrant Family," reprinted in *The Wisconsin Magazine of History* 29, no. 2 (December 1945): 219.

18. Stevenson, *Amateur Emigrant*, 139.

19. Stevenson, *Amateur Emigrant*, 139.

20. Clarke, *American Railway*, 251.

21. Quoted in Kvale, "Emigrant Trains," 248.

22. Dolf Sternberger, *Panorama, oder Ansichten vom 19. Jahrhundert*, 3rd ed. (Hamburg: Claassen and Goverts, 1955), 50, quoted in Wolfgang Schivelbusch, *The Railway Journey: The Industrialization of Time and Space in the Nineteenth Century* (Berkeley: University of California Press, 1986), 61.

23. Schivelbusch, *Railway Journey*, 64; italics in original.

24. Remeeus, "Journey of an Immigrant Family," 220.

25. Stevenson, *Amateur Emigrant*, 118–19.

26. Remeeus, "Journey of an Immigrant Family," 217. The extra $24 Remeeus spent is the equivalent of nearly $900 in today's currency; one dollar in 1854 equals around $37.50 in 2024.

27. "Castle Garden's Monopoly: Cogent Reasons for the Abolition of the Emigration Commission," *The World*, July 27, 1887, 5. Reprinted in Pamela Reeves, *Ellis Island: Gateway to the American Dream* (New York: Crescent Books, 1991), 26.

28. Einar J. Anderson, "Voyage of the Immigrant and How It Has Changed," *Swedish-American Historical Bulletin* 2, no. 3 (August 1929): 100, and Kvale, "Emigrant Trains," 245.

29. Kvale, "Emigrant Trains," 247.

30. Stevenson, *Amateur Emigrant*, 126.

31. Weyeneth, "Architecture of Racial Segregation," 19.

32. See R. David McCall, "'Every Thing in its Place': Gender and Space on

America's Railroads, 1830–1899" (master's thesis, Virginia Polytechnic Institute and State University, 1999).

33. See H. Roger Grant, *The North Western: A History of the Chicago & North Western Railway System* (DeKalb: Northern Illinois University Press, 1996).

34. Chicago & North Western Railway (C&NW), *The Care of the Immigrant in the New Passenger Terminal* (Chicago: Chicago & North Western Railway, 1912). Chicago & North Western Railroad Archives, Berwyn, IL.

35. Immigration Association of California, *California* (Chicago & North Western Railway, 1882), 1.

36. C&NW, *Care of the Immigrant in the New Passenger Terminal*, 9.

37. Grace Abbott, director of the Immigrants' Protective League and resident at Hull House, wrote a letter commending the Chicago & North Western for its "really thoughtful provision for the comfort of the immigrants passing through Chicago." The Chicago & North Western reprinted the letter in its booklet, *The Care of the Immigrant in the New Passenger Terminal*, 26.

38. *Grand Central Passenger Station, Harrison St. and Fifth Ave. Chicago, U.S.A.*, pamphlet. Wisconsin State Historical Society Library, Madison. Quote reprinted in Kvale, "Emigrant Trains," 275. Grand Central was the smallest of Chicago's passenger rail terminals. It serviced the Baltimore & Ohio Railroad, the Chicago Great Western Railway, the Minneapolis, St. Paul and Sault Ste. Marie Railway, and the Pere Marquette Railroad Company.

39. Droege, *Passenger Terminals and Trains*, 29.

40. C&NW, *Care of the Immigrant in the New Passenger Terminal*, 13, 15, 21.

41. Kraut, *Silent Travelers*.

42. "The Immigrant," Editorial, *The North Western* (March 1912): 15.

43. "The Immigrant," 15.

44. See Davis, "Henry Van Brunt and White Settler Colonialism in the Midwest," in *Race and Modern Architecture*, 99–115. Quote from 102.

45. "The Immigrant," 15.

46. Droege notes the Kansas City's Union Station "is an unusual one [because] it handles practically no suburban traffic but the number of through passengers is out of all proportion to the size of the city." Droege, *Passengers and Terminals*, 93.

47. These railroad companies were the Atchison, Topeka & Santa Fe; the Chicago & Alton; the Chicago, Burlington & Quincy; the Chicago, Rock Island & Pacific; the Chicago, Milwaukee & St. Paul; the Missouri Kansas & Texas; the Missouri Pacific; the St. Louis & San Francisco; the Union Pacific; the Wabash; the Chicago Great Western; and the Kansas City Southern.

48. The headhouse measured 510 feet by 150 feet and the length of the building over the tracks measured 410 feet by 165 feet. The central pavilion measured six stories high while the side wings are half that height. Droege, *Passenger Terminals and Trains*, 93. The building remains standing today, although passenger service to the station ceased in 1985.

49. "The New Kansas City, MO., Union Passenger Station," *Railway Gazette* 57, no. 18 (1914): 801.

50. "New Kansas City, Mo., Passenger Terminal," *Railway Gazette* 54, no. 21 (1913): 1121.

51. "The New Kansas City, MO., Union Passenger Station," *Railway Gazette* 57, no. 18 (1914): 800, and Droege, *Passenger Terminals and Trains*, 94.

52. For more on the Pullman cars see Joseph Husband, *The Story of the Pullman Car* (Chicago: A. C. McClurg, 1917; reprint Grand Rapids: Black Letter Press, 1974), and White, *American Railroad Passenger Car*, 245–66.

53. Stevenson, *Amateur Emigrant*, 155–56.

54. Stevenson, *Amateur Emigrant*, 155.

55. See White, *American Railroad Passenger Car*, 400–413.

56. Atchison, Topeka & Santa Fe (AT&SF) pamphlet, "Fast Time. Free Sleeping Car for Emigrants. Santa Fe Route. Atchison, Topeka & Santa Fe Railroad, circular No. 7-A," April 15, 1884. See also Kvale, "Emigrant Trains," 247–53, for description of emigrant sleeper cars.

57. Bianculli, *Trains and Technology*, 34 and Kvale, "Emigrant Trains," 251–52.

58. Stephen E. Ambrose, *Nothing Like It in the World: The Men Who Built the Transcontinental Railroad, 1863–1869* (New York: Simon and Schuster, 2000); David Howard Bain, *Empire Express: Building the First Transcontinental Railroad* (New York: Viking, 1999); Lewis H. Haney, *A Congressional History of Railways in the United States*, 10th ed. (New York: A. M. Kelley, 1968); and John Hoyt Williams, *A Great and Shining Road: The Epic Story of the Transcontinental Railroad* (New York: Times Books, 1988).

59. Kvale, "Emigrant Trains," 249–50.

60. Remeeus, "Journey of an Immigrant Family," 215.

61. AT&SF, "Fast Time. Free Sleeping Car for Emigrants. Santa Fe Route. Atchison, Topeka & Santa Fe Railroad, circular No. 7-A," April 15, 1884.

62. C&NW, *Care of the Immigrant in the New Passenger Terminal*, 13.

63. Stevenson, *Amateur Emigrant*, 159.

64. Stevenson, *Amateur Emigrant*, 161–62.

65. Mackenzie and Richards, *Railway Station*, 152.

66. See Francis Paul Prucha, *Documents of United States Indian Policy*, 3rd ed. (Lincoln: University of Nebraska Press, 2000); David Wallace Adams, *Education for Extinction: American Indians and the Boarding School Experience, 1875–1928* (Lawrence: University Press of Kansas, 1995); Brian W. Dippie, *The Vanishing American: White Attitudes and US Indian Policy* (Lawrence: University Press of Kansas, 1991); and Frederick E. Hoxie, *A Final Promise: The Campaign to Assimilate the Indians, 1880–1920* (Lincoln: University of Nebraska Press, 1984).

67. See Weyeneth, "Architecture of Racial Segregation"; Mia Bay, "Traveling by Train: The Jim Crow Car," in *Traveling Black: A Story of Race and Resistance*, 63–106; and Andrew Sandoval-Strausz, "Travelers, Strangers, and Jim Crow: Law, Public Accommodations, and Civil Rights in America," *Law and History Review* 23, no. 1 (2005): 55 pars.

68. Kvale, "Emigrant Trains," 263–65, 267–68.

69. For a discussion on gender and race in the context of transportation, see Richter, *Home on the Rails*; Barbara Welke, *Recasting American Liberty: Gender, Race, Law and the Railroad Revolution, 1865–1920* (New York: Cambridge University Press, 2001); Patricia Hagler Minter, "The Failure of Freedom: Class, Gender, and the Evolution of Segregated Transit Law in the Nineteenth-Century South," *Chicago-Kent Law Review* 70 (1995): 993–1009; and McCall, "Everything in Its Place."

70. MacKenzie and Richards, *Railway Station*, 137–39.

71. For simplicity's sake, however, I use the terms *first-class* and *second-class*, unless specifically referencing a particular accommodation such as the ladies' car.

72. William Dean Howells, ed., "English and American Railways," *Harper's Monthly* 71, no. 423 (August 1885).

73. McCall, "Every Thing in Its Place," 18–20.

74. Stevenson, *Amateur Emigrant*, 129.

75. George A. Crofutt, *Crofutt's Overland Tours* (Chicago: H. J. Smith, 1889), 17. See also *History of Pottawattamie County, Iowa* (Chicago: O. L. Baskin, 1883), 54, for biographical information on Thomas Swobe.

76. Frederick E. Shearer, *The Pacific Tourist: J. R. Bowman's Illustrated Transcontinental Guide of Travel, from the Atlantic to the Pacific Ocean . . . A Complete Traveler's Guide of the Union and Central Pacific Railroads* (New York: J. R. Bowman, 1882), 11.

77. Stevenson, *Amateur Emigrant*, 135.

Chapter 4: Midwest Settlements

Subheadings are from Stevenson, *Amateur Emigrant*, 150, 150, 160, 144, 159, and 172, respectively.

1. Stevenson, *Amateur Emigrant*, 145.

2. Stevenson, *Amateur Emigrant*, 143–46.

3. Stevenson, *Amateur Emigrant*, 145–46.

4. For more on the Krimmer Mennonite Brethren and their journey, see Jerry Barkman, "From Crimea to Kansas," *Oregon Mennonite Historical and Genealogical Society* 11, no. 1 (February 1998): 1–5.

5. Quote from an essay written by Wiebe, reprinted in Glenn D. Bradley, *The Story of the Santa Fe* (Boston: R. G. Badger, 1920), 122.

6. G. S. Harris to J. W. Brooks, July 21, 1872, George Harris, Private In-Letters, September 1869–October 1872, Burlington Archives, Newberry Library, Chicago. The Burlington & Missouri River Railroad Company was incorporated in Iowa in 1852 and in Nebraska in 1869. In 1872, the company was acquired by the Chicago, Burlington & Quincy Railroad (CB&Q) to serve as a subsidiary. For simplicity's sake, this company is hereafter referred to in the text as the Burlington Railroad, although footnotes will clarify which branch is referenced.

7. See Manu Karuka, *Empire's Tracks: Indigenous Nations, Chinese Workers, and the Transcontinental Railroad* (Berkeley: University of California Press, 2019).

8. This passage is from a section entitled "Progressive Settlement." Chicago, Burlington & Quincy Railroad, *Burlington Route: Cheap Lands West of the Missouri River* (Chicago: Poole Brothers, 1892).

9. See Jeffrey Ostler, *Surviving Genocide: Native Nations and the United States from the American Revolution to Bleeding Kansas* (New Haven, CT: Yale University Press, 2019).

10. See Shari M. Huhndorf, *Going Native: Indians in the American Cultural Imagination* (Ithaca, NY: Cornell University Press, 2001).

11. MacKenzie and Richards, *Railway Station: A Social History*, 151. See Tony Bennett, "The Exhibitionary Complex," in *Grasping the World: The Idea of the Museum*, edited by Donald Preziosi and Claire Farago (Burlington, VT: Ashgate, 2004) for a discussion of the ways in which ethnic displays and entertainment served to emphasize the power of the white viewer over Indigenous peoples.

12. Stevenson, *Amateur Emigrant*, 151.

13. Stevenson, *Amateur Emigrant*, 151–54.

14. Stevenson, *Amateur Emigrant*, 150.

15. See H. Craig Miner and William E. Unrau, *The End of Indian Kansas: A Study of Cultural Revolution, 1854–1871* (Lawrence: Regents Press of Kansas, 1978), 25–54; Paul Wallace Gates, *Fifty Million Acres: Conflicts over Kansas Land Policy, 1854–1890* (Ithaca, NY: Cornell University Press, 1954); and Francis Paul Prucha, *American Indian Treaties: The History of Political Anomaly* (Berkeley: University of California Press, 1994), 235–87.

16. This was in addition to the lands granted to individuals under the Homestead Act of 1862, which totaled over 270 million acres, or ten percent of area of the United States.

17. Illinois Central, *Charter of the Illinois Central Railroad Company and Other Documents* (Chicago: 1878), Illinois Central Archives, Newberry Library, Chicago.

18. Paul W. Gates, *The Illinois Central Railroad and its Colonization Work* (1934; New York: Johnson Reprint Corporation, 1968), 122–26.

19. The majority of investment capital for the western railroads and subsequent townsite development came from the Northeast, especially financiers from New York and Boston. John C. Hudson, "Towns of the Western Railroads," *Great Plains Quarterly*, Paper 1672 (1982), 45.

20. See John W. Reps, *Cities of the American West: A History of Frontier Urban Planning* (Princeton, NJ: Princeton University Press, 1979).

21. All of the Associate's thirty-three towns utilized a version of this plan, with Kankakee, Illinois, proving to be their most successful. By 1856, two years after the town's establishment, the population numbered 1,200, and by 1858 it had increased to nearly 3,000 people. Gates, *Illinois Central Railroad and Its Colonization Work*, 126–27. For a history of the general development of the railroad town over time, see Hudson, "Towns of the Western Railroads."

22. Hudson, "Towns of the Western Railroads," 51.

23. George B. Hibbard, *Land Department of the Northern Pacific Railroad Company* (n.p., 1873), 9, Ayer Collection, Newberry Library, Chicago.

24. Letter to the Editor, *American Settler*, February 1, 1872, Foreign Agencies, Burlington & Missouri, Scrapbook of English Clippings, 1871–1872, Burlington Archives, Newberry Library, Chicago.

25. Hudson, "Towns of the Western Railroads," 42.

26. "The Shaping of Towns," *American Architect and Building News* 2 (June 23, 1877): 195–96.

27. See, for example, the Atchison, Topeka & Santa Fe Railway Company, *Railroad Lands in Central and Southwestern Kansas on Eleven Years' Credit* (Topeka: Kansas Magazine Publishing, 1873).

28. John Waugh to the editor of the *People's Journal*, August 7, 1872, Scrapbook of English Clippings, 1871–1872, Foreign Agencies, Burlington & Missouri (Neb.), Newberry Library, Chicago.

29. Ralph W. Hidy, et al., *The Great Northern Railway: A History* (Boston: Harvard Business School Press, 1988), 21. Six dollars in 1872 is the equivalent of nearly $155 in 2024.

30. "Agreement between Chester B. Rushmore and the Illinois Central," April 28, 1853, May 24, 1853, and January 31, 1854; "Agreement between James Sumpter and Co. and the Illinois Central," March 11, 1854, Illinois Central Archives, Newberry Library, Chicago.

31. C. B. Nelson to G. S. Harris, August 6, 1871, G. S. Harris, In-letters, 1869–1872, Foreign Agencies, Burlington & Missouri (Iowa), Volume 2, Newberry Library, Chicago.

32. Fred Gerhard, *Illinois As It Is* (1857), quote reprinted in Carlton J. Corliss, *Main Line of Mid-America: The Story of the Illinois Central* (New York: Creative Age Press, 1950), 82–83.

33. Gates, *Illinois Central Railroad and Its Colonization Work*, 170–72, 188–224.

34. Paul W. Gates, "The Campaign of the Illinois Central Railroad for Norwegian and Swedish Immigrants," *Norwegian-American Studies* 6 (1931): 66–88.

35. AT&SF, *Railroad Lands in Central and Southwestern Kansas on Eleven Years' Credit.*

36. A. King to G. S. Harris, November 14, 1871, G. S. Harris, In-letters, 1869–1871, Burlington Archives, Newberry Library, Chicago.

37. "Agreement between Burlington & Missouri River Railroad Company in Nebraska and the Board of Emigrant Mission of the City of New York," March 5, 1877, Burlington Archives, Newberry Library, Chicago.

38. J. N. Abbott to Touzalin, July 3, 1878, Burlington Archives, Newberry Library, Chicago.

39. Richard C. Overton, *Burlington West: A Colonization History of the Burlington Railroad* (Cambridge, MA: Harvard University Press, 1941), 336–37.

40. *Nebraska State Journal* (Lincoln, Nebraska), July 17, 1871, and April 28, 1871. Quotes reprinted in Overton, *Burlington West*, 336–37.

41. *Omaha Daily Herald*, December 4, 1872. In Canada, it was the Dominion government, as opposed to private companies, who established temporary lodgings for settlers throughout the country. See Monteyne, *For the Temporary Accommodation of Settlers.*

42. Hibbard, *Land Department of the Northern Pacific Railroad Company*, 9.

43. Perceval Lowell to J. D. MacFarland, June 20, 1887, Agreements with Agents and Colonists, ca. 1877–1881, Burlington & Missouri River Railroad (Neb.), Burlington Archives, Newberry Library, Chicago.

44. Keith L. Bryant, *History of the Atchison, Topeka and Santa Fe Railway* (New York: Macmillan, 1974), 66–67.

45. "The English Press on Nebraska," Scrapbook of Newspaper Clippings, Burlington Archives, Newberry Library, Chicago.

46. Kristina Gray, *First Wave of Immigration from Ukraine to North Dakota at the Turn of the Twentieth Century*, Chester Fritz Special Collections, University of North Dakota, April 29, 2005), 11. The Gray, Kristina Papers, General Collection, Immigration History Research Center, University of Minnesota.

47. Gray, *First Wave of Immigration from Ukraine to North Dakota at the Turn of the Twentieth Century*, 11.

48. Commissioner of Statistics, *Minnesota: Its Resources and Progress; Its Beauty, Healthfulness and Fertility; and its Attractions and Advantages as a Home for Immigrants* (Minneapolis: Tribune Printing, 1871).

49. Commissioner of Statistics, *Minnesota: Its Resources and Progress*, 51–53.

50. Scrapbook of English Clippings, 1871–1872, Foreign Agencies, Burlington & Missouri River Railroad (Nebraska), Burlington Archives, Newberry Library, Chicago. It is worthwhile to note, however, that there were more social welfare programs available in the United Kingdom than in the United States at this time.

51. After one lecture in England, for example, Charles Schaller of the Burlington & Missouri River Railroad wrote to the land commissioner that they received four or five applications for land the next day. Schaller to G. S. Harris, August 26, 1871, G. S. Harris In-letters, September 1869–December 1872, vol. 2, Foreign Agencies, Burlington & Missouri (Iowa), Burlington Archives, Newberry Library, Chicago.

52. *The Daily Post*, October 13, 1871; *Liverpool Mercury*, October 9, 1871; and *The Daily Post*, October 13, 1871, G.S. Harris In-letters, September 1869–December 1872, vol. 2, Foreign Agencies, Burlington & Missouri (Iowa), Burlington Archives, Newberry Library, Chicago.

53. In 1871, the European Commissioner of the Burlington Railroad, Charles Schaller, wrote to the company's land commissioner that "Dawson has a meeting in Birmingham on Thursday next arranged by the Good Templars with a view to set up a large colony for the spring. [. . .] We may rely on fifty or seventy families of those understanding farming—Dawson shows his views of Iowa and Nebraska upon the terms of the Society providing advertising and printing so that it will cost us nothing and we shall reap all benefits [. . .]." Schaller to Harris, August 22, 1871, G. S. Harris In-letters, September 1869–December 1872, vol. 2, Foreign Agencies, Burlington & Missouri (Iowa), Burlington Archives, Newberry Library, Chicago.

54. Harris to Hollub, November 2, 1869, reprinted in Overton, *Burlington West*, 303.

55. Henrietta Jessen to Eleonore and Dorea Williamsin, February 20, 1850. Reprinted in Theodore Blegen, trans. and ed., "Immigrant Women and the American Frontier: Three Early 'America Letters,'" *Norwegian American Studies and Records* 5 (1930): 21–22.

56. Burlington & Missouri River Railroad, "Emigration to Nebraska: Advantages of Organized Colonization," Circular, 1871. Burlington Archives, Newberry Library, Chicago.

57. Hibbard, *Land Department of the Northern Pacific Railroad Company*, 9.

58. D. E. Jones to Daniel M. Lord, Esq. of the *Interior* (Chicago), October 4, 1871. G. S. Harris, Private In-letters, September 1869–October 1872, Burlington Archives, Newberry Library, Chicago.

59. [Illegible] to Superintendent C. E. Perkins, June 17, 1878, Agreements between Agents and Colonists, ca. 1877–1881, Burlington Archives, Newberry Library, Chicago.

60. See Wally Kroeker, *An Introduction to the Russian Mennonites* (Intercourse, PA: Good Books, 2005), 5–22.

61. Kroeker, *Introduction to the Russian Mennonites*, 9–12.

62. The first technique was to plow the fallow land in the fall and the second was to cut the grain high on the stalk at harvest time. Both of these methods would trap the snow on the field during winter instead of having it blow over, thus increasing the supply of moisture to the soil during the spring thaw. Overton, *Burlington West*, 123n33.

63. David Aidan McQuillan, "Adaptation of Three Immigrant Groups to Farming in Central Kansas, 1875–1925" (PhD diss., University of Wisconsin–Madison, 1975), 70–71.

64. In Mennonite villages, a farmer's youngest son usually inherited the land and the oldest learned a trade or established farms on surplus lands outside of the village. See McQuillan, "Adaptation of Three Immigrant Groups to Farming in Central Kansas, 1875–1925," 60–85. Although military conscription is often cited as the main reason why the Mennonites left Russia, it was, in fact, the ownership laws

that ultimately forced Mennonites to leave, since the Russian government eventually agreed to let Mennonites perform other duties in exchange for military service, such as work in forestry or in hospitals. Robert Collins, *Kansas, 1874: Triumphs, Tragedies and Transitions* (n.p.: CreateSpace, 2011), 129.

65. Funk was editor of *Herald der Wahrheit.* He would later sponsor many benefit campaigns and institutions to aid the Mennonites in America. Alberta Pantle, "Settlement of the Krimmer Mennonite Brethren at Gnadenau, Marion County," *Kansas Historical Quarterly* 13, no. 5 (February 1945): 260, n. 5.

66. Overton, *Burlington West*, 83.

67. *Congressional Record*, 1873, Vol. II, pt. 1, 3264.

68. *Congressional Record*, 1873, Vol. II, pt. 1, 3299.

69. [Illegible] to C. E. Perkins, June 17, 1878, Burlington Archives, Newberry Library, Chicago.

70. Reprinted in C. Henry Smith, *The Coming of the Russian Mennonites* (Berne, IN: Mennonite Book Concern, 1927), 84.

71. US Ambassador E. Schuyler wrote to the Secretary of State, Hamilton Fisk, concerning the requests of the Mennonites. The Department of State replied that "it is not to be doubted that they [the Mennonites] would be deserving of welcome in this country. As Russian law, however, forbids emigration or its encouragement, it would not be advisable for this government to interfere in the matter until the disposition of that government which you proposed to ascertain shall be known." Instruction No. 136, April 22, 1872, reprinted in Georg Leibbrandt, "The Emigration of the German Mennonites from Russia to the United States and Canada, 1873–1880, Part I," *Mennonite Quarterly Review* 7 (1932): 225.

72. Quoted in Hale Holden, "The Burlington in Nebraska," address given January 29, 1925, n.p., 6–7. Burlington Archives, Newberry Library, Chicago.

73. Holden, "The Burlington in Nebraska," 6–7. Burlington Archives, Newberry Library, Chicago.

74. Recollections of the delegation's journey are reprinted in Smith, *Coming of the Russian Mennonites*, 116–19. Quote from 117.

75. Smith, *Coming of the Russian Mennonites*, 118. Agent Touzalin had previously worked for the Santa Fe Railroad and succeeded in reorganizing the company's land and immigration departments; he left abruptly in 1874 due to conflict with the Santa Fe's new president, Thomas Nickerson. No doubt it was difficult for Touzalin to lose the Mennonite settlement to his former employer. Touzalin, in fact, had been the one to hire Schmidt as general foreign agent in 1873 while he still worked for the Santa Fe Railway. For more on Touzalin's work with the Santa Fe Railroad, see Bryant, *History of the Atchison, Topeka and Santa Fe Railway.*

76. McQuillan, "Adaptation of Three Immigrant Groups to Farming in Central Kansas, 1875–1925," 139. See also Smith, *Coming of the Russian Mennonites*, 132–193, for a discussion of each of these settlements.

77. In 2024, $2.50 is the equivalent of around $69. While the majority of Mennonites settled in Kansas, others arriving from Russia did, in fact, select the Burlington's lands in Nebraska as well as the Northern Pacific lands in the Dakota Territory, and still others formed colonies in Canada.

78. Georg Leibbrandt, "The Emigration of German Mennonites from Russia to the United States and Canada, 1873–1880, Part II," *Mennonite Quarterly Review* 7

(1933): 29, 32–33; McQuillan, "Adaptation of Three Immigrant Groups to Farming in Central Kansas, 1875–1925," 140.

79. The agricultural village model in some of these communities only lasted for a few years; if one of the families of the settlement relocated, their section of land would no longer form part of the communal system.

80. The word *saraj* is a Low German spelling of a Russian word for "shed."

81. *Marion County Record* (Marion, Kansas), January 16, 1875.

82. The protagonist in Ole Rølvaag's literary masterpiece *Giants in the Earth*, published in Norwegian as two volumes in 1924–1925 and translated into English in 1927, constructs a sod byre-dwelling. The novel provides vivid descriptions of the interior of such a structure. This architectural form was also common in the Netherlands, from where the Mennonites had originally migrated. As architectural historian Shirley Dunn points out, byre-dwelling had been utilized by the Dutch since at least the seventeenth century. See Shirley W. Dunn, "Influences on New York's Early Architecture," *Dutch Barn Preservation Society Newsletter* 16, no. 2 (Fall 2003).

83. *Daily Companion* (Atchison, Kansas), May 4, 1882.

84. Many of the Mennonites had been engaged in silk production in Russia. In 1887, the governor of Kansas passed legislation allowing $13,000 for the "purpose of establishing, maintaining and conducting a silk station of Kansas." The station was located in Peabody, Kansas, and workers raised silkworm eggs for free distribution to residents interested in growing cocoons. Many settlers sold the cocoons back to the station but on account of the high costs of running the facility and paying its employees (wages were much lower in foreign silk-producing countries), the station closed in 1897. Frank Blackmar, ed., *Kansas: A Cyclopedia of State History, Embracing Events, Institutions, Industries, Counties, Cities, Towns, Prominent Persons, Etc. . . .* (Chicago: Standard Publishing, 1912), 694–96.

85. M. A. Carleton, "Hard Wheats Winning their Way," *United States Department of Agriculture* (1914): 398.

86. See Collins, *Kansas, 1874*, 140–51, for more on agricultural developments in Kansas prior to the Mennonites' arrival. On the rise of wheat in Kansas, see James C. Malin, *Winter Wheat in the Golden Belt of Kansas* (University of Kansas Press, 1944); J. C. Stevenson and P. M. Everson, "The cultural context of fertility transition in immigrant Mennonites," in *Fertility and Resources*, edited by John Landers and Vernon Reynolds (New York: Cambridge University Press, 1990); and Gary M. Paulsen and James P. Shroyer, "The Early History of Wheat Improvement in the Great Plains," *Agronomy Journal* 100, no. Supplement 3 (2008): S-70–S-78.

87. Collins, *Kansas, 1874*, 146.

88. Paul Erik Olsen, "Visions of Freedom: Impressions of America in Nineteenth Century Denmark," in *Danish Emigration to the U.S.A.*, edited by Birgit Flemming Larsen and Henning Bender and trans. by Karen Veien (Aalborg, Denmark: Danes Worldwide Archives, 1992), 42.

89. Dan Perekrestenko, oral interview, 1940. General Manuscripts, Box 3, The Gray, Kristina Papers, General Collection, Immigration History Research Center, University of Minnesota.

90. Chambers of Commerce of Alliance, Hemingford, Marsland, Crawford, and Whitney in conjunction with the Burlington Railroad, *Northwestern Nebraska* (n.p.: n.d.). Burlington Archives, Newberry Library, Chicago.

Chapter 5: San Francisco

Subheadings are from Stevenson, *Amateur Emigrant*, 148, 165, 165, 163, and 172, respectively.

1. Stevenson, *Amateur Emigrant*, 161.
2. Stevenson, *Amateur Emigrant*, 164–66.
3. Stevenson, *Amateur Emigrant*, 159.
4. Stevenson, *Amateur Emigrant*, 159.
5. Stevenson, *Amateur Emigrant*, 160.
6. Stevenson, *Amateur Emigrant*, 163.
7. Stevenson, *Amateur Emigrant*, 161.
8. Stevenson, *Amateur Emigrant*, 162.
9. Stevenson, *Amateur Emigrant*, 155.
10. Stevenson, *Amateur Emigrant*, 163.
11. J. S. Holliday, *The World Rushed In: The California Gold Rush Experience* (Norman: University of Oklahoma Press, 2002), and Kenneth N. Owens, ed., *Riches for All: The California Gold Rush and the World* (Lincoln: University of Nebraska Press, 2002).
12. Leland Stanford, *Central Pacific Railroad Statement Made to the President of the United States, and the Secretary of the Interior, on the Progress of the Work, October 10, 1865* (Sacramento: H. S. Crocker, 1865).
13. Stevenson, *Amateur Emigrant*, 161. The terms *Mongols* and *Mongolians* were used well into the twentieth century as a synonym for the Chinese, although the terms occasionally encompassed other East Asians and South-East Asians as well. Here, Stevenson likely uses *Mongols* for dramatic effect as the term does not appear elsewhere in the book.
14. Stanford University's Chinese Railroad Workers in North America Project (CRRW), led by codirectors Gordon H. Chang and Shelley Fisher Fishkin, is a rich resource that seeks to give voice to the Chinese migrant laborers, and has resulted in several publications, including Gordon H. Chang and Shelley Fisher Fishkin, eds. *The Chinese and the Iron Road: Building the Transcontinental Railroad* (Stanford, CA: Stanford University Press, 2019), and Gordon H. Chang, *Ghosts of Gold Mountain: The Epic Story of the Chinese Who Built the Transcontinental Railroad* (New York: Houghton Mifflin Harcourt, 2019). To explore payroll records digitized and interpreted by the CRRW, see the Payroll Records Gallery at Stanford University Libraries, https://exhibits.stanford.edu/crrw.
15. Mark Kanazawa, "Immigration, Exclusion, and Taxation: Anti-Chinese Legislation in Gold Rush California," *Journal of Economic History* 65, no. 3 (September 2005): 779–805.
16. Stevenson, *Amateur Emigrant*, 161.
17. See Nayan Shah, "Perversity, Contamination, and the Dangers of Queer Domesticity," in *Contagious Divides: Epidemics and Race in San Francisco's Chinatown* (Berkeley: University of California Press, 2001), 77–104.
18. For more on the interethnic and interracial dynamic between the Chinese and Irish, see Barry Patrick McCarron, "The Global Irish and Chinese: Migration, Exclusion, and Foreign Relations Among Empires, 1784–1904," PhD diss., Georgetown University, 2016.
19. See Lee, *At America's Gates*, 6–7.
20. Cited in Robert S. Chang, *Disoriented: Asian Americans, Law, and the Nation-State* (New York: New York University Press, 1999), 82.

21. Lee, *At America's Gates*, 124. Lee notes that conditions were not any better at other west coast ports.

22. Richard Taylor to the Commissioner-General of Immigration, March 25, 1909, File 52999/44, Subject Correspondence, 1906–1932, Records of the US Immigration and Naturalization Service, Record Group 85, National Archives, Washington, DC.

23. F. H. Larnard to Assistant Secretary of Commerce and Labor, November 23, 1908, File 52770/21, Subject Correspondence, 1906–1932, Records of the US Immigration and Naturalization Service, Record Group 85, National Archives, Washington, DC; P.A. Surgeon to Collector of Customs, January 13, 1909, File 52999/44, Subject Correspondence, 1906–1932, Records of the US Immigration and Naturalization Service, Record Group 85, National Archives, Washington, DC.

24. *Chinese World*, January 22, 1910, as cited in Him Mark Lai, "Island of Immortals: Chinese Immigrants and the Angel Island Immigration Station," *California History* 57, no. 1 (Spring 1978): 91.

25. The petition was presented to Prince Tsai Tao on the occasion of his journey to San Francisco. *Chung Sai Yat Po*, May 2, 1910, Box 948, File 52961, Subject and Policy Files, 1893–1957, Records of the US Immigration and Naturalization Service, Record Group 85, National Archives, Washington, DC.

26. *Chung Sai Yat Po*, May 2, 1910, Box 948, File 52961, Subject and Policy Files, 1893–1957, Records of the US Immigration and Naturalization Service, Record Group 85, National Archives, Washington, DC.

27. The boycott lasted nearly a year but came to an end when the US government pressured the Qing government to revoke its support. Yong Chen, *Chinese San Francisco: A Trans-Pacific Community, 1850–1943* (Stanford, CA: Stanford University Press, 2000), 148–61; Lee, *At America's Gates*, 125–26; Lai, "Island of Immortals," 89.

28. Lee, *At America's Gates*, 123–25; Wu Ting-fang to John Hay, December 26, 1900, Notes from the Chinese Legation in the US to the Dept. of State, Records of the US Department of State, Record Group 59, National Archives, Pacific Region, San Bruno, CA; Files 54152/75, 55597/912, 54152/75, 52961/24-B, and Policy Files, 1893–1957, Records of the US Immigration and Naturalization Service, Record Group 85, National Archives, Washington, DC.

29. US Department of Commerce and Labor, Bureau of Immigration, *Annual Report of the Commissioner-General of Immigration for the Year Ended June 30, 1907* (Washington, DC: Government Printing Office, 1908), 143–44.

30. Chinese immigrants often hired some of San Francisco's best attorneys, many of whom also worked for the Chinese consulate and for the Chinese Six Companies. See Lee, *America's Gates*, 138–41. For other changes made in the enforcement of the Chinese exclusion laws, see US Department of Commerce and Labor, Bureau of Immigration, *Compilation from the Records of the Bureau of Immigration of Facts Concerning the Enforcement of the Chinese-Exclusion Laws: Letter from the Secretary of Commerce and Labor, Submitting, in Response to the Inquiry of the House, a Report as to the Enforcement of the Chinese-Exclusion Laws* (Washington, DC: Government Printing Office, 1906), 28–45.

31. US Department of Commerce and Labor, Bureau of Immigration, *Annual Report of the Commissioner General of Immigration for the Year Ended June 30, 1902* (Washington, DC: Government Printing Office, 1903); Act of June 30, 1903 (32 Stat. 1112); US Dept. of Commerce and Labor, Bureau of Immigration, *Treaty, Laws, and Regulations Governing the Admission of Chinese* (Washington, DC: Government Printing Office, 1903). For

more on the Bertillon system see Rhodes, *Alphonse Bertillon, Father of Scientific Detection*, and John Higham, *Strangers in the Land: Patterns of American Nativism, 1860–1925* (New Brunswick, NJ: Rutgers University Press, 2002), 149–57.

32. F. H. Larned to Secretary of Commerce and Labor, January 28, 1909, File 5220/71, Subject and Policy Files, 1893–1957, Records of the US Immigration and Naturalization Service, Record Group 85, National Archives, Washington, DC; *San Francisco Call*, September 9 and November 29, 1908; Lee, *At America's Gates*, 125.

33. Cited in Lee and Yung, *Angel Island*, 11.

34. Report from Victor H. Metcalf, December 30, 1904, Box 49, Folder 51456/1–15, Subject and Policy Files, 1893–1957, Records of the US Immigration and Naturalization Service, Record Group 85, National Archives, Washington, DC.

35. See Lee and Yung, *Angel Island*, for the experiences of other nationalities that entered the country through Angel Island.

36. *Report of the Commissioner-General of Immigration, 1903*, 63.

37. In the 1830s, the Spanish governor of California granted the land to Antonio Maria Osio for use as a cattle ranch, hoping that the island's function as a meeting place for smugglers and as a dueling range would cease if it was in private ownership. Valerie Natale, "Angel Island: 'Guardian of the Western Gate,'" *Prologue: Quarterly of the National Archives and Records Administration* 30, no. 2 (Summer 1998): 125.

38. The US Public Health Service eventually moved its headquarters to San Francisco, although the quarantine station itself remained in use until 1946. US Department of Commerce and Labor, Bureau of Immigration, *Annual Report of the Commissioner General of Immigration for the Year Ended June 30, 1928* (Washington, DC: Government Printing Office, 1929), and Natale, "Angel Island," 126.

39. It is unclear whether there was any prior relationship between Mathews and Sargent or if Mathews had ties in Washington, DC, that may have secured him a meeting with Sargent.

40. Letter from Mathews to Sargent, March 24, 1905, Box 49, Folder 51456/16–34, Subject and Policy Files, 1893–1957, Records of the US Immigration and Naturalization Service, Record Group 85, National Archives, Washington, DC.

41. Letter from Sargent to the Secretary of Commerce and Labor, March 30, 1905, Box 49, Folder 51456/16–34, Subject and Policy Files, 1893–1957, Records of the US Immigration and Naturalization Service, Record Group 85, National Archives, Washington, DC.

42. Letter from Senator George C. Perkins to George B. Cortelyou, Secretary Department of Commerce and Labor, April 29, 1904, Box 49, Folder 51456/1–15, Subject and Policy Files, 1893–1957, Records of the US Immigration and Naturalization Service, Record Group 85, National Archives, Washington, DC. For more on the cottage plan, see Carla Yanni, *The Architecture of Madness: Insane Asylums in the United States* (Minneapolis: University of Minnesota Press, 2007), 79–104.

43. The Angel Island cottages were destroyed in 1971 as part of a training exercise for Marin County firefighters.

44. US Department of Commerce and Labor, Bureau of Immigration, *Report of the Commissioner-General of Immigration for the Year Ended 1908* (Washington, DC: Government Printing Office, 1909), 144–45.

45. US Department of Commerce and Labor, Bureau of Immigration, *Report of the Commissioner-General of Immigration for the Year Ended 1908*, 144.

46. *Chinese World*, January 22, 1910, reprinted in Lai, "Island of Immortals," 91.

47. Down Town Association to Hon. Julius Kahn, February 18, 1910, Box 948, Folder 52961/24, Subject and Policy Files, 1893–1957, Records of the US Immigration and Naturalization Service, Record Group 85, National Archives, Washington, DC.

48. Lee, *At America's Gates*, 33, and Shah, *Contagious Divides*, 184.

49. Him Mark Lai, Genny Lim, and Judy Yung, "Poem 8," *Island: Poetry and History of Chinese Immigrants on Angel Island, 1910–1940* (Seattle: University of Washington Press, 1991), 40.

50. Lai, Lim, and Yung, *Island: Poetry and History*, 73.

51. Lee and Yung, *Angel Island*, 56.

52. Lai, "Island of Immortals," 95.

53. M. W. Glover to Acting Commissioner of Immigration, November 21, 1910, File 52961/26F, Central Office Subject Correspondence and Case Files, Entry 9, Records of the US Immigration and Naturalization Service, Record Group 85, National Archives, Washington, DC.

54. *San Francisco Chronicle*, August 18, 1908.

55. *San Francisco Chronicle*, August 18, 1908.

56. E. S. Fuller of Standard Wire Mattress Company to Bureau of Immigration, Washington, DC, July 30, 1908. Box 50, MLR A1–9, Folder 51456/58, Subject and Policy Files, 1893–1957, US Immigration and Naturalization Service, Record Group 85, National Archives, Washington, DC.

57. Telegram from North to the Bureau of Immigration, Washington, DC, August 11, 1908. Box 50, MLR A1–9, Folder 51456/58, Subject and Policy Files, 1893–1957, US Immigration and Naturalization Service, Record Group 85, National Archives, Washington, DC.

58. Letter from Commissioner North to the Commissioner General of Immigration, August 13, 1908. Box 50, MLR A1–9, Folder 51456/58, Subject and Policy Files, 1893–1957, US Immigration and Naturalization Service, Record Group 85, National Archives, Washington, DC.

59. Commissioner General F. H. Larned to Standard Wire Mattress Company, August 12, 1908. Box 50, MLR A1–9, Folder 51456/58, Subject and Policy Files, 1893–1957, US Immigration and Naturalization Service, Record Group 85, National Archives, Washington, DC.

60. Lee and Yung, *Angel Island*, 36, and Architectural Resources Group, *Historic Structures Report: Hospital Building, Angel Island Immigration Station* (Prepared for the National Park Service, California State Parks, Angel Island Immigration Station Foundation, 2002), 36, 44.

61. See Annmarie Adams, *Medicine by Design: The Architect and the Modern Hospital, 1893–1943* (Minneapolis: University of Minnesota Press, 2008). On the miasma theory of contagion and architecture, see Yanni, *Architecture of Madness*, 33–34.

62. Shah, *Contagious Divides*, 179–203.

63. Lee and Yung, *Angel Island*, 37–38.

64. Lai, "Island of Immortals," 94.

65. *Chinese World*, January 30, 1922, and Lai, "Island of Immortals," 94.

66. Letter from Mathews to Sargent, January 4, 1906, Box 49, Folder 51456/16–34, Subject and Policy Files, 1893–1957, US Immigration and Naturalization Service, Record Group 85, National Archives, Washington, DC.

67. Letter from Sargent to Mathews, January 17, 1906, Box 49, Folder 51456/16–34, Subject and Policy Files, 1893–1957, US Immigration and Naturalization Service, Record Group 85, National Archives, Washington, DC.

68. Gareth Hoskins, "Place to Remember: Scaling the Walls of Angel Island Immigration Station," *Journal of Historical Geography* 30 (2004): 687.

69. Luther C. Steward, Acting Commissioner, Immigration Service San Francisco, to Commissioner General, Immigration Service Washington, DC, December 19, 1910, Subject and Policy Files, 1893–1957, US Immigration and Naturalization Service, Record Group 85, National Archives, Washington, DC.

70. Architectural Resources Group, "Hospital Building," 25; Lee and Yung, *Angel Island*, 38.

71. Memorandum from the Secretary of the Bureau of Immigration, October 21, 1913, and Memorandum from the Bureau of Immigration, April 12, 1915, Box 1833, Folder 53620/175, Subject and Policy Files, 1893–1957, US Immigration and Naturalization Service, Record Group 85, National Archives, Washington, DC.

72. Jacqueline Huey, Carolyn Huey Jung, Stephen Sam Huey, and Cynthia Huey Chin, "Stories from our Father, Sam Herbert Huey (aka Sam Shu Huey), and Angel Island Immigrant," *Immigrant Voices* (San Francisco: Angel Island Immigration Station Foundation, 2013).

73. Dong Kingman, *Paint the Yellow Tiger*, excerpted in "Angel Island Memories," *Immigrant Voices*.

74. Lee, *At America's Gates*, 128.

75. Lai, Lim, and Yung, *Island: Poetry and History*, 16.

76. Lai, Lim, and Yung, *Island: Poetry and History*, 75.

77. Quote by Mrs. Woo, age 23 in 1940, printed in Lai, *Island: Poetry and History*, 73.

78. Lai, Lim, and Yung, *Island: Poetry and History*, 75.

79. Quoted in Lee and Yung, *Angel Island*, 39.

80. For statistics on the length of detainment and the persons detained, see Robert Barde and Gustavo J. Bobonis, "Detention at Angel Island," *Social Science History* 30:1 (Spring 2006): 103–36.

81. Notably, Chinese traveling in cabin (first) class had a slightly shorter detainment period than those traveling in second class, and significantly shorter than those traveling in steerage. Therefore, for Chinese immigrants who purchased a higher-class ticket in the hope of avoiding detainment, the strategy only worked if they purchased first-class tickets. Barde and Bobonis, "Detention at Angel Island," 121–26.

82. US Department of Commerce and Labor, Bureau of Immigration, *Annual Report of the Commissioner-General of Immigration for the Year Ended June 30, 1909* (Washington, DC: Government Printing Office, 1910), 129. During the exclusion period, the highest estimates of those using false papers occurred during the 1920s and 1930s. It is impossible to accurately provide exact numbers of those who entered the country illegally, as many would never have admitted it. Lee, *At America's Gates*, 190–91. Lee also notes that Commissioner North was obsessed with Chinese criminal behavior, and published two articles on Chinese criminal gangs in the period after his retirement from immigration service.

83. See Lee and Yung, *Angel Island*, 84–90.

84. Interview #23, Angel Island Oral History Project, Ethnic Studies Library, UC Berkeley, quoted in Lee and Yung, *Angel Island*, 84.

85. Samuel Backus to Commissioner-General of Immigration, November 1, 1911, File 52961/24-E, Central Office Subject Correspondence and Case Files, Entry 9, Records of the US Immigration and Naturalization Service, Record Group 85, National Archives, Washington, DC.

86. "Memorandum," c. 1905, by Frank P. Sargent, File 52704/12, Subject Correspondence 1906–1932, Records of the US Immigration and Naturalization Service, Record Group 85, National Archives, Washington, DC.

87. Lai, "Island of Immortals," 94.

88. Lai, "Island of Immortals," 99. Not all poems about detainment on Angel Island were inscribed on the walls. One Chinese detainee sent a long poem to the *Chinese World* newspaper, where it was printed on March 16, 1910. It was later printed in *Xinning Magazine*. The poem, written in the classical style, featured heroic figures who had overcome adversity. See Judy Yung, Gordon H. Chang, and Him Mark Lai, eds., *Chinese American Voices* (Berkeley: University of California Press, 2006), 118–24, and Lai, Lim, and Yung, *Island: Poetry and History*.

89. Lai, Lim, and Yung, *Island: Poetry and History*, 23.

90. Lai, Lim, and Yung, *Island: Poetry and History*, 25.

91. Lai, Lim, and Yung, *Island: Poetry and History*, 152.

92. Lai, Lim, and Yung, "Poem 24," *Island: Poetry and History*, 60.

93. See Lai, Lim, and Yung, *Island: Poetry and History*.

94. Maria Sakovich, "When the 'Enemy' Landed at Angel Island," *Prologue* 41, no. 2 (Summer 2009): 27.

95. San Francisco Immigration Commissioner Edward White and his staff conducted interrogations for more than eight hundred German, and later, Austrian and Hungarian, alien enemies and at least sixty-three resident aliens of varying nationalities. Sakovich, "When the 'Enemy' Landed at Angel Island," 26–28.

96. Natale, "Angel Island," 133.

97. During the entire ordeal, only two people were harmed. "A Mystery Fire on Angel Island," *San Francisco Chronicle*, August 13, 1940, 26, and Lee and Yung, *Angel Island*, 300.

98. Cited in Natale, "Angel Island," 133–34.

99. A. Warner Parker to the Commissioner-General of Immigration, August 21, 1915, File 53438/54, Central Office Subject Correspondence and Case Files, Entry 9, Records of the US Immigration and Naturalization Service, National Archives, Washington, DC, and Lee and Yung, *Angel Island*, 38.

100. Lee and Yung, *Angel Island*, 299. The German sailors of the *Columbus* had been at Angel Island since January 1940 after they were rescued by the Americans from British capture in the Atlantic Ocean. After the fire they were sent to a facility near Roswell, New Mexico, until the war's end. John Soennichsen, *Miwoks to Missiles: A History of Angel Island* (San Francisco: Angel Island Association, 2001), 141–50; John Joel Culley, "A Troublesome Presence: World War II Internment of German Sailors in New Mexico," *Prologue: Quarterly of the National Archives and Records Administration* 28 (Winter 1996): 279–95; and Natale, "Angel Island," 134.

101. Elaine Low, *An Unnoticed Struggle: A Concise History of Asian American Civil Rights Issues* (San Francisco: Japanese American Citizens League, 2008), 3–4.

102. Stevenson, *Amateur Emigrant*, 172.

Epilogue: The Journey Today

1. See Chang, Davis, and Wilson, eds., *Race and Modern Architecture.*

2. Poem Number 31, Lai, Lim, and Yung, *Island: Poetry and History*, 66.

3. As of 2020, roughly seven hundred miles of fencing have been built along the nearly two-thousand-mile southwest border. Known as the "Border Wall," in actuality it is a series of walls and fences designed to prevent pedestrian or vehicular traffic (or both) in areas with higher numbers of illegal crossings. These barriers range in material and design, from walls of scrap metal to steel mesh panels to steel or concrete bollard fences, and are meant to be climb-proof. The Sandia Fence, for example, extends vertically for ten feet and then angles in toward the climber on the Mexican side "using gravity and the weight of the climber against them." Blas Nuñez-Neto and Stephen Viña, *Border Security: Barriers Along the US International Border* (Congressional Research Service Report, September 21, 2006), 17.

4. "United States Immigration Detention," Global Detention Project, accessed May 18, 2022, https://www.globaldetentionproject.org/countries/americas/united-states.

5. While not from an architectural history perspective, the intersection of immigration and mental health is thoroughly addressed in Dinesh Bhugra and Susham Gupta, eds., *Migration and Mental Health* (Cambridge: Cambridge University Press, 2010).

6. US Immigration and Customs Enforcement, "Fact Sheet: 2009 Immigration Detention Reforms," US Department of Homeland Security, 2009; Dora Schriro, Immigration and Customs Enforcement, "Immigration Detention Overview and Recommendations," US Department of Homeland Security, October 6, 2009.

7. In the last two hundred years, more than eighty million immigrants settled in the United States, and the country has also been a leader in resettling refugees. Erika Lee, *America for Americans: A History of Xenophobia in the United States* (New York: Basic Books, 2019), 3.

BIBLIOGRAPHY

Archives

Chicago & North Western Railroad Archives, Berwyn, Illinois

Chinese Railroad Workers Digital Materials Repository, Stanford University Libraries

Ellis Island, New York, New York
Bob Hope Memorial Library Archives and Special Collections
Oral History Library

Ethnic Studies Library, University of California, Berkeley
Angel Island Oral History Project

Hays T. Watkins Research Library, Baltimore & Ohio Museum, Baltimore, Maryland
Baltimore & Ohio Railroad Company Annual Reports
Baltimore & Ohio Railroad Company Meeting Minutes

H. Furlong Baldwin Library, Maryland Historical Society, Baltimore, Maryland
Baltimore & Ohio Railroad Company Annual Reports

National Archives and Records Administration, Washington, DC
Record Group 85, Records of the US Immigration and Naturalization Service

National Archives and Records Administration, College Park, Maryland
Record Group 85, Records of the US Immigration and Naturalization Service

Newberry Library, Chicago, Illinois
Edward E. Ayer Collection
Everett D. Graff Collection
Chicago, Burlington & Quincy Railroad Collection
Illinois Central Railroad Collection

New York Public Library, New York, New York
Archives and Manuscripts Collection
William Williams Collection

New York State Archives, Albany, New York
Annual Reports of the Commissioners of Emigration of the State of New York, 1855–1890

University of Minnesota Library, Minneapolis, Minnesota
Charles S. Frost Papers, Northwest Architectural Archives
The Kristina Gray Papers, General Collection, Immigration History Resource Center

Sources

Abrams, Kerry. "Polygamy, Prostitution, and the Federalization of Immigration Law." *Columbia Law Review* 105, no. 3 (April 2005): 641–716.

Adams, Annmarie. *Medicine by Design: The Architect and the Modern Hospital, 1893–1943*. Minneapolis: University of Minnesota Press, 2008.

Adams, David Wallace. *Education for Extinction: American Indians and the Boarding School Experience, 1875–1928*. Lawrence: University Press of Kansas, 1995.

Ambrose, Stephen E. *Nothing Like It in the World: The Men Who Built the Transcontinental Railroad, 1863–1869*. New York: Simon and Schuster, 2000.

Anderson, Einar J. "Voyage of the Immigrant and How It Has Changed." *Swedish-American Historical Bulletin* 2, no. 3 (August 1929): 70–103.

Angel Island Association, Angel Island Immigration Station Foundation, California Historical Society, and Paul Q. Chow. "Angel Island: A Historical Perspective." http://www.americansall.com/PDFs/02-americans-all/13.9.pdf.

Anzaldúa, Gloria. *Borderlands/La Frontera: The New Mestiza*. 1987. 2nd ed. San Francisco: Aunt Lute Books, 1999.

Architectural Resources Group. *Historic Structures Report: Hospital Building, Angel Island Immigration Station*. Prepared for the National Park Service, California State Parks, Angel Island Immigration Station Foundation, 2002.

"Architecture Appreciations III: The New York Immigrant Station on Ellis Island." *Architectural Record* 12 (December 1902): 730–32.

Atchison, Topeka & Santa Fe Railroad. "Fast Time. Free Sleeping Car for Emigrants. Santa Fe Route. Atchison, Topeka & Santa Fe Railroad, circular No. 7-A," April 15, 1884.

Atchison, Topeka & Santa Fe Railway Company. *Railroad Lands in Central and Southwestern Kansas on Eleven Years' Credit*. Topeka: Kansas Magazine Publishing, 1873.

Bain, David Haward. *Empire Express: Building the First Transcontinental Railroad*. New York: Viking, 1999.

"Baltimore and Ohio Railroad." *American Railroad Journal* 24, no. 7 (February 15, 1868): 177.

Barde, Robert Eric. *Immigration at the Golden Gate: Passenger Ships, Exclusion, and Angel Island*. Westport, CT: Praeger, 2008.

Barde, Robert, and Gustavo J. Bobonis. "Detention at Angel Island: First Empirical Evidence." *Social Science History* 30, no. 1 (Spring 2006): 103–36.

Barkman, Jerry. "From Crimea to Kansas." *Oregon Mennonite Historical and Genealogical Society* 11, no. 1 (February 1998): 1–5.

Barnum, P. T. *The Life of P. T. Barnum*. London: Sampson Low, 1855.

Bay, Mia. "From the 'Ladies Car' to the Colored Car: Black Female Travelers in the Segregated South." In *The Folly of Jim Crow: Rethinking the Segregated South*, edited by Stephanie Cole and Natalie Ring, 150–75. College Station: Texas A&M Press, 2012.

Bay, Mia. *Traveling Black: A Story of Race and Resistance*. Cambridge, MA: Belknap Press of Harvard University Press, 2021.

Bell, Ian. *Dreams of Exile: Robert Louis Stevenson*. New York: Henry Holt, 2015.

Bender, Barbara, ed. *Landscape: Politics and Perspectives*. Providence, RI: Berg, 1993.

Bennett, Tony. "The Exhibitionary Complex." In *Grasping the World: The Idea of the Museum*, edited by Donald Preziosi and Claire Farago, 413–41. Burlington, VT: Ashgate, 2004.

Benton-Cohen, Katherine. *Inventing the Immigration Problem: The Dillingham Commission and Its Legacy*. Cambridge, MA: Harvard University Press, 2018.

Berg, Walter Gilman. *Buildings and Structures of American Railroads*. New York: Wiley and Sons, 1893.

Bergquist, James M. *Daily Life in Immigrant America, 1820–1870*. Westport, CT: Greenwood Press, 2008.

Berry, Bridget. *Female Immigration Depot: 1848–1886*. Sydney: Historic Houses Trust of New South Wales, 2005.

Beyer Blinder Belle / Anderson Notter Finegold. *Historic Structure Report: Ellis Island Statue of Liberty National Monument, New York–New Jersey*. Volume 1: The Main Building. US Department of the Interior, National Park Service, 1988.

Bhugra, Dinesh, and Susham Gupta, eds. *Migration and Mental Health*. Cambridge: Cambridge University Press, 2010.

Bianculli, Anthony. *Trains and Technology: The American Railroad in the Nineteenth Century*. 2 vols. Newark: University of Delaware Press, 2001.

Bjork, Kenneth O. *West of the Great Divide: Norwegian Migration to the Pacific Coast, 1847–1893*. Northfield, MN: Norwegian-American Historical Association, 1958.

Blackmar, Frank W., ed. *Kansas: A Cyclopedia of State History, Embracing Events, Institutions, Industries, Counties, Cities, Towns, Prominent Persons, Etc.* . . . Chicago: Standard Publishing, 1912.

Blegen, Theodore, trans. and ed. "Immigrant Women and the American Frontier: Three Early 'America Letters.'" *Norwegian American Studies and Records* 5 (1930): 14–29.

Boardman, James. "A Citizen of the World." In *America, and the Americans*. London: A. & R. Spottiswoode, 1833.

Board of Councilmen of New York City. *Report of the Special Committee on the Use of Castle Garden as an Emigrant Depot, March 17, 1856*. Document No. 12. New York: McSpedon & Baker, 1856.

Boland Erkkila, Catherine. "American Railways and the Cultural Landscape of Immigration." *Buildings and Landscapes: Journal of the Vernacular Architecture Forum* 22, no. 1 (Spring 2015): 36–62.

Boland Erkkila, Catherine. Review of *For the Temporary Accommodation of Settlers: Architecture and Immigrant Reception in Canada, 1870–1930*, by David Monteyne, *Buildings and Landscapes: Journal of the Vernacular Architecture Forum* 31, no. 1 (Spring 2024): 80–82.

Booth, Bradford A., and Ernest Mehew, eds. *The Letters of Robert Louis Stevenson*. Vol. 3, August 1879–September 1882. New Haven, CT: Yale University Press, 1994.

Bradley, Glenn D. *The Story of the Santa Fe*. Boston: R. G. Badger, 1920.

Brown, Dee. *Bury My Heart at Wounded Knee: An Indian Perspective of the American West*. New York: Pocket Books, 1970.

Brownstone, David M., Irene M. Franck, and Douglass L. Brownstone. *Island of Hope, Island of Tears*. New York: Rawson, Wade, 1979.

Bryant, Keith L. *History of the Atchison, Topeka and Santa Fe Railway.* New York: Macmillan, 1974.

Cannato, Vincent J. *American Passage: The History of Ellis Island.* New York: Harper Collins, 2010.

Carleton, M. A. "Hard Wheats Winning Their Way." *United States Department of Agriculture*, 1914.

Chang, Irene, Charles L. Davis II, and Mabel O. Wilson, eds. *Race and Modern Architecture: A Critical History from the Enlightenment to the Present.* Pittsburgh, PA: University of Pittsburgh Press, 2020.

Chang, Iris. *The Chinese in America: A Narrative History.* New York: Penguin, 2004.

Chang, Gordon H. *Ghosts of Gold Mountain: The Epic Story of the Chinese Who Built the Transcontinental Railroad.* New York: Houghton Mifflin Harcourt, 2019.

Chang, Gordon H., and Shelley Fisher Fishkin, eds. *The Chinese and the Iron Road: Building the Transcontinental* Railroad. Stanford, CA: Stanford University Press, 2019.

Chang, Robert S. *Disoriented: Asian Americans, Law, and the Nation-State.* New York: New York University Press, 1999.

Chen, Yong. *Chinese San Francisco: A Trans-Pacific Community, 1850–1943.* Stanford, CA: Stanford University Press, 2000.

Chicago, Burlington & Quincy Railroad. *Burlington Route: Cheap Lands West of the Missouri River.* Chicago: Poole Brothers, 1892.

Chicago & North Western Railway. *The Care of the Immigrant in the New Passenger Terminal.* Chicago: Chicago & North Western Railway, 1912.

Citizen of Baltimore. *A History and Description of the Baltimore and Ohio Railroad.* Baltimore: John Murphy, 1853.

Clarke, Thomas Curtis, et al. *The American Railway: Its Construction, Development, Management and Appliances.* New York: Charles Scribner's Sons, 1889.

Cohen, Naomi W. "Commissioner Williams and the Jews." *American Jewish Archives Journal* 61, no. 2 (2009): 99–126.

Cohn, Raymond L. *Mass Migration Under Sail: European Immigration to the Antebellum United States.* New York: Cambridge University Press, 2009.

Collins, Robert. *Kansas, 1874: Triumphs, Tragedies and Transitions.* n.p.: CreateSpace, 2011.

Commissioner of Statistics. *Minnesota: Its Resources and Progress; Its Beauty, Healthfulness and Fertility; and Its Attractions and Advantages as a Home for Immigrants.* Minneapolis: Tribune Printing, 1871.

Conzen, Michael P., ed. *The Making of the American Landscape.* Boston: Unwin Hyman, 1990.

Cooley, Charles. *Social Organization: A Study of the Larger Mind.* New York: Scribner's Sons, 1909.

Corliss, Carlton J. *Main Line of Mid-America: The Story of the Illinois Central.* New York: Creative Age Press, 1950.

Cowen, Philip. *Memories of an American Jew.* New York: International Press, 1932.

Cresswell, Tim, and Gareth Hoskins. "Place, Persistence, and Practice: Evaluating Historical Significance at Angel Island, San Francisco, and Maxwell Street, Chicago." *Annals of the Association of American Geographers* 98, no. 2 (2008): 392–413.

Crofutt, George A. *Crofutt's Overland Tours.* Chicago: H. J. Smith, 1889.

Cronon, William. *Nature's Metropolis: Chicago and the Great West*. New York: W. W. Norton, 1991.

Culley, John Joel. "A Troublesome Presence: World War II Internment of German Sailors in New Mexico." *Prologue: Quarterly of the National Archives and Records Administration* 28 (Winter 1996): 279–95.

Cunningham, John T. *Ellis Island: Immigration's Shining Center*. Charleston, SC: Arcadia, 2003.

Daniels, Roger. *Coming to America: A History of Immigration and Ethnicity in American Life*. 2nd ed. New York: Harper Collins, 2002.

Dillingham, William Paul. *A Dictionary of Races or Peoples*. Washington, DC: Government Printing Office, 1911.

Dilts, James D. *The Great Road: The Building of the Baltimore and Ohio, the Nation's First Railroad, 1828–1853*. Stanford, CA: Stanford University Press, 1993.

Dinnerstein, Leonard, and David M. Reimers. *Ethnic Americans: A History of Immigration*. 5th ed. New York: Columbia University Press, 2009.

Dippie, Brian W. *The Vanishing American: White Attitudes and US Indian Policy*. Lawrence: University Press of Kansas, 1991.

Directors of the Port of Boston, Massachusetts. *Supplementary Report to the General Court, March 31, 1915*. Cambridge, MA: n.p., 1915.

Droege, John. *Passenger Terminals and Trains*. New York: McGraw Hill, 1916.

Dunn, Shirley W. "Influences on New York's Early Architecture." *Dutch Barn Preservation Society Newsletter* 16, no. 2 (Fall 2003).

Esslinger, Dean R. "Immigration through the Port of Baltimore." In *Forgotten Doors: The Other Ports of Entry to the United States*, edited by M. Mark Stolarik, 61–74. Cranbury, NJ: Associated University Presses, 1988.

Fairchild, Amy L. *Science at the Borders: Immigrant Medical Inspection and the Shaping of the Modern Industrial Labor Force*. Baltimore: Johns Hopkins University Press, 2003.

Fessenden, Nicholas. "Norddeutscher Lloyd and Baltimore: A Transatlantic Partnership." *The Report: A Journal of German-American History* 48 (2020): 47–55.

Frazier, John W., Eugene L. Tettey-Fio, and Norah F. Henry, eds. *Race, Ethnicity, and Place in a Changing America*. 3rd ed. Binghamton: State University of New York Press, 2016.

Gates, Paul Wallace. "The Campaign of the Illinois Central Railroad for Norwegian and Swedish Immigrants." *Norwegian-American Studies* 6 (1931): 66–88.

Gates, Paul Wallace. *Fifty Million Acres: Conflicts over Kansas Land Policy, 1854–1890*. Ithaca, NY: Cornell University Press, 1954.

Gates, Paul Wallace. *The Illinois Central Railroad and Its Colonization Work*. 1934. Reprint, New York: Johnson Reprint Corporation, 1968.

Githens, Herbert J. et al. *A Reuse Plan for the Central Railroad of New Jersey Marine Terminal*. Newton, NJ: Historic Conservation and Interpretation, 1980.

Gothard, Jan. "Wives or Workers? Single British Female Migration to Colonial Australia." In *Women, Gender, and Labour Migration: Historical and Global Perspectives*, edited by Pamela Sharpe, 145–62. New York: Routledge, 2001.

Grand Central Passenger Station, Harrison St. and Fifth Ave. Chicago, U.S.A. n.p., n.d. Pamphlet. Wisconsin State Historical Society Library, Madison.

Grant, H. Roger. *The North Western: A History of the Chicago & North Western Railway System*. DeKalb: Northern Illinois University Press, 1996.

Greenfield-Sanders, Timothy, dir. *Toni Morrison: The Pieces I Am*. New York: Magnolia Pictures, 2019. DVD.

Greer, Adam C. "National Parishes within Ethnic Enclaves: The Gradual Process of Americanizing Catholic Immigrants to Baltimore." Master's thesis, Georgetown University, 2010.

Groth, Paul. *Living Downtown: A History of Residential Hotels in the United States*. Berkeley: University of California Press, 1999.

Groth, Paul, and Chris Wilson, eds. *Everyday America: Cultural Landscape Studies after J. B. Jackson*. Berkeley: University of California Press, 2003.

Groth, Paul, and Todd W. Bressi, eds. *Understanding Ordinary Landscapes*. New Haven, CT: Yale University Press, 1997.

Hagen, Norris C. *A Life in Garnet*. Unpublished manuscript, 1941. Manuscript Series, 4/23–4/25, North Dakota Institute for Regional Studies Records, University Archives, North Dakota State University, Fargo.

Hale, Grace E. *Making Whiteness: The Culture of Segregation in the South, 1890–1940*. New York: Vintage Books, 1999.

Haney, Lewis H. *A Congressional History of Railways in the United States*. 10th ed. New York: A. M. Kelley, 1968.

Harman, Claire. *Myself and the Other Fellow: A Life of Robert Louis Stevenson*. New York: Harper Collins, 2005.

Heaps, Willard. *The Story of Ellis Island*. New York: Seabury Press, 1967.

Heitman, Danny. "*Treasure Island* Author Robert Louis Stevenson Was a Sickly Man with a Robust Imagination." *Humanities* 36, no. 4 (July/August 2015).

Hepp, John Henry. *The Middle-Class City: Transforming Space and Time in Philadelphia, 1876–1926*. Philadelphia: University of Pennsylvania Press, 2003.

Hibbard, George B. *Land Department of the Northern Pacific Railroad Company*. n.p., 1873.

Hidy, Ralph W. et al. *The Great Northern Railway: A History*. Boston: Harvard Business School Press, 1988.

Higham, John. *Strangers in the Land: Patterns of American Nativism, 1860–1925*. New Brunswick, NJ: Rutgers University Press, 2002.

History of Pottawattamie County, Iowa: Containing a History from the Earliest Settlement to the Present Time . . . Biographical Sketches; Portraits of Some of the Early Settlers, Prominent Men, Etc. . . . Chicago: O. L. Baskin, 1883.

Holdsworth, Deryck W. "Geography: Buildings as Settings for Seeing Systems and Networks." *Journal of the Society of Architectural Historians* 65, no. 1 (March 2006): 18–20.

Holliday, J. S. *The World Rushed In: The California Gold Rush Experience*. Norman: University of Oklahoma Press, 2002.

Hoskins, Gareth. "A Place to Remember: Scaling the Walls of Angel Island Immigration Station." *Journal of Historical Geography* 30 (2004): 685–700.

Howe, Daniel Walker, ed. *Victorian America*. Philadelphia: University of Pennsylvania Press, 1976.

Howells, William Dean, ed. "English and American Railways." *Harper's Monthly* 71, no. 423 (August 1885).

Hoxie, Frederick E. *A Final Promise: The Campaign to Assimilate the Indians, 1880–1920*. Lincoln: University of Nebraska Press, 1984.

Hubbard, A. C. "To the Editor of the American." Archives of Maryland Polonia, Series XII. Emigration/Immigration, Special Collections Langsdale Library, University of Baltimore.

Hudson, John C. "Towns of the Western Railroads." *Great Plains Quarterly*, Paper 1672 (1982): 41–54.

Huey, Jacqueline, Carolyn Huey Jung, Stephen Sam Huey, and Cynthia Huey Chin. "Stories from our Father, Sam Herbert Huey (aka Sam Shu Huey), and Angel Island Immigrant." *Immigrant Voices*. San Francisco: Angel Island Immigration Station Foundation, 2013.

Huhndorf, Shari M. *Going Native: Indians in the American Cultural Imagination*. Ithaca, NY: Cornell University Press, 2001.

Hungerford, Edward. *The Story of the Baltimore & Ohio Railroad, 1827–1927*. 2 vols. New York: G. P. Putnam's Sons, 1928.

Husband, Joseph. *The Story of the Pullman Car*. 1917. Reprint, Grand Rapids, MI: Black Letter Press, 1974.

"The Immigrant." Editorial. *The North Western* (March 1912): 15.

Immigration Association of California. *California*. Chicago & North Western Railway, 1882.

Jacobson, Matthew Frye. *Whiteness of a Different Color: European Immigrants and the Alchemy of Race*. Cambridge, MA: Harvard University Press, 1998.

Kanazawa, Mark. "Immigration, Exclusion, and Taxation: Anti-Chinese Legislation in Gold Rush California." *Journal of Economic History* 65, no. 3 (September 2005): 779–805.

Kapp, Friedrich. *Immigration and the Commissioners of Emigration of the State of New York*. New York: Nation Press, 1870.

Karuka, Manu. *Empire's Tracks: Indigenous Nations, Chinese Workers, and the Transcontinental Railroad*. Berkeley: University of California Press, 2019.

Keith, Robert C. *Baltimore Harbor: A Pictorial History*. 3rd ed. Baltimore: Johns Hopkins University Press, 2005.

Kingman, Don. "Angel Island Memories." *Immigrant Voices*. Angel Island Immigration Station Foundation, 2013.

Kraut, Alan M. *Silent Travelers: Germs, Genes and the Immigrant Menace*. Baltimore: Johns Hopkins University Press, 1995.

Kroeker, Wally. *An Introduction to the Russian Mennonites*. Intercourse, PA: Good Books, 2005.

Kvale, Nicole Ingrid. "Emigrant Trains: Migratory Transportation Networks through Germany and the United States, 1847–1914." PhD diss., University of Wisconsin–Madison, 2009.

Lai, Him Mark. "Island of Immortals: Chinese Immigrants and the Angel Island Immigration Station." *California History* 57, no. 1 (Spring 1978): 88–103.

Lai, Him Mark, Genny Lim, and Judy Yung. *Island: Poetry and History of Chinese Immigrants on Angel Island, 1910–1940*. 1980. Reprint, Seattle: University of Washington Press, 1991.

Lampton, William J. "The Vicissitudes of a Problem." *The Scrapbook* I (1906): 1106–1109.

Lee, Erika. *America for Americans: A History of Xenophobia in the United States*. New York: Basic Books, 2019.

Lee, Erika. *At America's Gates: Chinese Immigration during the Exclusion Era, 1882–1943*. Chapel Hill: University of North Carolina, 2003.

Lee, Erika, and Judy Yung. *Angel Island: Immigrant Gateway to America*. New York: Oxford University Press, 2010.

Leibbrandt, Georg. "The Emigration of the German Mennonites from Russia to the United States and Canada in 1873–1880, Part I." *Mennonite Quarterly Review* 6 (1932): 205–26.

Leibbrandt, Georg. "The Emigration of German Mennonites from Russia to the United States and Canada, 1873–1880, Part II." *Mennonite Quarterly Review* 7 (1933): 5–41.

Low, Elaine. *An Unnoticed Struggle: A Concise History of Asian American Civil Rights Issues*. San Francisco: Japanese American Citizens League, 2008.

Luckey, George B. "America's Largest Immigrant Pier." *Book of the Royal Blue* 7, no. 10 (July 1904): 1–10.

Luibhéid, Eithne. *Entry Denied: Controlling Sexuality at the Border*. Minneapolis: University of Minnesota Press, 2002.

Lukacs, John. "Bancroft: The Historian as Celebrity." *American Heritage* 12, no. 6 (1961): 65–68.

Lupkin, Paula. "Mapping Macro-Circulation: Building, Banking, and Railroad Networks in the Great Southwest." Paper presented at the Annual Meeting of the Society of Architectural Historians, Buffalo, New York, April 10–14, 2013.

Lupkin, Paula. "Rethinking Region along the Railroads: Architecture and Cultural Economy in the Industrial Southwest, 1890–1930." *Buildings and Landscapes: Journal of the Vernacular Architecture Forum* 16, no. 2 (2009): 16–47.

Mackenzie, John, and Jeffrey Richards. *The Railway Station: A Social History*. New York: Oxford University Press, 1986.

Malin, James C. *Winter Wheat in the Golden Belt of Kansas*. Lawrence: University of Kansas Press, 1944.

Markel Howard, and Alexandra Minna Stern. "The Foreignness of Germs: The Persistent Association of Immigrants and Disease in American Society." *Milbank Quarterly: A Multidisciplinary Journal of Population Health and Health Policy* 80, no. 4 (December 2002): 757–88.

Master Car Builders' Association. *The Car-Builder's Dictionary*. New York: The Railroad Gazette, 1888.

McCall, R. David. "'Every Thing in Its Place.' Gender and Space on America's Railroads, 1830–1899." Master's thesis, Virginia Polytechnic Institute and State University, 1999.

McCarron, Barry Patrick. "The Global Irish and Chinese: Migration, Exclusion, and Foreign Relations among Empires, 1784–1904." PhD diss., Georgetown University, 2016.

McQuillan, David Aidan. "Adaptation of Three Immigrant Groups to Farming in Central Kansas, 1875–1925." PhD diss., University of Wisconsin–Madison, 1975.

Miller, Kerby A. *Emigrants and Exiles: Ireland and the Irish Exodus to North America*. New York: Oxford University Press, 1985.

Miner, H. Craig, and William E. Unrau. *The End of Indian Kansas: A Study of Cultural Revolution, 1854–1871*. Lawrence: Regents Press of Kansas, 1978.

Minter, Patricia Hagler. "The Failure of Freedom: Class, Gender, and the Evolution of Segregated Transit Law in the Nineteenth-Century South." *Chicago-Kent Law Review* 70 (1995): 993–1009.

Monteyne, David. *For the Temporary Accommodation of Settlers: Architecture and Immigrant Reception in Canada, 1870–1930*. Montreal: McGill-Queen's University Press, 2021.

Moreno, Barry. *Castle Garden and Battery Park*. Charleston, SC: Arcadia, 2007.

Moreno, Barry. *Ellis Island*. Charleston, SC: Arcadia, 2003.

Morrissey, Katherine. *Mental Territories: Mapping the Inland Empire*. Ithaca, NY: Cornell University Press, 1997.

Morrissey, Katherine G., and John-Michael H. Warner, eds. *Border Spaces: Visualizing the U.S.–Mexico Frontera*. Tucson: University of Arizona Press, 2018.

Natale, Valerie. "Angel Island: 'Guardian of the Western Gate.'" *Prologue: Quarterly of the National Archives and Records Administration* 30, no. 2 (1998): 125–35.

"New Kansas City, Mo., Passenger Terminal." *Railway Age Gazette* 54, no. 21 (1913): 1121.

"The New Kansas City, MO., Union Passenger Station." *Railway Age Gazette* 57, no. 18 (1914): 801.

Novotny, Ann. *Strangers at the Door: Ellis Island, Castle Garden, and the Great Migration to America*. Riverside, CT: Chatham Press, 1971.

Nuñez-Neto, Blas, and Stephen Viña. "Border Security: Barriers Along the US International Border." US Border Patrol. Congressional Research Service Report, September 21, 2006.

O'Kelly, Patrick. *Advice and Guide to Emigrants Going to the United States of America*. Dublin: William Folds, 1834.

Olsen, Paul Erik. "Visions of Freedom: Impressions of America in Nineteenth Century Denmark." In *Danish Emigration to the U.S.A.*, edited by Birgit Flemming Larsen and Henning Bender and translated by Karen Veien, 13–24. Aalborg, Denmark: Danes Worldwide Archives, 1992.

Osanna, Dan. *Cultural Resources Inventory: Angel Island Immigration Station Building Stabilization, Poem Restoration and Site Improvement Project*. Northern Service Center, Department of Parks and Recreation, November 2002.

Osgood, Joseph. "Central Railroad Company of New Jersey." *Coupler* (April 1949): Supplement.

Ostler, Jeffrey. *Surviving Genocide: Native Nations and the United States from the American Revolution to Bleeding Kansas*. New Haven, CT: Yale University Press, 2019.

Overton, Richard C. *Burlington West: A Colonization History of the Burlington Railroad*. Cambridge, MA: Harvard University Press, 1941.

Owens, Kenneth N., ed. *Riches for All: The California Gold Rush and the World*. Lincoln: University of Nebraska Press, 2002.

Pantle, Alberta. "Settlement of the Krimmer Mennonite Brethren at Gnadenau, Marion County." *Kansas Historical Quarterly* 13, no. 5 (February 1945): 259–85.

Paoni, Matthew Carl. "Dixie's Arms Are Open: The Promotion of Settlement in the Postbellum-Era of the South, 1870–1920." PhD diss., Johns Hopkins University, 2010.

Parrot, Charles. "The Central Railroad of New Jersey, Jersey City Terminal," Hudson County, New Jersey. National Register of Historic Places Inventory-Nomination Form. Washington, DC: National Park Service, 1975.

Paulsen, Gary M., and James P. Shroyer. "The Early History of Wheat Improvement in the Great Plains." *Agronomy Journal* 100, Supplement 3 (2008): S-70–S-78.

Petit, Jeanne D. *The Men and Women We Want: Gender, Race, and the Progressive Era Literacy Test.* Rochester, NY: University of Rochester Press, 2010.

Pierce, Harry H. *Railroads of New York: A Study of Government Aid, 1826–1875.* Cambridge, MA: Harvard University Press, 1953.

Pitkin, Thomas M. *Keepers of the Gate: A History of Ellis Island.* New York: New York University Press, 1975.

Pope, Robert. "Grand Central Terminal Station, New York." *Town Planning Review* 25 (1911): 55–64.

Prucha, Francis Paul. *American Indian Treaties: The History of Political Anomaly.* Berkeley: University of California Press, 1994.

Prucha, Francis Paul. *Documents of United States Indian Policy.* 3rd ed. Lincoln: University of Nebraska Press, 2000.

Raynsford, Anthony. "Swarm of the Metropolis: Passenger Circulation at Grand Central Terminal and the Ideology of the Crowd Aesthetic." *Journal of Architectural Education* 50, no. 1 (September 1996): 2–14.

Reemus, John. "The Journey of an Immigrant Family from the Netherlands to Milwaukee, 1854." Edited by Henry S. Lucas. *Wisconsin Magazine of History* 29, no. 2 (December 1945): 201–23.

Reeves, Pamela. *Ellis Island: Gateway to the American Dream.* New York: Crescent Books, 1991.

Reps, John W. *Cities of the American West: A History of Frontier Urban Planning.* Princeton, NJ: Princeton University Press, 1979.

Rhodes, Henry T. F. *Alphonse Bertillon, Father of Scientific Detection.* New York: Greenwood Press, 1968.

Richter, Amy. *Home on the Rails: Women, the Railroad, and the Rise of Public Domesticity.* Chapel Hill: University of North Carolina Press, 2005.

Robins, Anthony. *Report of the Landmarks Preservation Commission: Ellis Island.* New York: Landmarks Preservation Commission, 1993.

Roediger, David R. *The Wages of Whiteness: Race and the Making of the American Working Class.* 4th ed. New York: Verso, 2022.

Roediger, David R. *Working Toward Whiteness: How America's Immigrants Became White.* Updated ed. New York: Basic Books, 2018.

Rølvaag, Ole Edvart. *Giants in the Earth: A Saga of the Prairie.* Translated from the Norwegian by Lincoln Colcord and O. E. Rølvaag. 1927. Reprint, New York: Harper Perennial, 1999.

Safford, Victor. *Immigration Problems: Personal Experiences of an Official.* New York: Dodd, 1925.

Sakovich, Maria. "When the 'Enemy' Landed at Angel Island." *Prologue* 41, no. 2 (Summer 2009): 26–33.

Salyer, Lucy. *Laws as Harsh as Tigers.* Chapel Hill: University of North Carolina Press, 1995.

Sandoval-Strausz, Andrew. "Travelers, Strangers, and Jim Crow: Law, Public Accommodations, and Civil Rights in America." *Law and History Review* 23, no. 1 (2005): 53–94.

Schivelbusch, Wolfgang. *The Railway Journey: The Industrialization of Time and Space in the Nineteenth Century*. Foreword by Alan Trachtenberg. Berkeley: University of California Press, 1986.

Schivelbusch, Wolfgang. "Railroad Space and Railroad Time." *New German Critique* 14 (Spring 1978): 31–40.

Schmidt, C. B. "Reminiscences of Foreign Immigration Work for Kansas." *Kansas Historical Collections* 9 (1905–1906): 485–97.

Schneider, Dorothee. *Crossing Borders: Migration and Citizenship in the Twentieth-Century United States*. Cambridge, MA: Harvard University Press, 2011.

Schotter, H. W. *The Growth and Development of the Pennsylvania Railroad Company*. Philadelphia: Allen, Lane and Scott, 1927.

Schriro, Dora, Immigration and Customs Enforcement. "Immigration Detention Overview and Recommendations." US Department of Homeland Security, October 6, 2009.

Sewell, Jessica Ellen. *Women and the Everyday City: Public Space in San Francisco, 1890–1915*. Minneapolis: University of Minnesota Press, 2011.

Shah, Nayan. *Contagious Divides: Epidemics and Race in San Francisco's Chinatown*. Berkeley: University of California Press, 2001.

Shamrock Society of New York. *Hints to Emigrants from Europe Intending to Make a Permanent Residence in the United States*. New York: Van Winkle and Wiley, 1816.

"The Shaping of Towns." *American Architect and Building News* 2 (June 23, 1877): 195–96.

Shaw, William H. *History of Essex and Hudson Counties, New Jersey*. Philadelphia: Everts and Peck, 1884.

Shearer, Frederick E. *The Pacific Tourist: J. R. Bowman's Illustrated Transcontinental Guide of Travel, from the Atlantic to the Pacific Ocean . . . A Complete Traveler's Guide of the Union and Central Pacific Railroads*. New York: J. R. Bowman, 1882.

Smith, C. Henry. *The Coming of the Russian Mennonites*. Berne, IN: Mennonite Book Concern, 1927.

Smith, Don H. "Castle Garden, the Emigrant Receiving Station in New York Harbor." *Nauvoo Journal* 10, no. 1 (Spring 1998): 41–52.

Smith, Richard Mayo. Review of "The Report of the Ford Committee." *Political Science Quarterly* 3, no. 3 (September 1889): 529–31.

Soennichsen, John. *Miwoks to Missiles: A History of Angel Island*. San Francisco: Angel Island Association, 2001.

Spickard, Paul, Francisco Beltrán, and Laura Hooton. *Almost All Aliens: Immigration, Race and Colonialism in American History and Identity*. 2nd ed. New York: Routledge, 2022.

Stanford, Leland. *Central Pacific Railroad Statement Made to the President of the United States, and the Secretary of the Interior, on the Progress of the Work, October 10, 1865*. Sacramento, CA: H. S. Crocker, 1865.

Stephenson, Kathryn. "The Quarantine War: The Burning of the New York Marine Hospital in 1858." *Public Health Reports* 119 (January–February 2004): 79–92.

Sternberger, Dolf. *Panorama of the Nineteenth Century*. Translated by Joachim Neugroschel. New York: Urizen Books, 1977.

Stevenson, J. C., and P. M. Everson. "The Cultural Context of Fertility Transition in Immigrant Mennonites." In *Fertility and Resources*, edited by John Landers and Vernon Reynolds, 47–61. New York: Cambridge University Press, 1990.

Stevenson, Robert Louis. "Across the Plains: Leaves from the Notebook of an Emigrant between New York and San Francisco." *Longman's Magazine* 2 (July–August 1883).

Stevenson, Robert Louis. *The Amateur Emigrant*. 1896. New York: Carroll and Graff, 2002.

Stevenson, Robert Louis. "Epilogue to an Inland Voyage." *Scribner's Magazine* 4 (August 1888): 250–56.

Stevenson, Robert Louis. *An Inland Voyage*. London: Kegan Paul, 1878.

Stevenson, Robert Louis. "The Silverado Squatters." *Century Illustrated Monthly Magazine* (November–December 1883).

Stevenson, Robert Louis. *Travels with a Donkey in the Cévennes*. New York: Charles Scribner's Sons, 1879.

Stilgoe, John. *Metropolitan Corridor: Railroads and the American Scene*. New Haven, CT: Yale University Press, 1983.

Stover, John F. *History of the Baltimore and Ohio Railroad*. West Lafayette, IN: Purdue University Press, 1987.

Svejda, George J. *Castle Garden as Immigrant Depot*. Washington, DC: National Park Service, 1969.

Swearingen, Roger G., ed. *The Amateur Emigrant*. 2 vols. Ashland, OR: Lewis Osborne, 1976–1977.

Taylor, Lonn, et al. *The Star-Spangled Banner: The Making of an American Icon*. New York: Harper Collins, 2008.

Tewksbury, George E. *The Kansas Picture Book*. Topeka, KS: A. S. Johnson, 1883.

Thomas, William G. *The Iron Way: Railroads, the Civil War and the Making of Modern America*. New Haven, CT: Yale University Press, 2011.

Tichenor, Daniel. *Dividing Lines: The Politics of Immigration Control in America*. Princeton, NJ: Princeton University Press, 2002.

"Torch Applied to Locust Point Terminals of the Baltimore and Ohio." *Baltimore and Ohio Employes [sic] Magazine* 5, no. 7 (November 1917): 7.

Trunk Line Association Commission, Passenger Department. *Contract, Organization, Agreements and Rules, 1885–86*. New York: Russell Brothers, 1887.

Turner, Frederick Jackson. *The Frontier in American History*. New York: Henry Holt, 1921.

"United States Immigration Detention." Global Detention Project. Accessed August 22, 2020. https://www.globaldetentionproject.org/countries/americas/united-states.

Unrau, Harlan D. *Historic Resource Study: Ellis Island Statue of Liberty National Monument, New York–New Jersey*. 3 vols. US Department of the Interior, National Park Service, 1984.

Unruh, John. *The Overland Emigrants and the Trans-Mississippi West, 1840–1860*. Champaign: University of Illinois Press, 1993.

US Immigration and Customs Enforcement. "Fact Sheet: 2009 Immigration Detention Reforms." US Department of Homeland Security, 2009.

Vlach, John Michael. *Back of the Big House: The Architecture of Plantation Slavery*. Chapel Hill: University of North Carolina Press, 1993.

Ware, W. Porter, and Thaddeus C. Lockard Jr. *P. T. Barnum Presents Jenny Lind*. Baton Rouge: Louisiana State University Press, 1981.

Welke, Barbara. *Recasting American Liberty: Gender, Race, Law and the Railroad Revolution, 1865–1920*. New York: Cambridge University Press, 2001.
Wepman, Dennis. *Immigration*. New York: Facts on File, 2002.
Weyeneth, Robert. "The Architecture of Racial Segregation: The Challenges of Preserving the Problematical Past." *Public Historian* 27, no. 4 (Fall 2005): 11–44.
White, John H. Jr. *The American Railroad Passenger Car*. Baltimore: Johns Hopkins University Press, 1978.
White, John H. Jr. *A History of the American Locomotive: Its Development, 1830–1880*. New York: Dover Publications, 1979.
Williams, John Hoyt. *A Great and Shining Road: The Epic Story of the Transcontinental Railroad*. New York: Times Books, 1988.
Woodward, C. Vann. *The Strange Career of Jim Crow*. New York: Oxford University Press, 2002.
Yanni, Carla. *The Architecture of Madness: Insane Asylums in the United States*. Minneapolis: University of Minnesota Press, 2007.
Yung, Judy, Gordon H. Chang, and Him Mark Lai, eds. *Chinese American Voices*. Berkeley: University of California Press, 2006.
Zangwill, Israel. *The Melting-Pot*. New York: Macmillan, 1921.

INDEX